THE
BUREAUCRATIZATION
OF THE WORLD

THE
BUREAUCRATIZATION
OF THE WORLD

BY HENRY JACOBY

TRANSLATED FROM THE GERMAN BY
EVELINE L. KANES

UNIVERSITY OF CALIFORNIA PRESS
BERKELEY   LOS ANGELES   LONDON

Original title: *Die Bürokratisierung der Welt: Ein Beitrag zur Problemgeschichte.*

Published by Hermann Luchterhand Verlag GmbH, Neuwied and Berlin, 1969, as No. 64 in the series *Soziologische Texte,* edited by Heinz Maus and Friedrich Fürstenberg

University of California Press
Berkeley and Los Angeles, California

University of California Press, Ltd.
London, England

Paperback Edition 1976
ISBN 0-520-03044-3
Library of Congress Catalog Card Number:
74-165224
Printed in the United States of America

2 3 4 5 6 7 8 9

CONTENTS

INTRODUCTION

The Basic Problem of our Times

The concept of bureaucracy and all that it entails has emerged as a central social issue in the mid-twentieth century. Complaint about its growing influence in the world arises from man's feeling that he no longer controls his own destiny. Each member of contemporary society is part of a large conglomerate whose self-expression and sense of existence depends on the operation of complicated governmental machinery. Such groupings possess little structure, and the individual finds nothing to help him become integrated into a community.

The term *bureaucracy* refers to the fact that man's existence is directed and controlled by central agencies; not only is he unable to escape from the regulation and manipulation, he seems to depend on it. The overpowering anonymity of the control and the impenetrability of large powerful administrative machines produce fear and discontent. In spite of universal education and increasing use of the printed word and electronic media, the individual finds it increasingly difficult to understand the machinery. He has less influence on what happens in society now than before, because he lacks the means of making his will known. Man's alienation from his own world is expressed in his dissatisfaction with bureaucracy.

However, the voice which complains also demands bureaucracy, demands central control, demands regulatory administration and protective machinery. Modern man has lost spontaneous self-help. Projects which help others have become rarer; people now depend on specialized agencies to which they can turn.

The true problem of our times resembles a closed sphere. Centralization of all functions and accumulation of power are on the inside; isolation

1

and impotence of the individual are on the outside. These opposites have consistently intensified each other. Thus the looser western interpersonal relations became, the more they depended on bureaucracy. As the feudal order—which had been both stable and protective—disappeared, people required increased guidance and assurance, obtainable only from organizations and central agencies staffed by professionals. The world became more individualistic, and as each individual assumed responsibility for himself, he was less secure and had greater need of a strong state and a competent government. Once each man acquired greater faith in individualism, and swept only in front of his own door, so to speak, he found he had to rely on a centrally directed professional cleaning system for public streets. As society became modernized—that is to say industrialized, intricate, technologized and interlocking—the modalities of control were shaped into one of their oldest forms: that of bureaucracy. Alfred Weber put it aptly: "Like the ancient Egyptians and Babylonians, who had their system of canals which could only be controlled bureaucratically, we modern men are surrounded by a logistical network of gigantic proportions, consisting of railways, postal, electrical and other services; we live and die through its functions, as did those ancient peoples through their canals; the systems are similar in that they require direction and rational organization by a central bureaucracy."

Although control of our complicated technological existence requires rational thought and action, in the final analysis things do not remain rational. Max Weber, who analyzed bureaucracy sociologically, certainly saw it essentially as expressing a rational form of government. He described its characteristics as being the continuous operation of regulated agencies, possessing specifically defined functions and the authority required for their enforcement, with a firm limitation on when and how force is to be used. But what characterizes our age is precisely the forceful transformation of rational administration into the irrational exercise of power, the lack of clearly defined limits to coercion, and the increasing competence of a state which arrogates independence to itself. We have become aware that this self-emancipated state power prefers to base itself on myth rather than on the rational needs of a technical civilization, and that such myth provides the individual—plagued by fears and feelings of impotence in his atomized mass society—with a reassuring and compensating faith. The craving for protection and authority arises among isolated members of an unstructured mass. Out of insecurity, and the sense of alienation from the systems of one's own civilization, grow those irrational tendencies to subjugate oneself to complete authority and to seek refuge in a closed secular myth.

The readiness to accept governmental authority exists even where this is not enforced by totalitarian bureaucratic methods. During a liberal era, a period when society is freed from its traditional binding structures, and even where these simply do not exist, a social climate develops which lends itself to bureaucratic manipulation. "In this democratic Republic," de Tocqueville writes in *Democracy in America,* "the master no longer says: 'You shall think as I do or you shall die,' but he says: 'You are free to think differently from me and to retain your life, your property, and all that you possess, but you are henceforth a stranger among your people.' "

In a totalitarian state like Hitler's Germany, or Stalin's Russia, every expression of ideas differing from the party line was forcefully stopped by the bureaucratic machine. What one has to consider apparently is that totalitarian states are not accidental manifestations, but rather extreme symptoms of a worldwide tendency. The extreme development of this tendency can be explained in terms of the historical characteristics peculiar to Germany and Russia, but it did not take place outside the world in which we live. The fact that in totalitarian nations those occupying key positions achieve direct and absolute control must not only change our concept of society, it must profoundly influence all efforts towards the expansion and reconstruction of democracy.

Although daily complaints about bureaucracy are due merely to the red tape in official business, or annoyance at not receiving satisfaction, they are the problem of our times and indicate that we need to develop new social conditions. These can best be understood if one looks for them where they have become established in their most extreme form—which does not necessarily happen everywhere. However, in all important nations the political machine is strong enough to assume complete authority over all functions of society in times of crisis. Where the state is not yet a fully developed mechanism, as in economically underdeveloped and nonindustrialized nations, the necessary "hothouse" development of the economy can only be achieved through the existence of a centralized and concentrated governmental authority. But if bureaucracy signifies the control of society, it is understandable why there are such loud complaints. These are the complaints of the middle class, which feels at every move that it has reached the limits of its power and that a change of guard is about to take place. They are the same discontents once voiced by the aristocracy, when the newly created bourgeoisie eroded their position in society and it became obvious that a cultural era was ending. The contemporary development of a new form of social organization also meets opposition from those segments of society which are socialist oriented to the extent that they are still aware of the original aim of the socialist movement: namely, the expansion of democracy beyond the state it had reached among the middle classes. The powerful reality of bureaucracy reminds the socialist of Max Weber's skeptical question: "In the face of governmental bureaucracy's growing indispensability and the powerful position it thus acquires, what guarantee can there be that there are forces able to contain and effectively control this monstrous system, which is constantly growing in power and importance? How can democracy continue to exist in this limited sense?"

Under the pressure of existing conditions, socialism has been led to cooperate somewhat in the growth of bureaucracy, or it has been forced into the position of defending middle-class culture against the very bureaucracy to which it gave birth and which is undermining it. In this way socialism's utopian message is lost; yet without it the world becomes impoverished. Utopian ideas have always provided an impetus for the western world. Contemporary intellectual life is steeped in uneasiness and hopelessness because the future has become obscure. The problem which burdens everyone, even those who are unaware, is how to break the vicious circle in which the government's increasing tendency to regulate everything reduces the individual's ability to determine his own life. On the one hand, the bureaucratic spirit which permeates society turns its functionaries into total representatives of an "it"; on the other hand, everyone is manipulated by the "it" whatever mythic form it may assume. It is a spirit which dehumanizes society because it leads to the complete alienation of man from his own social existence. This existence becomes the object of an all-encompassing machinery, and Max Weber appears to be justified when he asks, "what can we put in place of this machinery to preserve a small part of mankind from this splintering of the soul, from the autocratic imposition of bureaucratic ideals?"

But first of all the history of this, our most urgent problem, has to be studied. In western history social functions have become the responsibility of the state in a continuous process of centralization and accumulation of power. Influential movements within society—whether conservative or revolutionary—originally encountered the bureaucratic manifestation with an enlightened optimism that is now disappearing.

To study the problem one must above all pursue presently neglected concepts which have been used at various times to come to terms with this social development.

It is the aim of this book to consider an essential phenomenon of our social existence in its entirety. While it is not intended to provide a historical review, examples are used to present the "ideal types" characteristic of its development. I shall not examine in detail either the wealth of existing historical data or national differences in its evolution. With a few exceptions, I have concerned myself with the intellectual and historical progress of the phenomenon during various periods of European-North American development. Naturally, the examples I present are subjective, but I have chosen them to provide essential concepts and points of view rather than an index of important thinkers. This is especially true of the vast contemporary literature (above all, that being produced in America), since a large number of recent publications are concerned with very specific aspects of the problem which fall outside the limits of this study. I was not concerned with investigating office procedures in the bureaucratic system, but with showing how that system—given national differences—has permeated society. I have tried to point out the complexity of the phenomenon, and in stressing democratic values and pointing to the danger they face in a world dominated by bureaucracy, I have also tried to look into the chances of their survival.

A detailed bibliography appears at the end of the book.

In conclusion, I should like to point out that I developed many of my ideas over a long period of collaboration with Professor Lewis A. Coser. Large sections of the manuscript were read by Professor Coser, and by Professor Paul J. Alexander of the University of California, to both of whom I am grateful for suggestions and encouragement.

The late Professor Friedrich Pollock, of the *Institut für Sozialforschung,* gave up the time needed to read, and to comment on, the finished manuscript, a gesture which proved invaluable to me.

PART ONE

THE BIRTH OF MODERN GOVERNMENT

1

THE DISSOLUTION OF AUTONOMOUS SPHERES OF INFLUENCE AND THE EARLY HISTORY OF BUREAUCRACY

Primitive Bureaucracies

Today's powerful administrative machinery, embracing highly industrial societies in its dense network and equipped to deal with every event and record every operation, actually developed over a long period of time. The idea one occasionally encounters that this controlled world came into being suddenly is false, although understandable. In the seventeenth and eighteenth centuries, the principles of bureaucratic administration were still considered revolutionary innovations. It was not until the nineteenth century's administrative expansion that the feeling of confronting a new phenomenon was justified—even if the actual change had occurred much earlier. If we really want to understand the system which directs and controls our lives in increasing measure by means of competent agencies, we have to find out how bureaucracy came into being. Only by studying the evolution of the administered world are we able to obtain an idea of bureaucracy's essential characteristics.

Although bureaucracy is not a European "invention," I intend to consider the history of European industrial societies in studying its development. Bureaucratic systems developed in all instances where large groups of men existed in large areas creating the need for a central agency to deal with problems. Alfred Weber wrote that the history of all great civilizations begins with the formation of a bureaucracy which supports and shapes men's whole existence. It was the priestly, hierarchically organized class of scribes which created and guarded the magic and sacred character of life in ancient Egypt and Babylonia, under the pharaohs or supreme monarchs. This class, founded on the economic productivity of the canal system, was probably the most totalitarian bureaucracy ever to have existed in history. The early great civilizations of China and India, which were also based on the economic use of canal systems on the Hoangho, Yangtze, Ganges and Indus rivers, revealed similar strong bureaucratic tendencies.[1]

In the same way, the Inca empire used a bureaucratic system to administer the construction of agricultural terracing, and established a communication network dependent on suspension bridges. Louis Baudin says of the Inca administrative officials that they were genuine representatives of the state. The Inca state, in order to achieve its economic balance, had to regulate the lives of its subjects down to the smallest detail, and thus endowed its representatives with far-reaching authority. They instituted statistical offices, supervised their subordinates' functions, saw that violations of the law were brought to justice, and compiled reports on everyone and everything for their superiors.[2]

When the Spanish invaded Peru and destroyed the Inca empire, they discovered a well-organized system of statistical data, using differently colored twines to indicate objects, and knots in the twines to represent numbers.

Statistics always provide evidence of a centralized administration; they form the basis for a centralized system of taxation. Jacques Pirenne indicates that under the V. dynasty in Egypt (2500-2350 B.C), taxation was determined by record offices, which centralized all information about citizens and their living conditions. A census was taken periodically. In this way the government possessed a record on each Egyptian, his property, the amount of his income, and the contract of hire or work which bound him to his owner or employer. All of Egypt was inventoried.[3] There was even a set time for sowing seed, determined by the flooding of the Nile, and regulations as to where and what to sow, and what percentage of the crop was to be delivered as tax. All of this required an experienced administrative bureaucracy whose structure, as Heichelheim points out, underwent various changes. It was influenced by Hellenism under Alexander, then by imperial Rome, and became more primitive in the Byzantine period. But at all times it was indispensable to the successful functioning of those civilizations. From Egypt, organizational influence spread to medieval governmental administrations of the Russian, as well

[1] Alfred Weber, "Bureaukratie und Freiheit," *Die Wandlung* (December 20, 1946).

[2] Louis Baudin, *Der Sozialistische Staat der Inka* (Hamburg, 1956). English edition, *A Socialist Empire: the Incas of Peru*, tr. Catherine Woods (Princeton, 1961).

[3] Jacques Pirenne, "L'Administration civile et l'organisation judiciaire en Egypte sous la Vᵉ dynastie," *Annuaire de l'Institut de Philologie et d'histoire orientales et slaves*, III (Bruxelles, 1935), 370-372.

as the Islamic Orient, and to some extent its effect was also felt in the Germanic and Romanic occident.[4]

Feudalism

After the fall of the Roman Empire, a type of society came into being which consisted of numerous small independent units showing little evidence of being controlled by a central administration or civil service. The French historian François Guizot noted three trends competing for control of society at the time. These were: man's basic freedom, the early attempts to establish a primitive monarchical system, and the emergent elements of feudalism.[5]

The primitive form of universal freedom allowed all free men to participate in the actions of nations, just as their strength was counted upon in times of need.[6] It permitted all to participate in deliberations, or be certain that those who did shared and represented their interests. This feeling was lost in the migrations of peoples and subsequent wars.

During the invasions of migrating groups a military hierarchy was established with specific leaders at its head. But this central royal power did not possess the machinery to enforce its authority. "Officials" were merely servants in the royal household, and the revenue of the king and his subordinates came from the land acquired in the conquered territories. The central power could not support itself.

At the beginning of the seventh century, the Franconian kings had to grant the liege lords the right to refuse entry into their domain to the king's representatives. This resulted in their financial, judicial and military autonomy.

Of the three competing trends Guizot mentioned, it was that of feudalism which became firmly established. While it was the king who was responsible for military leadership, no army existed because finances were lacking. The imposition of taxes led to revolts (for example, among the Franks in the sixth and seventh centuries), for such payments could be imposed only on the conquered and dominated. As Henri Pirenne puts

---

[4] F. M. Heichelheim, *Wirtschaftsgechichte des Altertums* (Leiden, 1939). English edition, *An Ancient Economic History: From the Paleolithic Age to the Migration of the Germanic, Slavic and Arabic Nations*, tr. Joyce Stevens (Leiden, 1958).

[5] François Guizot, *Histoire des origines du gouvernement représentatif* (Bruxelles, 1851). English edition, *History of the Origin of Representative Government in Europe*, tr. Andrew R. Scoble (London, 1861).

[6] G. W. F. Hegel, *Die Verfassung Deutschlands*, ed. Hermann Heller (Leipzig, 1922). An English translation is included in *Hegel's Political Writings*, tr. T. M. Knox (Oxford, 1964).

it: "The demesnial revenues of the prince replenished only his privy purse. It was impossible for him to increase his resources by taxes, and his financial indigence prevented him from taking into his service revocable and salaried agents. Instead of functionaries, he had only hereditary vassals, and his authority over them was limited to the oath of fidelity they gave him."[7]

Therefore, the military power of the central leadership—whether of king or emperor—depended on the vassals' or liege lords' willingness to put themselves and their followers at the ruler's disposal. Similarly, royal justice could not be exercised permanently over a larger territory without the aid of an administrative organization and consequently had to be delegated to the liege lords. As the seigneurs received not only land but also jurisdiction over it from the king, the latter's power decreased. Even the right of coinage, which had been its prerogative, was lost to the crown. Some three hundred vassals, according to Henri Pirenne, had appropriated the right of coinage under the early Capetians.[8] After all, the king had only been chosen as first among his peers. When Hugues Capet was crowned in 987, the title of king was awarded him because he had the largest feudal estate. However, at the time of Pépin's coronation in 751, the royal title was acquired by the holder of the highest office.[9]

The fundamental reason for the existence of the feudal vassalic system was the defense of the established agrarian society. Of this system Herder writes: "The barbarian feudal monarchy was actually a weak system . . . ; it was founded mainly to conduct wars and thus had to maintain perpetual campaigns to be effective, or degenerate into chaos and self-destruction."[10] But it was precisely in the pursuit of its military tasks that the feudal system destroyed itself. As offensive weaponry improved with the use of armed cavalry and armor, and with the establishment of castles which aided defense, higher revenues were required. However, medieval agriculture was unable to increase its production. The power and income of a seigneur could only be enlarged by the acquisition of new territory and demesnes. This led to constant struggles and feuds. The desire for the acquisition of power conflicted with the principle involving its distribution.

At the same time, the development of an economy based on commodities began to displace the feudal nobility's authority. As soon as wealth

[7] Henri Pirenne, *Medieval Cities* (New York, 1956), p. 161.

[8] Henri Pirenne, *Economic and Social History of Medieval Europe* (New York, 1937), p. 112.

[9] Georges d'Avenel, *Richelieu et la monarchie absolue* (Paris, 1884).

[10] J. G. von Herder, *Ideen zur Philosophie der Geschichte der Menschheit*, 2 vols. (Berlin, 1952), I. 603. English edition, *Outlines of a Philosophy of the History of Man*, tr. John Godfrey (London, 1800).

ceased to consist only of landed property, but included money and goods, the nobility no longer had a monopoly of wealth. With the increase in the barter of goods and resultant demand, self-supporting agricultural economy no longer sufficed. The political autonomy of a powerful demesne was only feasible as long as it was self-sufficient.

The new principle of social survival and the new type of wealth developed along with the towns. As their economic power grew, medieval cities tried to become independent of the feudal lords, to the point where they formed their own spheres of influence. The town became an independent municipal authority or, in the words of French historians, a *seigneurie municipale.* In these medieval towns it was the business of the burgesses to concern themselves with the administration of finance, law, trade and crafts; they constituted that group of people from which government officials were later to evolve.

Within the cities the guilds formed their own spheres of power which protected their members' independence and maintained equality among them. In establishing wool houses, oil mills, dye houses and sawmills for communal use, the guilds perpetuated the role of the rural parishes with their control over woods and pastures. The guilds were in no way mere representatives of interests in the sense of modern professional organizations. They formed a real sphere of life into which one was born, and which encompassed the totality of life, work and play. "Technical progress," writes Henri Pirenne, "took on the appearance of disloyalty."[11] He was speaking of the social structure of the guilds, which prevented guild members from competing with each other or harming one another by using new methods to produce goods more cheaply. To escape the restrictions and authority of the guilds, capital accumulated in trade was sent to the country in order to produce goods to satisfy increasing demand. Thus, goods were no longer manufactured for a specific customer but rather for an anonymous market.

The coexistence and conflicts of the feudal system's numerous small entities, and the social and economic contrasts which arose, promoted the growth of a third force, namely, *the centralized authority of the state in the form of the monarchy.*

The Birth of the French Monarchy

In connection with Robertson's history of Charles V, Herder describes how

[11] Henri Pirenne, *Economic and Social History of Medieval Europe,* p. 184.

The power of the monarchy increased together with that of the mercenary class, while at the same time individual feudal groups lost their authority. How the monarchy was able to enlarge its privileges and revenues; how it subjugated and controlled its internal enemies; and by what means it broadened its frontiers; all of this is shown in the middle and recent periods of French history. In this respect, France must be considered the precursor of all Europe.[12]

Indeed, the classical development of the modern state can be traced most clearly in the example of France.

The prerequisite for a true governmental system in society and the central enactment of its functions—previously carried out by independent authorities—is the availability of a competent group of people. The outward manifestation of a central authority consists of a specific building housing "offices" out of which this group of people can operate.

As previously noted, in a feudal monarchy the king was merely the first among peers on whom devolved the execution of his orders. Hence the formula for royal decrees: *"Avec le conseil commun et l'assemblement des évêques et des grands"* ("With the Common Council and the Assembly of Bishops and Nobles"). Then there is the recurrent phrase of St. Louis, "We and our barons consider." The *curia regis* or royal council consisted of these barons, but already at the end of the twelfth century, the first *officiers du roi* (officials of the king) were admitted to the council. Since their participation in the council was part of their professional duty, they attended constantly, whereas the nobility appeared infrequently, as it meant leaving their seigneuries. A monarchy which wants to exercise its autonomous power needs a dependent body of people, whose position in society consists in the fulfillment of assigned duties. It is the rise of such a class of functionaries which heralds the birth of bureaucracy. The duty of personal service to the king was separated from political administrative functions. Growing administrative responsibilities were concentrated in the *bureaux de la Chancellerie* (the chancellory offices) and in the hands of *notaires secrétaires* (secretary-notaries).

The small but rapidly growing class of *legistes* (men of law) and *plumitifs* (scribes) in France—their number increased from thirty in 1316 to 105 in 1356—did not lack self-confidence because of its lowly origin. It knew itself to be the king's representative and identified itself with his authority. Guillaume de Nogaret, who belonged to this class, wrote that "the *légistes* are not members of the aristocracy, but they are the king's knights." Already in 1283, Philippe de Rémi, sire de Beaumanoir, could say that

[12] Herder, *op. cit.,* I, p. 497.

14

"The King is sovereign over all the nobility; only he can issue edicts, he is in overall charge of the churches, and all worldly justice is in his hands." In this way the légistes propagated the centralization of authority with which they identified. Pierre Dubois, a royal advocate around the year 1300, demanded that all property belonging to the church be confiscated in behalf of the king, and suggested that the latter assume hegemony over the entire Christian world. The establishment of authority and the desire for supremacy were simultaneous developments.[13]

Specialization

In the King's administrative offices, division of labor was instituted at an early stage. Administrative specialization became necessary as the central executive acquired the responsibility and authority which had belonged to autonomous feudal powers. The Council of the French king developed three separate sections in the course of the thirteenth century: one for justice, one for finance (controlled by accountants known as *gens de comptes*), and a third one which constituted the Great Council. At the same time, an administrative network began to develop, which transmitted authority from the center to the rest of the country. Whereas previously the king's messenger or representative brought royal orders to the people, these orders were now enforced by officials in charge of financial, legal and military matters. A hierarchical system developed, with a fast-expanding base, which gave rise to a class of petty officials.

In his description of the monarchical administrative system, Adolphe Cheruel mentions the *prévots* who became local functionaries, but who originally took care of the royal demesnes. They were supervised by *baillis* and *sénéchaux*, who were responsible for each province's military, legal and financial administration. The collection of taxes was taken away from them later on, because specialized officials were entrusted with the distribution and collection of revenues.[14]

Under the prevailing communication system, it was difficult to control the growing number of petty officials—*lieutenants, sergents* and *bedeaus*—through whom power was increasingly centralized. In 1303, the increase was already such that a royal decree ordered—vainly!—the dismissal of four out of every five officials. A popular preacher, the Augustine Brother

---

[13] Emile Marie Joseph Gustave Dupont-Ferrier, *La Formation de l'état francqis et l'unité française, des origines au milieu du XVIᵉ siècle* (Paris, 1934), pp. 10, 12, 15, 44, 50, 51 and 52.

[14] Adolphe Cheruel, *Histoire de l'administration monarchique en France depuis l'avénement de Philippe-Auguste jusqu'à la mort de Louis XIV*, 2 vols. (Paris, 1855), I, p. 50.

Nicolas de Byart, said of these officials that they lie in wait until they can steal another's property like the wolf who devours the sheep.

In 1285, King Philippe le Bel sent out *controlleurs* to investigate complaints about these officials. However, he had to admit eventually that his investigations revealed nothing. That is how it was always to be in the future. Some were to terrorize those who complained, others were to pay them to keep silent, and there were those who, thanks to powerful friends, were to obtain favors from governmental departments. Cheruel writes of this period: "It became necessary to pay the troops and the vast hierarchy of officials which had developed under the French monarchy. This led to those fiscal measures which inspired great hatred for Philippe le Bel."[15] It was not until the middle of the sixteenth century that a regular supervisory system of regional officials by *commissaires* was established. In 1553, there were only six *commissaires,* but two years later their number had increased to twenty. At first they travelled from place to place, but soon they became permanently established in their districts.

Revenues to maintain the monarchy were obtained slowly and against the resistance of other social groups. The income from each seigneury belonged to the seigneur, who did not want his peasants to become impoverished for the benefit of any authority but his own. While it was true that the central organization of defense was the king's responsibility, this required funds; however, the feudal lords demanded their share of any taxes that had to be imposed. The king could obtain larger revenues, as required for wars and other expensive undertakings, only by appealing to autonomous feudal territories. He did this by calling an assembly of the general estates. The appeal was directed above all at the *seigneuries municipales,* the towns, where money was in more liquid form than in the country. However, the wealthier the town, the more it emphasized its independence. Taxes could be obtained only with their consent.[16]

The judicial and military systems also came under the jurisdiction of independent authorities. In feudal society, each of the smallest entities was responsible for its own legislation (insofar as it could be said to exist), and for the administration of justice. Augustin Thierry speaks of the "crumbling" of legislative and judicial systems—there being seigneurial, communal and clerical justice. According to Marc Bloch, the rivalry between these three groups turned royal justice into a sort of arbitration, a court of appeal to which the weaker side turned. However, after a

---

[15] *Ibid.,* p. 50.

[16] Before the feudal era, the Germans regarded taxation as a form of servitude. In 584, in Paris, when the freemen were asked to pay a head tax, there was a rebellion.

period in which the clerks seldom forgot the written law of the Roman past, and when common law came to predominate with local variations, systematic legislation gradually began to replace varying local practices.[17]

Military service was not originally an obligation towards a central authority; it was the common responsibility of able-bodied members of a community. The free man bore arms. However, the growing cost of equipment (which soon included a horse, after mounted nomads invaded Europe), forced the peasants to seek the feudal lords' protection and to forego their freedom and independent status. Military protection was, in fact, the feudal aristocracy's real function in society. Once this proved too difficult due to lack of funds (often compelling knights to commit acts of robbery), it became the crown's responsibility. Those who wished to avoid military duty could do so only through the payment of money, which enabled the king to pay mercenaries, who now became the king's army.

But the establishment of a paid army required regular revenues. Voluntary contributions from independent territories were irregular and could not be estimated in advance. Hence it became necessary for the central government to enforce a system of taxation. An edict issued by the French king in 1439 decreed that no feudal lord could collect taxes without royal permission. Because no efficient administrative system for revenue collection and disbursement existed, the levy of taxes was leased out to the highest bidders. Tax revenues and income obtained from royal desmesnes were administered by the royal accounting office. The former were administered as "extraordinary" finances until 1523, although they had already amounted to thirty times the "ordinary" finances in the middle of the previous century. By the second half of the sixteenth century, the bureaucratic structure of financial officialdom, consisting of *intendants* of finance with the *surintendants* above them, had been more or less developed.

Centralization of Administration

The process by which autonomous entities lost their authority to a central administrative apparatus was nowhere smoothly continuous. Federations were created in France as early as the thirteenth century to counteract the usurpatory demands of the crown. Where the latter

---

[17] Marc Bloch, *La Société féodale* (Paris, 1939). English edition, *Feudal Society,* tr. L. A. Manyon (Chicago, 1961).

17

had to retreat, royal officials bore the brunt. Augustin Thierry writes that the most daring among them were often destroyed by the groups they had injured.

In the fourteenth century, the French States General set up a control commission for taxation. The town burghers reacted with bloody revolts against regular payment of taxes. But this development merely furthered formation of a centralized system. The large number of independent aristocratic authorities lost their influence and their functions, as improved war technology, such as artillery, required greater funds. Their means were exhausted by the luxuries their status required. Barons had to enter the service of the royal court and army. The feudal structure disintegrated as lesser liege lords became directly dependent on the king, and the upper aristocracy lost its sovereignty over its vassals.

Even the autonomous towns increasingly lost their independence. In their endeavors to become independent of the feudal lords, the towns allied themselves with the crown, but once they acquired too much freedom, the latter looked to the lords for support against the towns. Military authority was taken away from the towns by French legislation in the fifteenth century, and they lost the right to administer their judicial and police systems during the sixteenth century. Eventually their finances, too, passed into the hands of the central administration.

As their wealth came to depend more and more on commerce, and as the barter of goods replaced self-sufficiency, the cities became increasingly interested in the development of a central authority. At stake was the security of traffic and markets, and the control and regulation of currency, weights and measures. The business-oriented bourgeoisie thus provided the state with a basis for funding a standing army, indispensable for the proper functioning of any governmental system.

The state therefore made it its business to protect the wealth of the middle class. Systems of coinage and measurement were developed. The exportation of raw material and the importation of finished goods were forbidden. Subsidies were given to certain enterprises and trade monopolies were distributed. Guild regulations, forbidding the expansion of businesses, were discontinued. Roads and canals were built, improved and maintained. Mercantilism was born. The state itself began operating businesses as royal gunpowder and porcelain factories were established.

Certain functions of society, which had been independent, now came under the jurisdiction of the state, giving rise to a class of people whose position in society was determined by office rather than heredity. By the sixteenth century, they were known in France as *la magistrature,* and the term *quatrième état*—fourth estate—gained currency. The bureaucracy stood out as a separate class, recognizable by its special long gown, the *robe longue.* The true nobility looked down on the *noblesse de robe,* as its higher officials were designated. D'Avenel mentions that the Prince de Rohan admitted, in the first half of the seventeenth century, that the *robes longues* had assumed greater importance than the true aristocracy.[18] But already in the middle of the sixteenth century, it was said that one could hardly go anywhere without meeting an official.[19] Just as they had once aspired to the clergy, sons of the bourgeoisie now wanted to become royal officials. The court saw this as a useful means of financing its luxuries; official positions were sold to fill the royal coffers.

[18] D'Avenel, *op. cit.*
[19] Dupont-Ferrier, *op. cit.*

THE FIRST
BUREAUCRATIC STATE:
THE ABSOLUTE MONARCHY

The Birth of the Modern State—400 Years of European History

The transfer of power and authority—territorial or corporative—from numerous small feudal bodies to a central administration which controlled all spheres of life, was part of a continuous process. The creation of this new kind of power affected people of all classes. It meant that duties and privileges were taken away from men known in their local regions, and entrusted instead to distant, impersonal offices. Decisions were no longer made at the local level where they were influenced by common tradition and customs. They were replaced by a central system of uniform, rational laws which applied universally. This system superseded a multitude of contradictory interests by creating an administrative authority possessing efficient methods and techniques.

Political systems of the Middle Ages had not achieved a permanent concentration of power because their hierarchical nature limited the liege lords' authority. This applied also to royal or imperial heads of state, who lacked an organization to enforce their will. Alliances among feudal powers were temporary and created for a specific purpose. Small entities were able to survice and remain militarily, judicially and financially independent in a society based largely on agrarian self-sufficiency. In these communities men led a traditional existence rooted in the past, with clear ideas of right and wrong. The dissolution of this complex world—a historical process which lasted 400 years—resulted in the growth of the absolute monarchy, the birth of the modern state.

A First Attempt to Form a Modern State

Indications of what the modern state was to be can be seen in the premature attempt of Emperor Frederick II to create an absolute monarchy—patterned after oriental models—out of the former Norman empire in Sicily and southern Italy. Jacob Burckhardt describes the attempt in some detail: "Especially after 1231, Frederick's decrees aimed at the creation of an omnipotent royal power, at the complete destruction of feudalism and at the transformation of the people into a powerless, unarmed and highly taxable populace. He centralized the entire legal system . . . people were denied the right to elect officials . . . Frederick attempted to take over all commerce along the shores of the Mediterranean."[1] All the characteristics of the modern state are revealed in Frederick's attempts to replace the feudal system, as has been pointed out by Ernst Kantorowicz. His army took on a professional appearance, as paid mercenaries increasingly replaced vassals. The Emperor personally appointed officials and courts to enforce the law. A central code of laws was developed. The constitution issued at Melfi in 1231 was a collection of laws and administrative regulations which have been termed the "birth certificate of modern bureaucracy." A university was established at Naples which differed from all previous ones in that it was concerned not with pure erudition but with purposes of the state; it was not a school for aspiring clerics but for training civil servants. The emperor appointed officials to carry out administrative regulations, and the old feudal ties of the nobility to the emperor were replaced by the ties of service at court or official duty. Knights' castles became state fortresses.

Frederick was also the first emperor who consciously aimed at controlling the minds of his subjects. For that reason, he paid particular attention to the political police system. The Emperor's economic policy was much admired; the grain trade, for example, was in large measure turned into a state monopoly. Large-scale traders could purchase grain only from the crown.

Frederick's concept of government was that the raison d'etat did not contravene divine or natural law—but was itself this law, which sums up the basic traits of the "first absolute monarchy of the West."[2]

The Absolute Monarchy

Adolph Wagner has observed that the bureaucratic image of the modern state was formed in the seventeenth century:

[1] Jacob Christoph Burckhardt, *Die Kultur der Renaissance in Italien* (Bern, 1943). English edition, *The Civilization of the Renaissance in Italy*, tr. S. G. C. Middlemore (New York, 1944).
[2] Ernst H. Kantorowicz, *Kaiser Friedrich der Zweite* (Berlin, 1927). English edition, *Frederick the Second*, tr. E. O. Lorimer (London, 1931).

A number of political events which had taken place earlier—such as the post-Reformation wars, and the economic results of the Age of Discovery—favored the extension of existing state functions and the development of new ones. Numerous important elements contributed to the increase in bureaucratic activities: the army, the internal national cultural policy, and the mercantilist economy. Above all, the planned policies of the welfare-police states of enlightened and unenlightened absolutism, and especially of despotism, played an active role in bureaucracy's growth. In France this required greater finances and revenues, which meant higher taxation to the degree that duties, royal privileges and monopolies . . . and finally the national debt itself proved insufficient.[3]

The connection between absolute monarchy and the feudal system from which it evolved has frequently been overemphasized by historians. They have thus obscured the deep rift in European society caused by the development of the modern state. This occurred because modern historicity was developed by the very middle class whose revolutionary struggle for ascendance had been waged simultaneously against the absolute monarchy and the remnants of feudalism.

Hegel rightly remarked that absolute monarchy, which had grown out of feudalism, at first retained feudal characteristics, but he pointed out that feudal vassals had become officials of a state whose laws they had to enforce.[4]

If one follows Herder's suggestion and continues to trace the progress of French history, it will be seen that some of the hereditary nobility did indeed accept official positions, and that it became their privilege to occupy positions of leadership in the army, at court and in provincial governments.[5] Once in the employ of the royal executive, the only difference between a seigneur and those around him was his higher rank in office. At the time of Louis XIV, court ceremony was changed to give high government officials precedence over those of noble birth.

The change in status of the French nobility has been aptly described by d'Avenel: Prior to Richelieu's time, the king demanded loyalty from his subjects; afterwards he insisted on submission. The aristocracy was compensated for the loss of its political rights by useful and prestigious offices. It was no longer in command, but it had a livelihood and the means of impressing its status on others. This was what was meant by their feudal rights. A noble could still acquire wealth if his political

---

[3] Adolph Wagner, "Finanzwissenschaft und Staatssozialismus," *Zeitschrift für die gesamte Staatswissenschaft*, XLIII (1887).

[4] G. W. F. Hegel, *Vorlesungen über die Philosophie der Geschichte* (Berlin, 1837). English edition, *Lectures on the Philosophy of History*, tr. J. Sibree (New York, 1956).

[5] J. G. von Herder, *Ideen zur Philosophie der Geschichte der Menschheit*, 2 vols. (Berlin, 1952). English edition, *Outlines of a Philosophy of the History of Man*, tr. John Godfrey (London, 1800).

activity conformed to the will of the king, but his wealth no longer depended on heredity.[6] In towns now deprived of their autonomy, elected magistrates were replaced by royal officials. Administration of the police system was also taken over by the crown. Again, according to d'Avenel:

> Just as Greek and Roman mythology created tutelary spirits for each town and household, and gods for every event in life, Richelieu's administration appointed officials to deal with every conceivable person or object. People, animals, goods, voyages, all negotiations of public or private life, all coming and going, the simplest activities, were matters for the administration: crossing a bridge, cutting a tree, a bale of hay. . . . Regulations existed for the most everyday affairs . . . bringing about the dread disease of bureaucracy for which no revolution has yet found a cure.[7]

Since tolls, taxes, and import and export duties had to be collected, comprehensive machinery for financial administration had to be established. Various departments were set up, each with specifically defined responsibilities and regional representatives—the *intendants*. In his memoirs, the Duke de Saint-Simon mentions that at the beginning of the eighteenth century, 80,000 people were employed in administering the salt tax. This may be an exaggerated figure, but the fact is that a vast number of officials were needed to combat the smuggling of salt.

It was customary to sell official positions and in many instances these positions were even made hereditary. Therefore, as each new office was created, it also provided a source of revenue for the government. The sale of offices, however, was responsible for the formation of a network of personal and local interests which bore a resemblance to the centrifugal tendencies of the feudal system. Administrative spheres of influence tended to become as "independent" as had the feudal ones of the past. The bureaucrat who paid close attention to local interests—in whose representation he had acquired proprietary rights—could not be transferred even though the central government disapproved of his actions. That is why Richelieu noted in his will that it would be necessary to send officials to the provinces to investigate the conduct of local judicial and financial officials. In a detailed study on the establishment of such *commissaires,* Otto Hintze writes:

> The commissaire was a specific agent of monarchical discipline and of the authority of the absolute state. By means of such agents, the administrative system was protected from the dangers of private interests until, in the seventeenth and eighteenth centuries, it acquired the essence of the modern *raison d'état.* . . .

[6] Georges d'Avenel, *Richelieu et la monarchie absolue* (Paris, 1884).
[7] *Ibid.*

An analogous repetition of the feudal system of commissioning can be found later in the tendency of holders of proprietary offices to consider them as rights rather than functions of public duty. Since they were entangled with local and class interests, district offices frequently became the focal point of insurmountable, passive resistance against orders from higher authorities. . . . Once the commissaire was no longer an officer of the king but a functionary, he represented a new type of civil servant reflecting the absolute state. While this new, single-minded type did not entirely replace that of the old officialdom, the two merged and after a long struggle a radical change was effected in the administrative system.[8]

Under Henry IV, it had been the function of the commissaire to accompany the army and to administer the conquered territories dictatorially. Later, under Louis XIV and Colbert, the commissaire became an intendant and played an integral role in the central administration. The origin and history of the intendant system have been discussed by Hanotaux, who points out that the indendant directly represented the central executive. The difference between delegation and jurisdiction had, however, already been noted in the sixteenth century by the French political philosopher Bodin. A jurisdiction established a legal claim; a delegate could be recalled at any time. Originally, such delegation was temporary, but gradually the office of intendant became permanent.[9] De Tocqueville summarized the importance of this position as follows: The central administration in Paris (in charge of the *contrôleur général*) had, in fact, only one representative in each province. However, in the eighteenth century there were still members of the aristocracy who were known as *provincial governors*. The honor of this title was still conceded to them, but they no longer possessed any power. It was the intendant who exercised real governmental authority. The intendant corresponded with all the ministers. He appointed a subdelegate to each canton, subordinate to him, whom he could recall, and who represented the government within this smaller district. France was governed by thirty intendants.[10]

[8] Otto Hintze, "Der Commissarius und seine Bedeutung in der allgemeinen Verwaltungsgeschichte: Eine Vergleichende Studie," in *Staat und Verfassung: Gesammelte Abhandlungen zur allgemeinen Verfassungsgeschichte,* ed. Gerhard Östreich (Göttingen, 1962).

[9] Albert Auguste Gabriel Hanotaux, *Origines de l'institution des intendants de province d'après des documents inédits* (Paris, 1884).

[10] Alexis de Tocqueville, *L'Ancien Régime et la révolution,* ed. I. P. Mayer (Paris, 1964), pp. 101–102. (Original publication date was 1856.) English edition, *De Tocqueville's L'Ancien Régime,* tr. M. W. Patterson (Oxford, 1956). Colbert who held the office of controleur général did not receive this title until 1665. His correspondence with the intendants reveals that there was practically no matter—from taxes to horse-breeding—on which they did not have to submit reports.

In his study of the commissaire system, Otto Hintze showed how it gave rise to a new regional officialdom all over Europe.[11] In France the intendant became the *préfet*. But in all those instances where the central authority mistrusted the existing bureaucracy and found it necessary to reassert its power, commissaires were appointed. The commissaire appeared as the representative of the French Revolutionary Convention, as the préfet under Napoleon and as the political commissar of Russia's revolutionary Bolshevist government.

The increasing identification of bureaucracy and the state was symbolized at the beginning of the sixteenth century by the introduction of ministerial counter-signatures of royal decrees. In addition, under Henry III (1575–1589), the King's Council, or *conseil du roi*, first became the *conseil d'état*, or Council of State.

Writing on the bureaucracy of absolutism, Paul Frölich comments: "The concept of absolutism as the personal rule of a monarch who enforces his will is a superficial one. It is bureaucracy which represents absolute authority, the monarch being the symbol at its head. . . . When powerful political leaders occupy the throne of an absolute monarchy they themselves are the bureaucratic heads."[12] It did not matter whether strong-willed monarchs like Henry IV, Gustavus Adolphus, or the Great Elector ruled, or whether important ministers such as Sully, Richelieu or Oxenstierna were in control. In the words of Carl J. Friedrich: "Behind these famous builders of the modern state stand the army and the bureaucracy, the nameless hundreds and thousands of faithful servants of the king and crown who in these decades emerge as the core of modern government."[13]

The Duke de Saint-Simon wrote Louis XV that the contrôleur général disposed of revenues as he wished, and that it was customary for ministers who sat with the King in Council not to learn of decrees and promulgations bearing the king's and their own signatures until criers announced them beneath their windows.

The cost of maintaining and expanding the army (according to d'Avenel approximately 50 percent of state revenues was spent on the military), and of supporting the bureaucratic machine, induced the state to acquire as much revenue as it could through taxation; but it also tried to increase the wealth on which the taxation was levied.

[11] Hintze, *op. cit.*

[12] Paul Frölich, *1789, die grosse Zeitwende: Von der Bürokratie des Absolutismus zum Parlament der Revolution* (Frankfurt-am-Main, 1957).

[13] Carl J. Friedrich, "Constitutionalism versus Absolutism," in *Synopsis: Festgabe für Alfred Weber* (Heidelberg, 1948), p. 138.

In the commercial centers of Italy, a political economy had developed guaranteeing the increase of wealth through encouragement of the production of goods to be exchanged against gold. This system prohibited exportation of raw materials required for the manufacture of these goods, and instituted measures to keep gold in the country. As Marx put it: "The various states of Europe scrambled for the patent of this discovery . . . They were not content to fleece their own people, indirectly by protective tariffs, directly by premiums upon export, and the like. In dependent neighbouring countries, industry was forcibly uprooted, as, for example, happened to the woolen manufacture of Ireland under English rule."[14]

To fully utilize the "patent," it was necessary to check the guilds' vested interests which stood in the way of the expanding production of goods. This could only be achieved by political measures, that is, by interfering in the cities' rights. The state itself finally had to finance production in order to increase the amount of exportable goods. "The primary capital of the industrialists was, to a great extent, directly obtained from the State treasury"[15]

The state also participated in trade monopolies to promote exports and to divert money into the treasury. Indeed, only through the authority of the state could the French minister Colbert induce wealthy Marseilles merchants to form a monopoly with their ships. He summarized the aims of the entire mercantilist economy in his *Lettres:* "Manufactured goods produce a return in the form of money; this is the sole object of commerce and the only means of enlarging the scope and power of the state."[16] This economic aim necessitated state legislation. Royal trade ordinances replaced guild, corporation and municipal regulations. Governmental control increased in the areas of coinage, weights and measures, and trade routes.

The economic bureaucracy of the state never doubted that all economic processes were controllable. As early as 1577 a royal decree tried to regulate industry and commerce in the whole of France. Industries were to be established or transferred; the quantity and quality of goods were to be controlled, and price increases in raw materials and finished goods were to be prevented. Severe sanctions were imposed to maintain prices and wages at a fixed level, and an inspection service was set up to supervise all necessary measures.

[14] Karl Marx, *Capital,* tr. E. and C. Paul, 2 vols. (London, 1962), II, p. 839.

[15] *Ibid.,* p. 839.

[16] Jean-Baptiste Colbert, *Lettres, instructions et mémoires,* ed. Pierre Clément, 9 vols. (Paris, 1861), Vol. II.

Lack of scientific understanding only served to increase faith in the omnipotent skills of bureaucratic management. Royal decrees vainly tried to stabilize the relationship between money, gold and silver. But it was a relationship which depended on the laws of the market, and manifested itself in undesired and unpredictable ways. Absolute monarchy never succeeded in overcoming its financial difficulties, so that the acquisition of money became its main concern. This meant increasing centralization. The intendants, the officials concerned with financial and tax administration, were the most powerful men in the country. However, the weak communications system continued to hamper efficient organization and control of national revenues and expenditures.

In their efforts to overcome the system's weaknesses the central authorities developed new, rational procedures. Colbert's administration introduced a type of public bookkeeping and a tax-roll system. Attempts were even made to create a uniform code of laws (the *ordonnance civile* of 1667 and the *ordonnance criminelle* of 1669).

In addition to the systematization of economic policy, the conduct of war became the responsibility of an organized, central system. Now it was the minister of war, and not the field commander, who took credit for military successes. For example, Louvois founded supply depots and set up storehouses in fortresses along the frontiers. Thus the French were able to rely on their provisions, while enemy troops had to loot and pillage to feed themselves, and were dependent on fresh fodder for their horses. What proved successful in one country was of course adopted by others.

Joseph Schumpeter has provided a succinct analysis of the historical role of absolute monarchy:

The wealth and power of [the] state was the unquestioned object of policy: maximum public revenue—for the court and the army to consume—was the purpose of economic policy. . . . Concern for the welfare of the classes on which that social system fed entered into that policy. . . . All this—precisely where concern for the welfare of manufacturers, farmers and laborers was most real— meant management of everything which in turn meant the rise of modern bureaucracy, a fact that is no less important than is the rise of the business class. The resulting economy was a Planned Economy; and it was planned, primarily, with a view to war.[17]

---

[17] Josef A. Schumpeter, *History of Economic Analysis* (New York, 1954), p. 147.

The Rise of Prussian Bureaucracy

The Brandenburg-Prussian State

Prussian bureaucracy has become proverbial. It is regarded as a unique example of state bureaucracy. The previous section of this chapter studied bureaucratic growth in the light of French historical development. To complete the survey, it is also important to trace the origins of the Prussian administrative system.

At the end of the seventeenth century, the Brandenburg-Prussian state consisted of some heterogeneous principalities, most of which had been united by the Hohenzollern princes through marriage. Feudal landowners were in control, especially in the east, and were responsible for the judiciary and the local police. The *Landstände* (territorial estates) supervised taxation and legislation, meeting in provincial diets (*Landtage*). Each province had its own provincial government and only indigenous inhabitants could hold office. Hans Rosenberg described Brandenburg's ruler as "scarely more than a super-Junker."[18]

The Thirty Years War had left the country devastated and the burgher class of the towns impoverished. The peasants were serfs and were bound to do forced labor. Due to existing political conditions on the continent, the Great Elector, Frederick William (1640–1688) needed a standing army to help defend his frontiers. This required a permanent source of revenues, but the *Stände* were unwilling to approve regular taxation because they felt the Elector's ruthless collection of taxes had ruined the country. In fact, the nobility refused to comply with the tax demands, arguing that they would be prevented from educating their children in a manner consistent with their status. This forced the Elector into using illegal methods to obtain the unauthorized taxes, for which he required officials who were independent of the local *Stände*. The officials appointed specifically to collect taxes (they operated from 1680 to 1722) were representatives of the war department. Each official was in total control of from six to fifteen towns.[19]

Former army officers were an important element in the tax administra-

---

[18] Hans Rosenberg, *Bureaucracy, Aristocracy and Autocracy: The Prussian Experience 1660–1815* (Cambridge, Mass. 1958), p. 31.

[19] Otto Hintze has pointed out the similarity in procedure for dealing with the municipalities in France and Prussia. In both cases, officials were first concerned with the investigation of debts. Then they began to administer the financial system, which led to the total disappearance of communal autonomy. In Prussia, the city treasuries eventually came under the control of fiscal agents, *Steuerräte*. See Otto Hintze, "Der Beamtenstand," in *Soziologie und Geschichte: Gesammelte Abhandlungen zur Soziologie, Politik und Theorie der Geschichte*, ed. Gerhard Ostreich (Göttingen, 1964).

tion and the army served as their model for professional conduct. Gustav Schmoller theorizes that the absence of a bourgeois business sense and the predominance of military discipline were important to the development of Prussian bureaucracy.[20] However, this did not prevent corruption and graft from being prevalent in the eighteenth century.

Development of the Bureaucratic Machine

Otto Hintze has shown how the first fiscal and administrative bureaucracy grew directly out of the system of war commissioners. The origin of the new Prussian administration was similar to that of the intendants in France. As traditional autonomous provincial governments were eliminated towards the end of the seventeenth century, a new central administration developed from the war commissioners who formed the War Board. They later combined with the older Domains Board to form the War and Domains Board (1723). Whereas in France the intendants acted as individual officials, their Prussian counterparts were collegiate. They nevertheless constituted a new administrative class superimposed on, and eventually replacing, the traditional provincial hierarchy.[21] In his conflict with the old hierarchy, the Great Elector attempted to subject the provinces to central authority. Individual provincial governments were given their own administrative, war, and fiscal departments, but these were directly responsible to the Berlin executive authority. Territorial and particularist tradition did, however, continue to exist for a long time, and the Elector's administrative officials were considered foreigners in the provinces.

Not until the reign of Frederick William I, the "soldier king" (1688–1740), did a real bureaucracy come into being. Frederick William established a standing mercenary army—the fourth largest army in Europe, although according to the size of its population Prussia only ranked thirteenth. This required increased taxation, and benefiting from the experience of his predecessor the Great Elector, he extended the excise tax to cover a greater number of goods. No doubt the Prussian administrative and tax systems were much influenced by those of France, and it may be assumed that a report of Ezechiel Spanheim—Ambassador of the Great Elector to the court of Louis XIV—was utilized to this end. Spanheim described the French system of indirect taxation on such items

---

[20] Gustav Friedrich von Schmoller, *Umrisse und Untersuchungen zur Verfassungs-Verwaltungs-und Wirtschaftsgeschichte* (Leipzig, 1898).
[21] Hintze, "Der Beamtenstand."

as timber, food and hats. He emphasized that the French governmental system allowed the king to exact levies as he pleased. Taxes on goods were collected partly upon entry into towns, partly upon manufacture, partly at the point of sale. A trained and steadily expanding bureaucracy was consequently required.[22] As Frederick William I was also interested in taxing the aristocracy as much as possible, he preferred to appoint members of the middle class to the highest administrative offices. In his instructions to his son, he pointed out that an official who served the king faithfully would have many enemies, particularly the entire nobility.[23]

Prussia did not become a bureaucratic state in the real sense until the time of Frederick II (1740–1786), although even then authority was shared by the bureaucrats and the landed aristocracy. The two groups alternately cooperated and fought as the king naturally tended to appoint aristocrats to the higher offices.

In a poor country like Prussia, the "tamed" nobility did not have the opportunities, as did the French nobles, of being appointed to the court in great numbers. Nor did income from their estates suffice to feed their families; they were consequently forced to seek other sources of income such as commissions in the army and high administrative positions. In one of his dispatches to London in 1772, the British Ambassador, Lord Malmesbury, reported that the Prussians were poor, conceited, ignorant and without principles. He commented that had they been rich, the aristocracy would not have consented to serve in subordinate positions with such enthusiasm and fortitude.[24] Many a personal tragedy was played out among those who undertook to serve in these subordinate positions. Joseph von Eichendorff had to submit to such a fate as the son of a bankrupt land-owning aristocrat. In his lyric poems he speaks of his nostalgia for the "old castle," where "father walks peacefully in the garden, and grandfather would not exchange his way of life for that of any king." The heroes of his romances were "good-for-nothings," who wandered through the world without a care, whereas von Eichendorff himself was shunted from one department to another as an auxiliary helper during his thirty years of civil service.[25] However, service in the

[22] Ezéchiel Spanheim, *Relation de la Cour de France en 1690,* ed. Emile Bourgeois (Paris, 1900).

[23] However, the king was not averse to selling offices to the highest bidders, to obtain money for his recruiting fund. This, in turn, led him to complain that officials worked hand in glove with the nobility.

[24] Quoted by Johannes Scherr, *Blücher,* 2 vols. (Leipzig, 1865), I, p. 129.

[25] Paul Stöcklein, *Joseph von Eichendorff in Selbstzeugnissen und Bilddokumenten* (Hamburg, 1963).

administration did permit members of the nobility to sabotage any reforms which ran counter to their class interests.

Unlike in France, where the proliferation of bureaucrats caused early complaints, Prussia's poverty prevented the appointment of a sufficient number of officials—at least from the civil servants' point of view. The constant financial crises of the state also required a special type of fiscal administration. Although the king considered aristocrats to be better human beings, it was to the middle class that he turned to head the fiscal hierarchy. This led to a situation where the prestige of office lured the aristocrat; it no longer came to him because of his prestigious birth.[26]

Special Characteristics of the Regime and its Bureaucracy

Where bureaucracy is in control there is usually an executive head who both concentrates and distributes power, whether he takes the form of an absolute monarch or a dictator. The fact that eighteenth century Prussian officials were at first known as "royal servants" (an expression which probably dates back to their having administered the royal desmenes), in no way affected their position in society. On the contrary, they were seen as the crown's representatives. Once the state superseded the king, towards the end of the century, these officials came to be known as "servants of the state"—the term "official" as used today first becoming current in the nineteenth century. The king soon realized the importance of identifying with the state, whether it was in the form of *l'état c'est moi* or *der erste Diener des Staates*. When Frederick II called himself the "first servant of the state" in 1752, he recognized himself to be in an executive position over his "royal servants."

Contemporary romantic reaction to the rise of bureaucracy indicates an awareness that the system contradicted the original concept of feudal monarchy. In 1798, the young Novalis wrote: "It is incorrect to call the King the first servant of the state. The king is not a citizen, hence he cannot be a servant of the state. Monarchy is distinguished by the belief in a man of superior birth, in the voluntary acceptance of an ideal man."[27] Indeed, Frederick was not the king envisaged in the dreams of the poet Novalis. He was the head of a bureaucratic regime, in which

---

[26] The importance of high office was already emphasized at the end of the seventeenth century by the bestowal of a noble title on the officeholder. Sons of such "functional" nobles often remained faithful to the bureaucratic career for generations. Frederick II recommended their employ, because they embodied a professional tradition.

[27] Novalis, "Glauben und Liebe oder Der König und die Königin," in *Auswahl und Einleitung*, ed. Walter Rehm (Frankfurt-am-Main and Hamburg, 1956).

all decisions were subject to his authority, in which nothing occurred without his knowledge and consent. The enlightened despotism embodied by Frederick has been outlined in the blustering style of the historian Johannes Scherr:

"Enlightened" despots, however seriously and conscientiously they performed their tasks, were basically no more than rational breeders of sheep. They knew of and recognized no other progress than the one they decreed. . . . The main fault of their system lay in its generalizations, pressing everything into the same mold, the low esteem for, or rather the decided contempt for the individuality of people and nations. . . .

No citizen could flourish in the shadow of this despotic authority, which was protected jealously and with the utmost vigilance. When, in his old age, the king complained in a fit of bitter resentment that he was tired of ruling over slaves, he forgot that it was he himself who had relentlessly accustomed his "nation prussienne" to a state of slavish obedience.[28]

This submission had even infiltrated into the internal system of the bureaucracy, for although it possessed authority as an entity, its individual members were subject to the same sovereign power they represented. Criticism within the administration was prohibited no less than was external criticism. After the Seven Years' War, when the fiscal administration opposed the royal intention of increasing the annual tax levy by two million talers, tax and customs officials were imported from France to administer the excise tax. The imposition of taxes on all commodities, in a country where manpower was scarce, led to demands for higher wages. When this made manufacturers and merchants complain, the king requested the collegial General Directory (the chief body of the central administration) to investigate these matters. The resulting memorandum to the king rightly emphasized that rising wages were the direct outcome of higher taxes on meat and drink, and also criticized taxation methods. In the margin of the report the king wrote in his own hand: "I am amazed at the impertinence of this memorandum. I excuse the ministers, because they are ignorant, but those who drafted this reply are malicious and corrupt, and must be given exemplary punishment. Otherwise I will never be able to control this rabble."[29] The following day the cabinet issued a decree informing the General Directory that the Fiscal Councillor Ursinus had been removed from office and sent to the Fortress at Span-

[28] Scherr, *op. cit.,* I, pp. 54, 55 and 57.
[29] Cited in Franz Mehring, *Die Lessing-Legende* (Berlin, 1963), p. 128. English edition, *The Lessing Legend,* abr. tr., A. S. Grogan (New York, 1938).

dau. The decree further warned all those who might express similar criticisms that they could expect to be confined there for life.

However, the relationship between the autocratic head and its bureaucracy had another side to it, of which Hans Rosenberg writes

In a political system of highly concentrated personalized authoritarianism, a well-established bureaucracy could accomplish a great deal by obstructiveness and trained mediocrity. The royal servants of Prussia ultimately made the king's power inferior to their own. . . . The bureaucratic nobility functioned as the political ally of the squirearchy. . . . With the use of forged evidence . . . they succeeded in completely thwarting Frederick's modest efforts to pave the way for . . . the abolition of service labor obligations on private estates.[30]

The distrust which existed between the autocratic sovereign and the increasingly powerful bureaucracy was reflected in the *Reglements* detailing each official's duty and the distribution of work in the system. At the same time, the collegial system facilitated mutual supervision among the officials, to the point where they informed on one another. Even ministers were secret agents who submitted confidential reports on their fellow ministers to a formally organized supervisory agency. Naturally this resulted in the formation of competing cliques.

Because the Reglements were kept strictly secret, bureaucratic officials became a special caste, a kind of state priesthood. The privileges they enjoyed—such as "exemption from the payment of most taxes and from the jurisdiction of the lower courts of law"—underlined the importance of their position.[31] In the eyes of the functionaries, such preferential treatment and special status were well merited; for those who served the state were its representatives and its personification.

The State and the Economy

With all the enthusiasm of a new institution, eighteenth century Prussian bureaucracy saw to it that all social functions, especially the economy, came under state control. The government instituted monopolies and privileges, fixed wages and prices, and established accounting systems. The import of numerous commodities was prohibited, and the export of wool was made subject to the death penalty. In the interests

---

[30] Rosenberg, *op. cit.,* pp. 194–195. It is interesting that the general principle is applicable to all autocratic regimes. See Wilhelm Ensslin, "The Emperor and the Imperial Administration," in N. H. Baynes and H. St. L. B. Moss, eds., *Byzantium: An Introduction to East Roman Civilization* (Oxford, 1948).

[31] Rosenberg, *op. cit.,* p. 101.

of state revenue and the financing of the army, factories and mining were developed. Poorly managed enterprises were warned to improve and even forced to change to more profitable operations. Immediately after Frederick's accession, a special department of commerce and manufacture was set up within the General Directory, and the first specialized ministry to be formed was that of Commerce.

As "first servant of the state," the King insisted he had authority over all private property. Without special authorization and a passport, no Prussian subject could change his place of residence. Novalis complained at the end of the eighteenth century: "Since the death of Frederick William I, no state has been run more like a factory than Prussia. Though a machinelike administration may be essential to the physical well-being, strengthening and efficiency of the latter, it cannot continue to develop on that basis alone."[32]

Bureaucratic Despotism

The joint authority, feudal and bureaucratic, on which eighteenth century Prussian absolutism was based, saw that its interest lay in the suppression of the drive for personal freedom and democratic rights. It therefore had recourse to police methods. The "police state," as Otto Hintze expressed it, replaced the older system with its feudal squirearchies run in the interests of the ruling class, but which in its rudimentary form was certainly a constitutional state.[33]

The pros and cons of the "police state" have been set out by Gustav Schmoller, the state-socialist who liked to emphasize the better features of Prussian bureaucracy: "The corrupt conditions of the feudal era could only be eliminated by means of a 'police state.' . . . But it was a harsh and relentless system. The type of eudaemonistic and socialistic welfare policy it established threatened to destroy the protected private sphere of individual freedom."[34]

The police-like autocracy practiced by the Prussian sovereign has been described by numerous persons writing in that period. In 1750, Sir Charles Hanbury Williams, England's Ambassador to Prussia, reported that it was unbelievable how concerned the *pater patriae* was for the welfare of his subjects. So much so that he interfered in their most private affairs, their marriages, the education of their children, and the management

[32] Novalis, *op. cit.*
[33] Hintze, "Der Commissarius."
[34] Schmoller, *op. cit.*

of their estates. All they had was freedom of thought. All classes felt coercion, and distrust was expressed on every face. Williams quoted Hamlet to the effect that "Denmark is a prison"; he found Prussia equally so, in the literal sense of the word.[35]

Similar unfavorable impressions were recorded by an Italian poet, and by several German writers. In his autobiography, Vittorio Alfieri compared Berlin to one big army barracks, and the whole Prussian state to a single enormous, unrelieved guardroom. About the same time, in 1769, Lessing wrote his friend Nicolai that Prussia was the most despotic state in Europe. Six years later, Wieland commented in a letter to Merk that he hoped heaven would preserve him from the fate of living under the rule of Frederick's "stick." Winckelmann always referred to Prussia as the "despotic country."[36]

Criticism of literature and science, as far as it was allowed to be practiced in Prussia, was subject to bureaucratic control. When the *Hallenser Intelligenzblatt* began publishing book reviews and scientific articles in 1729 the King decreed that all professors of the medical, philosophical and law faculties had to take turns in submitting articles. These were due no later than each Thursday, and were to be written in clean, legible handwriting. Above all, scholars were asked to provide the public with "useful" truths. But the most clear-cut expression of the despotic attitude towards the critically minded individual was Frederick's decree of 1784. It has been quoted by Jürgen Habermas:

A private individual is not entitled to pass judgment on the actions, proceedings, laws, decrees and instructions of the sovereigns and their courts, their state servants, collegia and tribunals. He may not find fault with them publicly, or make known or distribute any such information which may have come to his knowledge. A private individual is incapable of passing judgment because he lacks full knowledge of the circumstances and motives."[37]

[35] Cited by Scherr, *op. cit.*, I, p. 128.
[36] Cited by Scherr, *op. cit.*, I, pp. 128–129.
[37] Cited by Jürgen Habermas, "Strukturwandel der Öffentlichkeit," *Politica*, IV (Neuwied, 1965).

THE RATIONALIST CONCEPT
OF THE STATE

Montchrétien's Treatise on Political Economy

Vilfredo Pareto once pointed out that it is not the intellectuals who create the prevailing philosophy of a period; they merely invest it with their authority.[1] Ideas which respond to strongly felt material needs can be disseminated even if no one listens to the intellectuals who are their best interpreters. A good example was the appearance of the first textbook on political economy in 1615, written and printed for the King of France by Antoine de Montchrétien. This extraordinary book, entitled *Traicté de l-Oeconomie Politique*, was never read by the king. It dealt in minutest detail with the economic activities which the state ought to undertake, but was entirely forgotten after the author was killed during a Huguenot rebellion. His ideas were borne out by subsequent events, although no one had paid attention to them at the time of their publication. Similar ideas had, however, already been expressed by Barthélemy Laffemas, who had been Henry IV's court tailor and later became his Minister of Commerce. They were eventually put into practice by Richelieu and Colbert.[2]

Montchrétien's main concern was to augment information available to the government by means of statistical surveys. In the last chapter of his book he implored the king to develop a more equitable system of taxation, since all unrest, rebellions and civil wars resulted from the extreme poverty of some of his subjects, and the extreme wealth of others. However, a just tax system required exact statistics on various professions and all sources of income.

In fact, the desire for statistics was the clearest expression of the drive toward global administration. When Colbert dispatched his *maîtres des*

[1] Vilfredo Pareto, "Réponse à René Johannet," *Cahiers Vilfredo Pareto*, no. 2 (1963). Letter originally written January 1, 1920.

[2] Barthélemy Laffemas, *Règlement général pour dresser les manufactures en ce royaume* (Rouen and Paris, 1597). Laffemas suggested that obligatory *bureaux de manufactures* be established which would provide arbitration of disputes as well as technical advice.

requêtes in 1664, to supervise the activities of the nobility, clergy and administrative officials, he also requested them to provide statistics on all financial and economic matters. He instructed them to work out a fairer system of taxation and to eliminate the cause of poverty. It was almost as if he wished to put Montchrétien's theories into practice.

Some Thoughts on the Nature and Tasks of the State

The emergence of the modern state naturally sparked new speculation on its nature and purposes, and the instrumentalities by which men could live together within a rational system. The new ideas, opposed as they were to the chaos of feudal tradition, actually favored an organized central authority to control the myriad competing local interests.

It took a long time, however, to resolve the incongruity between the desire to analyze the world statistically and the results actually obtained. For example, although torture, the galley and even hanging were stipulated in Milan, in 1749, to punish falsified harvest reports, the declared amount of grain was about a million bushels below that actually harvested.[3]

Practically speaking, rational thought and concepts developed in those administrative offices where the affairs of state were conducted. Activities dealing with road and bridge building, construction of fortresses and the science of war, all of them early concerns of central administration, encouraged the growth of rational concepts.

The declining feudal world regarded bureaucratic "pen-pushers" with contempt, but the emerging business-oriented bourgeois class, the growth of mechanized industry and consequent division of labor, all encouraged the spirit of rationalism. Bookkeeping and regulated work were of common concern to state institutions and the rising business class, as were currency systems and weights and measures. Pascal—who felt the world required despotic governments because it was corrupt—invented a calculating machine for the purpose of computing taxes.

Thomas Hobbes Contrasts the Rational "Artificial" State with the Natural State of Anarchy

The political concept of the omnipotent state as necessary to the rational organization of social life was first articulated strongly

[3] Giovanni Valentino Mattia Fabroni, *Dei provvedimenti annonarj* (Firenze, 1817).

and logically by Thomas Hobbes, who was later seen as the apostle of true evil by the feudal system's last great admirer, Karl Ludwig von Haller, the Swiss philosopher.[4]

It has been debated whether Hobbes is to be considered a defender of absolute monarchy, or a prophet of bourgeois rationalism. What is important, however, is that he developed a complete theory of the state. Within the context of his time, his concepts were too advanced. He saw the absolute monarchy as only one of several possible systems, for his central concern was the power of the state considered apart from the form in which it was expressed. It was his belief that each society required the guidance of a powerful central authority.

One and a half centuries later, Karl Ludwig von Haller proposed a romantic and utopian theory of the natural social state versus the illusion of the artificial civic one. Hobbes, however, saw the "natural" state as an expression of unbearable anarchy, in contrast to which he developed his idea of the "artificial" state: "For by Art is created that great LEVIATHAN . . . which is but an Artificiall Man; though of greater stature and strength than the Naturall, for whose protection and defence it was intended."[5]

It was Hobbes' intention to invest the state with total authority and thus prevent the civil wars which were part of the feudal or "natural" system, for reason requires that we strive for peace. Hobbes' Leviathan, the mortal god, was to be the instrument that would ensure peace. Only a sovereign state could serve as arbiter between individuals and groups who disagree. Society needed a uniform authority, whatever its form, which would demand obedience. This central power could brook no individual opinion since a man's conscience and judgment were subject to error. Even religion was to be controlled by the state, for no one could serve two masters. This would also apply to political parties, since their existence led to civil war, and since each party potentially was the seed of a new state in the bosom of the old one.

While Hobbes' doctrine rejected feudalism, it by no means favored a bourgeois concept of property, which he considered tolerable only as long as it was subject to state control. For the state to function properly it had to regulate all activities of its subjects: the will of the state had to control the will of the people. Only certain liberties were to be permit-

---

[4] See Chapter IV for further discussion of Karl Ludwig von Haller's *Restauration der Staatswissenschaft* (Winterthur, 1816).

[5] Thomas Hobbes, *Leviathan or the Matter, Forme and Power of a Common-Wealth Ecclesiasticall and Civill*, ed. W. G. P. Smith (Oxford, 1965), p. 8.

ted to the citizens: the ability to buy and sell, to make contracts with others, the choice of profession and the education of children. Foreign trade, however, was to be administered by the state.

Hobbes subscribed to a mercantilist, or more accurately, state-socialistic economic theory. He was basically suspicious of the merchant, whom he considered to be guilty of rebellious tendencies because: "His grievances are but taxes, to which citizens, that is merchants, whose profession is their private gain, are naturally mortal enemies, their only glory being to grow exclusively rich by the wisdom of buying and selling."[6]

He saw land and labor as the basis for the wealth of society. Since, according to the law of nature, everybody had a share in the land, the state was to regulate its distribution. Hobbes conceived of labor as an exchangeable commodity. Those who were incapable of work were not to be left to the charity of private institutions, but were to be provided for by the state. Those who were able-bodied were to be forced by law to work.

Hobbes' concept of the absolute state was nevertheless founded on good faith. He did not see himself as a defender of tyranny, but as a believer in the rule of reason. It was left to later writers, such as Feuerbach in the eighteenth century and Vialatoux in our era, to suggest that Hobbes' ideas advocated the suppression of individual freedom, that they would lead to despotism and the totalitarian state. Their projected fears that rational authority could be transformed into an irrational force if pushed to extremes, have been borne out by events in the twentieth century.[7]

The State as "Work of Art" and Promoter of Welfare

The theory of a rational state power, whether based on Hobbes' philosophical premises or the political and economic considerations of Montchrétien, was developed in the seventeenth century in the belief that it best served the purposes of a well-organized society. Montchrétien was convinced that state control of the economy would enrich the country and lead to a more just distribution of its wealth. Hobbes was also a serious, moral person; and if he treated the science

[6] Thomas Hobbes, *Behemoth* (London, 1680), (New York, 1962).
[7] Paul Johann Anselm von Feuerbach, *Anti-Hobbes, oder aber die Grenzen der höchsten Gewalt und das Zwangsrecht der Bürger gegen den Oberherrn* (Erfurt, 1798); and J. Vialatoux, *La Cité de Hobbes: Théorie de l'Etat totalitaire* (Paris, 1935).

of politics with mathematical detachment (as did Spinoza and other learned men of his time), he did so because he felt it was necessary for the promotion of peace and the public good.[8]

Whatever were the brutality, corruption and other defects of absolute monarchy, it did result in the theory of an intricate administrative network which operated to the benefit of all. This image was projected not only by apologists and propagandists of royal power, but also by those utopian visionaries who wanted to create the best of all possible worlds. Utopian visions accompanied the development of the modern state. They were rationalistic in nature, very different from the chiliastic ecstasies of the religiously inspired rebellions agitating the dying medieval world. Once the traditional patchwork of autonomous local powers was replaced by an increasingly centralized and coordinated governmental system, once the state was seen as a "work of art," the idea of a "perfectible" work of art inevitably followed.

Such a perfect "work of art" was described by Tommaso Campanella, a Calabrian monk and imprisoned rebel, in his *Civitas solis poetica: idea reipublicae philosophicae,* 1643.[9] His *City of the Sun* was to be governed by an all-powerful ruler, the *Great Metaphysicus,* whose authority even extended to the selection of marriage partners and to sexual relations. Bureaucratic control was also present on the island Utopia of Sir Thomas More, the archetype of all utopias, where the inhabitants' movements were subject to permission from the authorities and to their possession of a passport.[10] In another ideal state, that of the Sevarambes, conceived by Denis Vairasse d'Allais, all men were equal under the law of nature. However, administrative officials responsible for the distribution of goods were better housed, fed and clothed than the average citizen.[11]

The concept of rational utilization of centralized state power also influenced political philosophies in the eighteenth century. Encyclopedists no less than Physiocrats set their hopes on enlightened despotism. Peru, China, Egypt and even the Russia of Catherine II became examples for

[8] For a discussion of Hobbes' moral stance, see Julius Lips, *Die Stellung des Thomas Hobbes zu den politischen Parteien der grossen englischen Revolution* (Leipzig, 1927), especially Introduction by Ferdinand Tönnies.

[9] Friedrich Meinecke, in *Die Idee der Staatsraison in der neueren Geschichte* (Berlin, 1925), points out that Campanella did not regard this "work of art" as an utopian Ideal but as something perfectly attainable. English edition, *Machiavellism: the Doctrine of raison d'état and its Place in Modern History,* tr. Douglas Scott (London, 1957).

[10] Sir Thomas More, *De optimo reipublicae statu deque nova insula Utopia* (1615).

[11] Denis Vairasse d'Allais, *Histoire des Sevarambes* (Paris, 1677).

the enlightenment, admired by men like Diderot, D'Alembert and Voltaire.[12]

In his study of prerevolutionary France, de Tocqueville commented that the Physiocrats wanted the state to transform the entire nation. Since they found no model around them conforming to their ideals, they looked for one in the heart of Asia. De Tocqueville claimed it was no exaggeration to say that every one of the Physiocrats included a eulogy of China in his writing.[13] This is borne out by the works of men like the Abbé Baudeau, or Johann Heinrich Gottlob von Justi. The latter compared European with the supposedly barbarian governments of Asia, but found Chinese administrations to be the best and most efficient for his purpose. Von Justi was able to point to the well-planned fiscal organization, and to the fact that in spite of their great numbers, the mandarins were considered to be the servants of the state and the fathers of their people and indeed functioned as such.[14]

In an earlier work, von Justi had already developed his idea of state officials acting as parents who were responsible for the moral and physical well-being of the population. He conceived of administration—known in his times as *Polizeiwissenschaft*—as the procedures and institutions whereby the wealth of the state is established on a permanent basis and is used efficiently to ensure universal prosperity and welfare. Von Justi saw administrative control as operating in three main areas: personal possessions, real estate, and the moral condition of the subjects. Above all, he was concerned that the government involve itself in the people's welfare by encouraging agriculture and manufacturing; by seeing that sufficient food was available at reasonable prices; and by providing for the aged and invalids unable to earn their living. He actually drew up a fully developed theory of the welfare state. The beautification of cities,

[12] Karl Marx pointed out that the tendency to see in Russia the protector of liberalism and national aspirations was nothing new. He alluded to the celebration of Catherine II as a standard-bearer of progress by a whole host of French and German representatives of the enlightenment. See Karl Marx, *Herr Vogt* (Berlin, 1953), p. 146. This pamphlet was first published in 1860.

[13] Alexis de Tocqueville, *L'Ancien régime et la révolution,* ed. I. P. Mayer (Paris, 1964), pp. 259–261. Original publication date was 1856. English edition, *De Tocqueville's L'Ancien Régime,* tr. M. W. Patterson (Oxford, 1956).

[14] See Nicolas Baudeau, *Première Introduction à la philosophie économique ou analyse des états policées, par un disciple de l'ami des hommes* (Paris, 1776); and Johann Heinrich Gottlob von Justi, *Vergleichungen der Europäischen mit den Asiatischen und anderen vermeintlich Barbarischen Regierungen* (Berlin, Stettin and Leipzig, 1762). The first to turn against the admiration of China, against the image of a government which submits all actions of its subjects to a fixed rule of conduct, was the Mainz Jacobin Georg Foster in a 1793 essay, "Über die Beziehung der Staatskunst auf das Glück der Menschheit."

obligatory fire insurance, public education, dowries for brides—nothing was forgotten. He was anxious, however, to distinguish between his system and that of the despotic state where, he pointed out, administration is limited to the collection of taxes on bread and meat, to the removal of wastes, the maintenance of street-lighting and the appointment of night-watchmen.

The question of public criticism was a problem for von Justi. While he felt constructive criticism to be necessary, he was against the expression of ideas which would interfere with the state's peaceful functioning. His remedy was to suggest a system of book censorship, to control what scholars wanted to *publish* although without infringing on their freedom of *thought.*[15]

The Age of Enlightenment seemed to have developed the outlines of a prudently administered welfare state, in which freedom was to be dispensed in cautious doses. The century which had elapsed between Hobbes' "Leviathan" and von Justi's "administration" had done much to produce the detailed theory of such a state. It was believed that as soon as the "philosophes" developed the principles of wise administration, sovereigns would adopt them and thus achieve happiness for their people.

---

[15] Johann Heinrich Gottlob von Justi, *Die Grundfeste zu der Macht und Glückseligkeit der Staaten oder ausführliche Vorstellung der gesamten Polizeiwissenschaft* (Königsberg and Leipzig, 1760).

REACTIONS TO BUREAUCRACY

In Defense of Feudalism

It was natural that the first attack on the centralized bureaucratic state should come from those whose authority had been taken away. For centuries the feudal barons had tenaciously resisted any encroachment on their power. Under Louis XIV, the old nobility had neither power nor political influence, the sum of their privileges being confined to their exemption from taxes. Their spokesmen complained about this "unnatural" state of affairs, but as they were forbidden to express their criticism in France, their writings were published in Holland. These aristocrats discovered similarities between absolute monarchy and the bureaucratic despotism of oriental society. Pamphlets appearing around 1686 bore titles such as *La Cour de France turkonisée*, or *Het France Turckye*. The latter claimed that France resembled Turkey in that no one owned anything and no one could undertake actions against the wishes of the king because the means for such action had been taken away from the people. Another illegal publication, which appeared in 1689, complained specifically about the repressive measures taken against the nobility by the royal intendants.

In a comprehensive history of the kings of France, published in the Hague five years after his death, Henri de Boulainvilliers showed that it was the aim of the monarchy to destroy the aristocracy. He not only compared French monarchical government to that of China and the Tatars, but concluded that Richelieu, and after him Louis XIV, had gone further towards destroying the nobility than any previous regime.[1] Another nobleman, the Duke de Saint-Simon (1675–1755), sent Louis XV an anonymous memorandum in which he listed all the privileges taken

[1] Henri de Boulainvilliers, *Histoire de l'ancien gouvernement de la France*, 3 vols. (La Haye and Amsterdam, 1727). English edition, *An Historical Account of the Ancient Parliaments of France, or States-General of the Kingdom*, 2 vols., tr. Charles Forman (London, 1739).

away from the aristocracy. He complained that the intendants' actions determined whether a prince on his estates could still be distinguished from his vassals or peasants. Saint-Simon cited all the offices which could easily be abolished, and he was most indignant that provinces were being administered by officials, or *les gens d'écriture* as he called them, instead of by feudal princes. As a true aristocrat, he himself had turned down the position offered him, only serving as Ambassador to Spain in an honorary capacity. Above all, he was vexed by the type of information required for statistical data, which had gone beyond such matters as property and population, and exposed the most important family secrets.[2]

Justus Möser—A Defender of Local Authority

The feudal nobility was not alone in expressing such criticism of the rational organization of the state. The problems of the new institutions were less clearly delineated in Germany, where the disintegration of the feudal system in the multitude of small principalities progressed more slowly. Justus Möser (1720–1794), a learned patrician, lawyer and official of the provincial Diet of Osnabrück, became a defender of traditional institutions against "abstract rationalism." He attacked the "current trend toward universally applicable laws and decrees," which "endanger common liberties," and contrasted "local common sense" with bureaucratic centralization. He accused the General Directory of trying to govern the country on the basis of academic theories, of wishing to give each councillor of the Directory authority over local officials. Greater diversity in legislation was essential, according to Möser, if freedom were to be preserved.

Möser proposed that local officials be controlled by a central administration with the help of "accurate charts and tables." This would not prevent each prince from having his own regulations, each small town from having its own administrative code, or each peasant community from enjoying its own particular privileges and rights. He also wanted judges to base their decisions on local laws and traditions. It was his criticism of centralization that too many general decrees were issued and too few of them enforced.[3]

---

[2] Louis de Rouvroy, Duke de Saint-Simon, *Mémoires* (Paris, 1947). English edition, *The Memoirs of the Duke of Saint-Simon on the Reign of Louis XIV, and the Regency,* tr. Bayle St. John (London, 1900).

[3] Justus Möser, *Patriotische Phantasien* (Berlin, 1778).

A Professor from Bern Blames the "Philosophes"

What the absolute monarchy had created and what it had destroyed was most clearly set forth by Ludwig von Haller some time after its demise in France and after its foundations had been shaken in all other countries under the onslaught of the bourgeoisie.[4] Von Haller criticized the bureaucratic state in terms not very different from those used by France's former feudal barons against the administration of Richelieu and Colbert. He was obsessed by the vision of an ideal feudal state, and because his orientation was toward the past he was able to provide sharp insights into the nature of the modern state. Going beyond the current battle over whether the state was to be ruled according to the principles of the *ancien régime* or the wishes of the bourgeoisie, he placed himself in hostile opposition to the whole idea of the modern state.[5] He understood the radical changes which had taken place and was prepared to place more blame on Louis XIV than on the Revolution.

While the politicians were fighting over who should administer taxes, and over who should be taxed and how, von Haller saw in taxation simply a newly invented evil. In his idealized feudal society, the prince as "independent lord of the manor" had no right to demand tribute from his subjects. Only in dire need was he allowed to ask for taxes, which his "free subjects" would then approve. The same held for military service. Service and assistance were matters for the local parliaments, and subject to contract. Von Haller considered Prussia under Frederick II to be the purest existing example of the artificial state, where the royal legal code turned human beings into civil slaves.[6]

Austria, under Joseph II, suffered from similar evils, according to von Haller. Administrative officials replaced princes in functions where they had no business to be. They no longer concerned themselves with administering the affairs of the emperor, but controlled the people and their private activities.

[4] Karl Ludwig von Haller, *Restauration der Staatswissenschaft oder Theorie des natürlichgesellschaftlichen Zustandes der Chimäre des künstlich-bürgerlichen entgegengesetzt* (Winterthur, 1816).

[5] Haller's liberal critics could not understand this attitude. One of his admirers, Karl Ernst Jarcke, remarked that the distorting superficiality of the liberals was revealed in the fact that with few exceptions his contemporaries considered von Haller to be the most extreme absolutist ever to have lived. See K. E. Jarcke, *Vermischte Schriften,* 3 vols. (München, 1839), I, p. 133.

[6] When Alexis de Tocqueville studied Frederick's code, he found that while it was still partially feudalistic in concept, essentially it reflected the principles of the absolute state. It no longer spoke of royal power but of state power. Above all, it supported the principle of universal taxation and centralized administration, and made the state responsible for helping the poor and keeping them at work. Frederick's successor revoked this code as being too revolutionary. See Alexis de Tocqueville, *L'Ancien régime et la révolution,* ed. I. P. Mayer (Paris, 1964), p. 345.

Von Haller could not countenance the head of the state as an expression of so-called universal will, or as the "first servant of the state." To him princes were free individuals who managed their own affairs, not those of others. He saw "natural states," in contrast to the new "artificial states," as consisting of "autonomous social spheres," and "independent relationships between services and communities." Von Haller blamed the "philosophes" whose mistaken theories had contributed to the establishment of the artificial state. But his main blame was reserved for Thomas Hobbes, whom he regarded as the true apostle of state sovereignty. He warned that the end result of such a system could only be what he called an "unlimited Césaro-Papacy," an omnipotent temporal and spiritual dictatorship.

The Enemies of Bureaucracy in Power

The question now arose as to whether the "anti-philosophes," those whose doctrine was opposed to the errors of the "philosophes," were in a position to restore the natural state—at least in those countries where their students and disciples were attaining political power. In France it was Bonald and de Maistre, both born in 1754, who expressed the doctrine of restoration. Bonald believed that the only effect of human intervention was simply to prevent society from coming into its natural state.[7] De Maistre held that the revolutionary spirit could be checked by disseminating the doctrine that society possessed an unchangeable natural order to which man must submit.[8]

At the very moment that disciples of these doctrines gained power, their reactions to man's impotence in the face of inevitable historic trends proved quite different from what had been expected. With the overthrow of Napoleon, a king had come to power in the person of Louis XVIII who represented the medieval concept that the king never dies. He consequently dated his reign from the death of Louis XVI's son, during the Revolution. It was not until 1820 however, after the assassination of the Duke de Berry, that the truly ultraradical proponents of the "natural state" like the Count de Villèle, sworn enemies of Napoleonic state structure, came into their own. This period has been examined in detail

[7] Louis Gabriel Ambroise de Bonald, "Théorie du pouvoir politique et religieux," in *Oeuvres,* 2 vols. (Paris, 1854).

[8] Joseph Marie de Maistre, "Etude sur la souveraineté," in *Oeuvres complètes,* 14 vols. (Lyon, 1884–1887).

by Alan B. Spitzer, who discusses the fate of Napoleon's administrative system under the "ultra" ministry:

The power that had at last been gathered into the hands of an ultra ministry resided most of all in the apparatus of the centralized administrative state so often criticized by its new masters. . . . the prefect [was] the most important local police official and political agent of the ministry at a time when the national administrative machine was operated with authentic Napoleonic rigor by former advocates of decentralization and local autonomies. . . . The parliamentary leader of the ultras, the Comte de Villèle, also decried (before assuming office) the political dangers of concentrating all power in Paris. In an eloquent speech on the budget for 1818 he deplored the conservation of "precisely the most appropriate administrative system for despotism that had ever been invented." . . . no government could resist the temptation to exploit this modern instrument of political direction and control. . . . the projects to reform the over-centralized Napoleonic state were not to be realized under the Bourbons.[9]

Another historian, Georges Weill, pointed out that the civil servant actually originated in the time of Napoleon. The *ancien régime* had used commissaires but they lacked solidarity; the provinces had their own officials—the magistrates—who did not consider themselves part of the group appointed directly by the king. Under Napoleon all officials were appointed by the state to whose central authority they owed allegiance. In the years 1814 and 1815, according to Weill, it was believed that the new bureaucracy would undergo serious setbacks in its confrontation with those who espoused decentralization. It was anticipated that the former provinces would be restored, but nothing came of this. In 1814, when Villèle suggested to the Duke d'Angoulème (the subsequent successor to the throne) that he return its ancient rights to the province of Languedoc, the Duke replied: "We prefer the departments to the provinces." In the Chamber, opponents of centralization existed on the right and left of the political spectrum. Royer-Collard is quoted by Weill as saying: "Centralization has turned us into an administered nation and put us in the hands of irresponsible officials who are themselves controlled by a central authority."[10]

Weill shows that some reform was attempted between 1821 and 1828, but that nothing came of it. No government likes to consent to the reduction of its own power, and ministers do not want to relinquish their authority. The Restoration actually became the golden period of bureau-

---

[9] Alan B. Spitzer, "The Bureaucrat as Proconsul: the Restoration Prefect and the *Police Générale*," *Comparative Studies in Society and History,* VII, no. 4 (1965), pp. 371-372.

[10] Georges Weill, *La France sous la monarchie constitutionelle (1814-1848)* (Paris, 1912), pp. 104-105.

cracy. The prefect chose members of the *conseil général,* and appointed the mayors; and it was he who, through an active and suspicious police system, spied on individuals considered to be dangerous.

What happened, in fact, was that the government of those ultraradical disciples of the theory of the "natural state," those representatives of feudal reaction, had surrendered to the bureaucratic state. Even the most violent *ressentiments* of a class which had long since lost the real basis of its power did not suffice to undo what had been done. Nor could hymns of praise to the good old times reverse this trend. Those idealized "days of yore" were portrayed by the German poet Joseph Freiherr von Eichendorff in "Der Adel und die Revolution," where he writes: "Those days were neither good nor old but a caricature of what had once been good. The sword had become the gallant's rapier, the helmet a wig, the lord of the castle had turned into a retired colonel. Long ago his ancestors had looted the merchants as they passed by the castle; now he lived on his lonely country estate, besieged and hemmed in by manufacturers."[11]

[11] Joseph Freiherr von Eichendorff, "Der Adel und die Revolution," in *Aus dem literarischen Nachlass* (Paderborn, 1866).

THE NINETEENTH CENTURY: INDIVIDUALISM VERSUS THE BUREAUCRACY

The Unrestrained Development of Economic Egoism and the Early Welfare State

As the economic bonds of feudalism were severed and the autonomy of medieval social institutions ended, two groups of isolated individuals were created: a mass of people without property, employment or homes, and a class of self-interested industrial entrepreneurs. A need was now felt for a central authority to control this new situation in which each man looked only to his own advancement.

In its development of industry and commerce, the mercantile protectionist system necessarily produced capitalist entrepreneurs. As the medieval economy based on handicrafts was replaced by a market economy, a new type of economic man was created. New legal concepts were developed to protect property acquired as a result of the growing economy, which found their most radical expression in article 16 of the Girondists' constitutional draft of 1793, namely: "Property rights permit every citizen to dispose of his property and income as he sees fit."

Hobbes anticipated nothing but chaos from a system which allowed bourgeois profit motives to dominate society. In *Behemoth*, he described merchants as self-seekers who saw taxation for the benefit of the state only as an obstacle to their own acquisition of wealth. German philosophers echoed Hobbes' fears of the acquisitive instinct and its consequences. Fichte regarded bourgeois economy as a permanent competitive struggle which would end in a dictatorial state; and Hegel believed it was incumbent upon the state to curb the economic self-interest developing in society.

Indeed, the bureaucracy found itself responsible for the two disparate classes of isolated individuals mentioned earlier. If only to prevent anarchy, it assumed this task during the earliest period of capital accumulation. Already, in the fifteenth and sixteenth centuries, England began providing for the vast number of wandering beggars and paupers. Elizabeth I instituted the famous Poor Law (1601)—largely for military considerations—which ensured the general right to work, the supply of tools and housing, and which allowed each agricultural laborer a cottage and at least four acres of land.[1] Under Henry IV of France, the peasant was protected against seizure of his livestock and tools. Later, Mazarin's administration established hospitals for the poor. Finally under Colbert the Parisian *Conseil de Police* was organized and the capital transformed into a modern city through guaranteed water supplies and public sanitation.

New administrative concepts concerning the role of government in law and order, and the availability of manpower for a mercantile economy, soon clashed with medieval attitudes towards work and life. Once feudal organizations were broken up, the enclosure system instituted and a market economy established, large numbers of beggars and tramps roamed the countryside, rejecting the new discipline of regular work, or else prepared to work only for their immediate needs. This led to their being tortured, hanged, shut away on galleys or sent to the workhouse. All rational thinkers of the sixteenth and seventeenth centuries recommended forced labor institutions, Lafférmas (Henry IV's councillor) no less than Hobbes.

Bureaucratic administrations used a dual system of force and welfare to establish order in the confusion resulting from the economic transformation of Europe. Even if force prevailed over welfare measures at first, the state was at last aware of its obligations for the welfare of the people.

Adolph Wagner, the so-called state or *Katheder* socialist, indicated that without being aware of it, the absolute welfare state laid the foundation for the principle of "the reproductivity of taxes." It did this by using government funds for necessary and useful administrative functions, by the provision of effective protection and legislation, and by promoting the best interests of the people. However, he did add that the absolute monarchy never did anything through the people themselves, but always acted paternalistically on their behalf.[2]

---

[1] It was a great day for the British middle class when the Poor Law was repealed in 1834.

[2] Adolph Wagner, "Finanzwissenschaft und Staatssozialismus," *Zeitschrift Für die gesamte Staatswissenschaft* (1887).

Other nineteenth century writers, among them the historian Sismondi and the English economist John Barton, concerned themselves with the changes brought about by the new economy. Reviewing Barton's two publications bearing on the English working class, Sismondi pointed out an apparent paradox.[3] He showed Barton maintaining that real wages had decreased between the middle of the eighteenth and the first decade of the nineteenth century, whereas England's population had increased by two-and-one-quarter million within a quarter of a century.[4] Sismondi commented that this demonstrated how the health of the working class had improved in an era when its economic condition had worsened. While improved medical science was in part responsible, Sismondi noted that medical attention required a certain income. General advances in science, he felt, and the ways in which the government made use of them, contributed to the greater well-being of the populace. The administrative system was responsible for such things as better building standards, the proper ventilation of houses, and the prompt removal of refuse. It also improved water supplies and prevented spoiled foodstuffs from reaching the market. In this way Sismondi explained that the life expectancy of the poor grew at the very moment when their economic level declined.

Alexis de Tocqueville Discovers the Continuity of the Bureaucratic System

At no time was the absolute monarchy primarily a welfare state. In fact its welfare policies were largely conducted by a police system. It was precisely during the "enlightened" period of the authoritarian regime that police measures became comprehensive and were supported by a system of permanent records.[5] As new methods developed in com-

[3] See John Barton, *Observations on the Circumstances which Influence the Condition of the Labouring Classes of Society* (London, 1817), p. 92; and *An Inquiry into the Causes of the Progressive Depreciation of Agricultural Labour in Modern Times, with Suggestions for its Remedy* (London, 1820), p. 128. See also Sismonde de Sismondi, "Observations," *Annales de législation et d'économie politique,* I (1822).

[4] The decline in real wages in England was related to the increase in prices resulting from the war against France in 1793, and the passage of the Speenhamland Act in 1795. The latter guaranteed everyone an income corresponding to a given quantity of bread. Although this assured the necessities of life, wages actually paid sank below the guaranteed minimum since workers were partially paid from public relief funds. It was not until the Poor Law reform of 1834 ended the Speenhamland Act that the freedom of the labor market was restored and the triumph of economic individualism assured.

[5] For example, in Austria a program was proposed in 1768 for training police officials, emphasizing the secrecy of their duties. It was precisely under the truly enlightened monarchies of Joseph II and Leopold II that such a police bureaucracy developed. See Denis Silagi, *Jakobiner in der Habsburger Monarchie: Ein Beitrag zur Geschichte des aufgeklärten Absolutismus in Österreich* (Wien, 1962).

merce and industry, administrative intervention became more difficult for bourgeois entrepreneurs to bear. They had the new intelligentsia on their side, who found that the state's authoritarian supervision and censorship were stifling. That is why the great transformation of society, which followed in the wake of the French Revolution, was celebrated all over Europe as the beginning of civil liberties and self-government for the people. The nineteenth century witnessed an upsurge of liberal ideas and attitudes; a man like Ludwig von Haller was regarded as a reactionary crackpot for wishing to return to a "natural state."[6] But his colleague Sismondi was one of those who expressed the prevailing feeling of vitality in their work. "The European," Sismondi wrote, "congratulates himself on being born into the nineteenth, and not one of the other earlier centuries."[7] It was evident that von Haller's contemporaries did not share his fears that the "artificial" state would turn into an omnipotent dictatorship.

With the exception of Russia and Turkey, authoritarian regimes were on the decline, and progress could no longer be halted. It was a time when the last remains of medieval ties and privileges were done away with; when links to land and guilds were broken; when markets expanded beyond old, narrow frontiers and there were no limits to capitalist enterprise. The famous Prussian edict of October 9, 1807, dealing with the free use of land and the emancipation of the peasants, stated in its preamble that it was in the interests of justice and the principles of a well-organized national economy that all barriers be removed which had prevented the individual from achieving the prosperity to which he was entitled by his own efforts.

Technical innovations and the spirit of rationalism now replaced fusty traditions. Representative of this progress was the bourgeoisie which began to occupy important administrative positions. Not much attention was paid to the fact that the concept of the modern state had outlived its creator—the absolute monarchy—and was doing well in the soil of the capitalist system. Balzac, however, did not fail to notice its growth. In his analysis of contemporary society, *Les Employés,* he wrote in 1838 that the bureaucracy was a gigantic power which had developed in 1789 as a result of the replacement of the sovereign by the state.

When de Tocqueville began to examine American democracy in 1832, he also looked into the origins of the bureaucratic state. He found that

---

[6] See Chapter IV, p. 00 (62) passim.

[7] Jean Charles Leonard Sismonde di Sismondi, "Du Prince dans les pays libres ou du pouvoir executif," *Annales de législation et d'économie politique,* I (1822).

the disappearance of traditional institutions, and the development of a system under which the individual concentrated exclusively on his own affairs, led to greater state control of social functions. General apathy toward public affairs "must almost compulsorily concentrate the direction of all men and the management of all things in the hands of the adminis-ctration."[8]

For a better understanding of modern democracy, de Tocqueville turned to the study of prerevolutionary France. To his surprise he discovered that the modern state had grown out of the ancien régime. The Revolution had not halted the process of centralization. On the contrary, it had continued and expanded the administrative system it took over from the absolute monarchy. The abolition of feudal privileges only helped to strengthen the trend toward central administration. De Tocqueville pointed out how at the beginning of the Revolution, Mirabeau had already stated that equality before the law did not contradict the true principle of the absolute state. Mirabeau had written to the king that such acts as the abolition of the nobility's privileges could only serve to strengthen royal power. (Richelieu would have been delighted by the idea of having a single class of subjects.) Mirabeau had also written that equality would facilitate the use of executive power; indeed, one year of the Revolution had accomplished more for royal authority than had all the many years of absolutism.[9]

In fact, more than half a century after the Revolution, de Tocqueville discovered that the bureaucratic administration had far greater authority than that exercised by the absolute monarchy. The latter had never been able to enforce its decrees effectively, but had succeeded in the negative task of destroying intermediate autonomous institutions which stood between the individual and the central power.

Another Frenchman, Dupont-White, was also impressed by the superiority of the liberal bourgeois administrative system over that of autocratic regimes.[10] He contrasted England with tsarist Russia, which was considered the dreaded enemy of liberal Europe in the midnineteenth century. He concluded that the liberal English governmental system was much more effective and comprehensive than that of Russia, which had far less authority over society.

[8] Alexis de Tocqueville, *De la démocratie en Amérique*, 4 vols. (Paris, 1835). English ediiion, *Democracy in America*, tr. Henry Reeve (New York, 1945).

[9] Alexis de Tocqueville, *L'Ancien régime et la révolution*, ed. I. P. Mayer (Paris, 1964), p. 65. Original date of publication was 1856. English edition, *De Tocqueville's L'Ancien Régime*, tr. M. W. Patterson (Oxford, 1956).

[10] Charles Brook Dupont-White, *L'individu et l'état* (Paris, 1857).

Karl Marx agreed with de Tocqueville's observation that while the forms of government changed, administrations continued uninterruptedly to accumulate more functions and responsibilities. He expressed his ideas in the pamphlet against Bonaparte, *Der Achzehnte Brumaire des Louis-Bonaparte:*

This executive authority, with its enormous bureaucratic and military organization, its extensive, ingenious state apparatus—an army of half a million officials side by side with another half-million soldiers—this terrible parasite which clings to the body of French society and clogs its pores, developed during the time of the absolute monarchy. . . . The first French Revolution . . . had to expand what the absolute monarchy had begun, namely centralization. . . . Napoleon completed the apparatus . . . All revolutions end by perfecting this machine, instead of destroying it. The political parties which vie with one another for control of the nation, look on the bureaucratic system as their prime booty.[11]

De Tocqueville's Analysis of the Bureaucratic State

The conclusions reached by de Tocqueville in his penetrating analysis of the American democratic system helped him formulate certain general theories regarding the importance of expanding governmental activity everywhere. He saw that the tendency of the modern state to make all men equal reflected democratic aspirations. However, he recognized that equality only facilitates the growth and influence of a central power. The influence and activity of the state is felt in all sectors of public life, from regulating trade and commerce and providing for the working class, to the construction of roads, canals and harbors.

De Tocqueville also pointed out the isolating effect the bureaucratic system had on the individual. Modern industry had thrown a multitude of individuals together, bereft of social ties except those of the family, and without local authorities to whom they could turn for protection. Because they needed some system of authority, they invested the centralized bureaucratic structure with ever greater powers. The administration of such an organization grew more and more complicated and required an increasing number of officials. De Tocqueville feared that the expansion of bureaucracy would end for Christian nations in a despotism comparable only to that existing in oriental society. He condemned the universal apathy which might put society in the hands of dictators.

[11] Karl Marx, "Der Achzehnte Brumaire des Louis-Bonaparte," *Die Revolution* (New York, 1852). Reprinted in Karl Marx-Friedrich Engels, *Werke* (Frankfurt, 1966), IV, *see* especially pp. 111–112. English edition, *The Eighteenth Brumaire of Louis Bonaparte* (Moscow, 1967).

A historical myth exists that bourgeois liberalism restrained state power. However, historical reality did not correspond to the ideal envisaged by liberal nineteenth century ideologists. The principal result of the bourgeois social system was the individual's emancipation from the fetters of feudal restrictions. Freedom of movement replaced bondage, personal freedom was substituted for dependence on a feudal master. Religious freedom led to more general freedom of thought and ended the clerical monopoly of knowledge. The abolition of the guild system allowed the individual his choice of profession and liberty in exercising it. But while the history of the decline of feudalism can be understood as liberation of the individual, one can wonder if this really served the best interests of the world. For the feudal ties were not merely restrictive; they also protected the individual.

Economic Liberalism Versus State Intervention

Because in the bourgeois-capitalist world the individual was left to his own devices insofar as his economic existence was concerned, he became self-centered and apathetic toward public affairs. This apathy, which de Tocqueville saw as one of the basic causes of the expansion of state power, was for Marx the expression of apolitical man, the passive product of a disintegrating society. However much the increase in state activities, centralization of social functions or the absolute monarchy impressed the Duke de Saint-Simon or Ludwig von Haller, one must retrospectively admit how weak and circumscribed this power actually was. For a long time the central authorities still found themselves in constant competition with local and regional powers, since their efficiency was hampered by the difficulties of communication. It was not until the emergence of the constitutional state that a rational bureaucratic system gained control over dying local autonomy. Writing at the end of the nineteenth century, Adolph Wagner pointed out that state activities were increasing rather than decreasing, as liberal theory would have required. In the fields of law, defense, culture and welfare, governmental activities increased at the same time that legislators endorsed economic liberalism. The growth of bureaucracy in a period of economic individualism was one of the greater ironies of history.

In the eighteenth century, Adam Smith had reproached Colbert with trying to organize the industry and commerce of a great nation as if they were departments of a public office. This was contrary to the liberal plan of equality, liberty and justice for all.[12]

The desire to pursue one's own interests without restraint was echoed over and over again by the lords of industry. They saw private business as an autonomous area which was not to be invaded by public administration. They achieved private independence on the basis of their capital, but it did not lead to their becoming a new feudal power. The industrial knight could not retire to his castle, since all interests were closely tied to those of society and the state. The state, in its turn, promoted industrialization where it deemed it profitable. This relationship between state and industry has been studied by Ulrich Peter Ritter with regard to Prussia.[13] He found that Prussian officials were not convinced by Adam Smith's theory of nonintervention. They believed that state promotion of industry was essential to prosperity.

Prussia with its powerful bureaucratic structure was by no means unique in its economic policy. In discussing the effects of economic intervention in England, Karl Polanyi found

There was nothing natural about *laissez-faire;* free markets could never have come into being merely by allowing things to take their course. Just as cotton manufactures—the leading free trade industry—were created by the help of protective tarriffs, export bounties, and indirect wage subsidies, *laissez-faire* itself was enforced by the state. The thirties and forties saw not only an outburst of legislation repealing restrictive regulations, but also an enormous increase in the administrative functions of the state, . . . It was the task of the executive to collect statistics and information, to foster science and experiment. . . . Benthamite liberalism meant the replacing of Parliamentary action by action through administrative organs.[14]

Some of the new administrative functions, according to Polanyi, were instituted because of the weakness and perils inherent in a self-regulating market system. Others resulted from the increasingly complex state of civilization. Numerous measures dealing with public health, security standards in factories and mines, and compulsory schooling led to the establishment of still more administrative machinery. But, he noted: "Most of those who carried these measures were convinced supporters of laissez-faire, and certainly did not wish their consent to the establishment of

[12] Adam Smith, *An Inquiry into the Nature and Causes of the Wealth of Nations* (London, 1776), IV, Chap. 9.

[13] Ulrich Peter Ritter, *Die Rolle des Staates in den Frühstadien der Industrialisierung* (Berlin, 1961).

[14] Karl Polanyi, *The Great Transformation* (Boston, 1957), p. 139.

a fire brigade in London to imply a protest against the principles of economic liberalism."[15]

Other essential reform measures were carried out in the face of bourgeois opposition. Society finally had to protect itself against the evils attendant on the Industrial Revolution. Humanitarians worked together with economic and political interests in opposition to economic individualism. In Prussia, the army demanded state regulation of child labor, claiming it lacked recruits because night work had ruined the health of the children. In England Tory politicians and the clergy cooperated in their fight for child protection and the Ten Hours Bill. These social movements produced governmental legislation in spite of resistance from factory owners. Factory inspection was introduced in England in 1833, and in Prussia in 1853. It was an era when the working class was made aware of its rights, and which saw the beginning of the trade union movement. On the Continent especially, workers' organizations forced the bourgeoisie to undertake reforms to prevent revolutionary reactions. Under Bismarck, a German social security system was inaugurated in 1881 by imperial decree.

At the close of the nineteenth century, European industrial nations possessed the basis for a centrally administered welfare state. From this point on, state concern for conditions of life resulted in official intervention in all areas of human existence, and ultimately mushroomed into the all-enveloping social security systems of the second half of the twentieth century.

---

[15] *Ibid.*, p. 146. *Cf.* also Herbert Spencer, *The Man versus the State* (New York, 1884), in which he accused the Liberals of betraying their principles by agreeing to that type of state intervention.

PART TWO

THE ADMINISTERED WORLD

BUREAUCRACY INVADES
THE ECONOMY

The State's New Responsibilities

The bourgeoisie, supporting new concepts of freedom of the individual and economic liberalism, was not willing to allow increased bureaucratic intervention. Economists were not the only ones to claim that the state had no business interfering in the economy; philosophers and poets expressed similar ideas. In Kant's posthumously published writings, one finds the observation that: "It is the nature of all governments to permit every man to take care of his own happiness, to see that he is free to do so in association with those around him. It is not the responsibility of government to organize the life of the private individual, only to help him achieve a harmonious existence." Goethe, in his famous conversations with Eckermann, came to a like conclusion. He expressed his conviction that the father should take care of his home, the craftsman see to his customers, the clergyman ensure brotherly love, and the government not interfere.[1] The spirit of the period spoke as clearly through Kant and Goethe as through Adam Smith.

Now that it was liberated from feudal privileges, from the limits of guild regulations, and from being in leading strings to governmental mercantilist economic policy, capitalist economy began to transform Western Europe into an industrial society. The welfare measures instituted by bureaucratic monarchies had brought about a population increase, leading to the overpopulation which permitted the expansion of capital industrial enterprise. But wherever capitalist enterprise flourished it came into conflict with bureaucracy. The new methods of production and distribution required freedom of action and the elimination of administrative barriers. The bourgeoisie, having attained wealth and culture, was no longer willing to subordinate itself to the bureaucracy of absolute

[1] Johann Peter Eckermann, *Gespräche mit Goethe in den letzten Jahren seines Lebens* (Wiesbaden, 1959), p. 570. Conversation dated October 20, 1830. English edition, *Conversations with Goethe in the last Years of his Life,* tr. S. M. Fuller (Boston, 1852).

monarchies. As Marx expressed it, "the entire civil, military and clerical bureaucracy of the absolute monarchy was unwilling to exchange its dominant position for one serving the bourgeoisie." Friedrich Engels added that "the bourgeoisie was therefore forced to destroy the power of this wanton, bullying bureaucracy. As soon as the bourgeoisie gains control over governmental administration and legislation, the bureaucracy loses its independence."[2]

Despite its opposition to bureaucratic expansion, Western bourgeoisie needed this type of central power. In the nineteenth century, the bourgeoisie encountered governmental systems which, except in America, had developed over centuries and had consequently acquired fundamental social functions for whose administration no other organizations existed, and which could no longer be performed spontaneously.

Although capitalist ownership represented a new force in society, it was neither a system of self-support, nor could it produce the basis for the completion of political and administrative tasks. However much the theoreticians and prophets of the new economic system supported laissez-faire, they also believed the central governmental authority and its machinery had a significant function. They were against governmental control of property, and its intervention in the production and exchange of goods. But even in this connection they were willing to make certain exceptions.

In *The Wealth of Nations,* Adam Smith saw the state as having three comprehensive responsibilities: first, the nation's external defense; second, the protection of the citizen against another's injustice; and third, the development of facilities which were beyond the competence of the private individual, or whose cost was greater than any eventual return on investment.

External military defense had to become the state's responsibility once national states and a capitalist economy were established. As soon as national rather than private interests competed in the international market, the economy required military backing. Alexis de Tocqueville had anticipated early on that it would be through the economy that bureaucracy would acquire great influence:

There is always a multitude of men engaged in difficult or novel undertakings, which they follow by themselves without shackling themselves to their fellows. Such persons will admit, as a general principle, that the public authority ought not to interfere in private concerns, but by an exception to that rule, each of

[2] Friedrich Engels, "Der Status Quo in Deutschland," in Karl Marx-Friedrich Engels, *Werke,* IV (Berlin, 1964).

them craves its assistance in the particular concern on which he is engaged and seeks to draw upon the influence of the government for his own benefit. . . . If a large number of men applies this particular exception to a great variety of different purposes, the sphere of the central power extends itself imperceptibly in all directions.[3]

Smith finally attributed judicial and police functions to central government because the bourgeois citizen was unable to defend his property physically in the manner of his feudal forebears, nor did he any longer possess enough political power to maintain small systems of justice.

A French exponent of Adam Smith's economic theories, Jean-Baptiste Say, also recognized the necessity for state intervention in certain areas. Taxation by the government, he felt, should be limited, otherwise it would lead to the development of too complex a machine which might misuse its power. He recommended that the state encourage and increase production by means of subsidies and other incentives. However, it was the third of Smith's proposed public administrative functions that Say particularly endorsed: the construction of roads and other public systems of communication.[4]

An improved communication system was essential to the centralization of executive control and the growth of a capitalist economy. An article in *The Economist,* published in London on January 26, 1856, in the heyday of laissez-faire and free trade, dealt with the pros and cons of the entire problem:

The episode of railways in our general history shocks our preconceived opinions. . . . There are . . . harbours to be made, huge ships and fleets to be built, combined systems of drainage and water supply to be executed. . . . How is the work to be done? Our reliance on private interest has failed. Must we imitate our continental neighbours and trust more than ever to Government? This is an important and serious question which practice answers affirmatively, and theory negatively.

The gap between liberal theories and the realities of capitalist development was already evident in the golden age of the market economy. In his book on England, Dupont-White pointed out still other increases in centralization. The entire banking system, he noted, which had been uncontrolled until 1844, was now subject to state law. The government had taken the administration of its Indian colonies away from the East India Company, and all the legislation enacted between 1823 and 1853

---

[3] Alexis de Tocqueville, *Democracy in America* (New York, 1945), II, p. 294, n. 1.

[4] The most important work of this French economist was *Traité d'économie politique* (Paris, 1803). English edition, *A Treatise on Political Economy,* tr. C. R. Prinsep (London, 1821).

served only to strengthen the power of the central executive. Dupont-White could not help admitting that while this legislation furthered the interests of the bourgeoisie, it was bound to have far-reaching effects on society as a whole.[5]

From Private Enterprise to an Organized Economy

Development of a capitalist economy involved increasing administrative absorption of social functions. The American economist, Henry Charles Carey, blamed this kind of traditional European interventionism for the difficulties which were arising in the market economy. Karl Marx criticized Carey for his interpretation: "Of course Carey did not investigate to what extent state intervention in the form of public debt or taxes grew out of the bourgeois system itself. For instance, such intervention occurred in England not as a result of, but because of the abolition of feudalism; and as for North America, there the power of the central executive increased with the centralization of capital." At the same time, Marx added: "Meanwhile Carey, who begins his thesis with the emancipation of American middle-class society from state control, concludes with the postulate of state intervention. He sees this as necessary to prevent outside interference with the consistent development of a bourgeois economy (as in fact happened). He is a protectionist."[6]

Private industry contributed greatly to the need for and development of a centralized administrative system. In a market economy, competition was the stimulus which brought about new methods in production, introduced new products and helped find new outlets. But competition tended to be a self-destructive, rather than creative force. Production began to be concentrated in the hands of joint stock companies, which required a central organization for such matters as a credit system and the administration of the money to be used as capital. Banking officials controlled the banks; private enterprise and creative business instincts were no longer appropriate in joint stock companies which required regulated administration. Karl Marx says of joint stock companies that they "turn the truly operative actual capitalist into a mere director, an administrator of outside capital." Once a business has developed into a sufficiently large concern, "it needs a director or manager to act as supervisor. Industrial managers, not industrial capitalists, are the backbone

[5] Charles Brook Dupont-White, *L'Individu et l'état* (Paris, 1857).

[6] Karl Marx, *Grundrisse der Kritik der politischen Ökonomie* (Berlin, 1953). English edition, *The Grundrisse*, ed. and tr. David McLellan (London and New York, 1971).

of our industrial system."[7] Originally the financial interests of the individual and that of a business concern had been synonymous; but, as Werner Sombart describes it, with the development of stock companies the financial aims of the individual were no longer the central concern of the economy.[8] Capital became something to be administered, the concern of an organization.

At first managers acted as the major-domos of the entrepreneurs but, as in the Franconian Empire, the major-domos eventually gained control. Industrial officials rose to important positions in the cartels and syndicates into which joint stock ventures organized themselves. By 1931, Ferdinand Fried could write that managing directors had replaced entrepreneurs, and that large monopolies of Germany such as the Steel Trust, the Chemical Trust, the DD-Bank, the compulsory Coal Syndicate, the Crude Steel Cooperative, and the banking combines all required organizers and administrators.[9]

In the nineteenth century, a businessman who had gained above average profits as a result of improved production and sales methods—until his competitors duplicated his success or surpassed him—was, so to speak a mobile element within society. As Eugen Schmalenbach puts it:

Freedom is an essential element in the life of a successful businessman and hence is a prerequisite to his effectiveness. He cannot bear to be restricted. In a free national economy, responsibility is a necessary correlate to freedom. Companies may construct, expand or rebuild plants; they may manufacture whatever they consider to be worthwhile, try to find ready markets and set prices they consider appropriate. But in a free national economy they must do all of this on their own responsibility. If one of their projects is unsuccessful, they have to bear the entire loss. They must even take into account the possibility of being completely ruined.[10]

However, when Edgar Salin investigated post World War I economy, he ascertained that "the twentieth century entrepreneur has lost the ability to face ruin." By then, it was frequently a managing director, rather than the owner of a business enterprise, who played the decisive role in the economy and its system of monopolies. He had his position and retained it. As Salin puts it: "The man who has been fortunate enough

---

[7] Karl Marx, *Capital*, tr. E. and C. Paul, 2 vols. (London, 1962).

[8] Werner Sombart, *Sozialismus und soziale Bewegung im 19. Jahrhundert* (Jena, 1897). English edition, *Socialism and the Social Movement in the 19th Century*, tr. Anson P. Atterbury (London and New York, 1898).

[9] Ferdinand Fried, *Das Ende des Kapitalismus* (Jena, 1931).

[10] Eugen Schmalenbach, *Der freien Wirtschaft zum Gedächtnis* (Köln and Opladen, 1949).

to achieve a position in these large monopolies is much more secure than he could have been under a free economic system."[11]

Schmalenbach, whose study appeared after World War II, concludes resignedly, "the tendency toward bureaucratic control in large concerns has turned a mass of employees into bureaucrats and officials. They have lost the spirit of enterprise."[12] But, of course, his conclusion merely completes a process which had been commented on in the twenties. Otto Heinrich von der Gablentz wrote:

It used to be the bookkeeper who was in charge; now there are accounting offices, and purchasing and sales departments. The engineer and his staff are now part of engineering departments, laboratories and experimental workshops. The technologies involved in each employee's work tend to obscure insight into the functions of the enterprise as a whole. Technicians, buyers, salesmen and stockroom clerks, all come to management with conflicting demands in the name of their departments. Each is responsible only for his own function and expects the company to act with this in mind. It is the beginning of the struggle for control. Once it is no longer possible to supervise the total operation, administration must be split up with some kind of control at the top. Only a carefully organized hierarchy can bring about the efficient operation of a business enterprise. . . . As early as 1872 the firm of Krupp issued a set of "General Regulations" which stated: "The growth of the plants and offices of this company makes it necessary . . . to define the rights, duties and limits of each office and position both in the firm as a whole and with respect to all other offices."[13]

Max Weber sees the development of bureaucracy as being first of all the process in which it becomes possible to supervise and compute the activities of an organized administrative system. He considers the basic characteristics of bureaucracy to be: a continuous operation of regulated official functions involving authority to assign and define their limits.[14] All of this was contained in the Krupp Regulations, which anticipated the organization of modern business.

Half a century after the Krupp Regulations appeared, Otto Hintze, the German historian, found that

If the political historian takes account of typical manifestations of modern economic activity in the capitalist age—such as administrative and auditing systems

[11] Edgar Salin, "Von den Wandlungen der Weltwirtschaft in der Nachkriegszeit," *Weltwirtschaftliches Archiv* (January, 1932).

[12] Schmalenbach, *op. cit.*

[13] Otto Heinrich von der Gablentz, "Industriebureaukratie," *Schmollers Jahrbuch*, II (1926).

[14] Max Weber, *Wirtschaft und Gesellschaft* (Tübingen, 1922), pp. 650–678. English edition, *Economy and Society: An Outline of Interpretive Sociology*, ed. Guenther Roth and Claus Wittich, tr. Ephraim Fischoff *et al.* (New York, 1968).

of large corporations, their competition and attempts to regulate or eliminate it by means of mergers, trusts and combines—he is constantly reminded of quite similar tendencies in the development of states. For instance, their rivalry, their attempts to federalize, their administrative agencies and their financial system. Above all, this view reveals modern governmental bureaucracy in quite a different light from that of the traditional, idealistically informed concept of the state.[15]

In such administrative systems, there is no autonomous area for the intuitively acting individual businessman. Control of a business and responsibility for it constitute the highest rung of a professional ladder. The term "professionalization of business leadership" was coined in America. Writing on this subject in 1945, Robert A. Gordon says:

Whatever his title, the chief executive in our largest corporations is not ordinarily the type of creative and aggressive business leader who is both famous and infamous in the annals of American industry. He is not the restless dynamic individual of an earlier generation who, owning his company, pioneered into new lines and "risked his shirt." . . . Rather, he is a professional executive doing a "management job." . . .

As a matter of fact, the prevalence of group, instead of individual, action is a striking characteristic of management organization in the large corporations. In many cases, committees of executives have partially supplanted individuals in the formulation and approval of major decisions.[16]

These same qualifications apply in Germany as Hans Paul Bahrdt shows in his investigation of bureaucracy in large corporations: "We are mistaken if we believe that it is the director who makes decisions. Decisions require adequate information. The director believes he is the one to make the final decision, in spite of the vast bureaucratic machine which prepares everything for him. He is only a traffic policeman who signals, he does not decide where the car is to go."[17] But where the thoroughfare is closed, the state is called on to help and, in the words of Edgar Salin, "The State is not in a position to withhold its aid."[18]

The state was even less able to ignore such requests for aid when they came from vast enterprises whose collapse would have had far-reaching effects on the whole economy, and on social and political life. During

---

[15] Otto Hintze, "Nationale und europäische Orientierung in der heutigen politischen Welt," (1925), in Soziologie und Geschichte: Gesammelte Abhandlungen zur Soziologie, Politik und Theorie der Geschichte, ed. Gerhard Ostreich (Göttingen, 1964).

[16] R. A. Gordon, Business Leadership in the Large Corporations (Washington, 1945), pp. 71 and 99.

[17] Hans Paul Bahrdt, "Fiktiver Zentralismus in den Grossunternehmungen," Kylos, 4 (1954).

[18] Salin, op. cit.

the years of the great Depression it was customary for governments to take action in the form of subsidies and other aids. In Germany this was known as "the socialization of bankruptcy." State intervention was called "the governing of the capitalist economic system." The fear was expressed that it would be Europe's capitalist-oriented statesmen, rather than its socialists, who would undermine and perhaps destroy the economy.[19]

State Intervention in the Economy

The state was forced to intervene extensively, in Europe as well as America, during the worldwide economic crisis of 1929. It did so by means of price supports, bulk purchasing, the limitation of production and the creation of jobs. The regulation of credit and interest rates, the increase of purchasing power, monetary controls and import and export quotas became the responsibility of appropriate offices. Many of these measures became permanent, thus enlarging and extending the state's role in the economy.

World War II and the problems it produced only furthered this process. The state had to maintain full employment and institute a monetary and credit policy to prevent an economic crisis; it participated in public investments and nationalized banks and industries. Departments were established to plan and direct the economy, and agriculture received aid in the form of subsidies and price support.[20]

But state action soon moved beyond internal economic affairs. Collapsing world markets—a result of the financial crisis—and post World War II anti-colonial revolutions became matters for governmental measures. In previous centuries, private export of capital to noncapitalist, nonindustrial nations had helped stabilize world economy. Now the export of capital was a state responsibility, undertaken partially by aid programs to "underdeveloped" countries.

Montchrétien, who had dedicated his treatise on political economy to the king and Marie de Medici in 1615, could hardly have anticipated to what extent his recommendation of state participation in the economy

---

[19] Arthur Salz, *Macht und Wirtschaftsgesetz: Ein Beitrag zur Erkenntnis des Wesens der Kapitalistischen Wirtschaftsverfassung* (Berlin and Leipzig, 1930).

[20] Agriculture, which was not part of the general progressive trend of all modern industrial states, and was not integrated into the prevailing economic system until the second half of the twentieth century, was now subject to more state regulation and received more state assistance than any other sector of the economy. Even if the agricultural producer appeared to be a free agent, he was in fact the object of comprehensive bureaucratic control.

would be realized in the second half of the twentieth century. Some three hundred years later, John Maynard Keynes maintained that conditions of crisis surely justified interference by the state with unemployment compensation, publics works, state credits and deficit budgets. He offered the consolation that these actions were justified on the basis of economic theory. But even he had not foreseen the full scope of governmental intervention in economic life.[21]

Montchrétien and Keynes both based their theories on the importance of state tax policy in the control of the economy. Of course they also recommended, or considered as necessary, other rational governmental measures—Keynes even spoke of the necessity of extensive socialization of investments—but they merely recognized the direction in which the economy was being forced to move. Keynes, in contrast to Montchrétien, was a successful writer, but no doubt Vilfredo Pareto's dictum could be applied in modified form—that it was not Keynes who·was responsible for state intervention, but that his reputation as an author was furthered by this trend.

In the decades since Keynes' work appeared, this trend has shown continuous progress. State credits, investments and expenditures have themselves increased to such an extent that their administration has considerable influence on the course of the economy.[22] In attempting to study the characteristics of the "new capitalism," Andrew Shonfield points out that government is becoming increasingly responsible for economic planning, not only with respect to what will occur, but also with respect to what *should* occur. It takes for granted that there be a predetermined yearly increase in national income, and uses output-input calculations to maintain a balanced economy. Shonfield sees economic planning as the most characteristic expression of the new capitalism, reflecting determination to take charge of rather than be driven by economic events. In Britain the same motivation "finally moved a Tory government, elected to office in the early 1950's with an almost fanatical market ideology, to adopt economic planning as a central theme of its domestic policy."[23]

---

[21] *See* the Foreword to John Maynard Keynes, *The General Theory of Employment, Interest and Money* (New York, 1936). *See also* Keynes' *The End of Laissez-Faire* (London, 1926).

[22] The public investments of the German Bundesrepublik increased from 13.7 billion marks in 1958 to 26.5 billion marks in 1963. In the United States more than one hundred federal institutions existed at the beginning of the 1960s for purposes of credits, insurance and state guarantees of all kinds. The amount of loaned public capital in June 1963 was estimated at $105 million, as against $11 million in 1945.

[23] Andrew Shonfield, *Modern Capitalism: The Changing Balance of Public and Private Power* (London, New York, Toronto, 1965), p. 221.

The Company as an Institution

The free market came into being in the nineteenth century as a vast autonomous sphere in which the economy's fate seemed to be determined by "natural" laws of supply and demand without bureaucratic manipulation. Price came to be the decisive factor in economic activity. But it was obvious after the crisis of 1929 that the decrease in prices of agricultural products and raw materials did not result in the expectations of increased industrial output and lower commodity prices.[24] This led to an investigation by the United States Senate which found that in addition to the traditional market, where supply and demand were balanced by a flexible price, there was a new administered market, where production and demand were equated at an inflexible administered price. "Administered prices" were set by large corporations. The transition from a free market to one that is coordinated bureaucratically had progressed to such extent that for the most part American economic activity was now carried on by large administrative systems.[25]

Where once it had been up to the entrepreneur to adjust his activities to the impersonal forces of the market, it was now the manager's task to use his business policy—which includes price policy—to establish market conditions.

The commodity market was not alone in losing its determining power; the capital market, too, lost its significance where the economy was managed by large organizations. The fact that the latter finance their own activities reduces the regulating function of the capital market. A company which has reached institutional size is only marginally concerned with the market to build up capital and investments.[26] Reversing former procedure, capital formation is dependent on investments planned by management. Capital created by spontaneous savings no longer "chooses" its investments. Interest rates are given increasingly less importance in calculations preceding investment. Large corporations use their profits for investment purposes on the basis of management decisions. These companies set their technical and financial goals for several years ahead. The free choice of business owners to invest profits according to interest

---

[24] Salin, "Von den Wandlungen der Weltwirtschaft . . ." *op. cit.*

[25] Gardiner C. Means, "Industrial Prices and their Relative Inflexibility," *U. S. Senate Document* 13, Seventy-fourth Congress, First Session (Washington, 1935), pp. 1 and 10.

[26] For example: between 1946 and 1953 new investments in the United States amounted to $150 million (financial and banking enterprises are not included). Out of this amount, 64 percent came directly from self-financing, and only 6 percent came from issuing stocks. The rest was lent by banks, or acquired in loans outside the market.

rates—once the essential consideration of the capital market—has been forced into the background.[27] In addition, the way in which companies have merged and become integrated has changed operations of the capital market into administrative procedures and located them elsewhere. The market has been superseded by management, and one-time private initiative has become an organizational function.

The amalgamation of companies has transformed them into permanent institutions. Their administration is similar to that of the state, so that nationalization makes very little difference to the nature of large corporations. For example, the nationalization and almost immediate denationalization of the British steel industry had no real effect on either manager or worker.

The institutionalization of companies has further excluded the businessman from being an autonomous agent in the economy. What has been called the "condition of entry" to an industry prevents new companies from entering those sectors of the economy controlled by a few large firms. The smaller company finds the costs too high, since "large amounts of absolute capital investment are required for efficiency."[28] The lack of this capital constitutes a barrier behind which the managers who control the economy operate.

The Manager's Image

The proportion of businessmen and capitalists involved in the leadership of major American companies decreased from 44 to 15 percent between 1900 and 1950. Around 1900, half of them owed their positions to the fact that they had founded the company, or invested their capital in it. Less than one-fifth of them had risen from the ranks of company employees. Half a century later, the situation was reversed: about one half had been employees and only one-eighth had participated in establishing or had invested capital in the firm.[29] In the same period, an ever smaller number of managers came from technical departments of companies. The popular conception of the technical specialist at the head of a modern business was no longer applicable; he was, in fact, replaced by an administrator.

[27] François Mombert, "Contribution à une théorique des incidences de l'impôt sur les sociétés," *Revue de science financière* (juillet, 1962), pp. 437–460.

[28] Joe S. Bain, *Barriers to New Competition: Their Character and Consequences in Manufacturing Industries* (Cambridge, Mass., 1962), p. 55.

[29] The figures are taken from the survey by Professor Mabel Newcomer, *The Business Executive: The Factors that Made Him, 1900-1950* (New York, 1955), table 45, p. 102.

To see how free forces operate in a capitalist market economy, one must understand the role played by the entrepreneur. In the same way, the new economy can most clearly be interpreted through the agency of the manager-administrator.[30] Insight into the growth and development of the manager's role in industry can be gained by studying the life of a man who devoted the greater part of it to one of America's largest corporations. Alfred P. Sloan's autobiography, covering the years he spent with General Motors, provides the opportunity.[31]

How does this man, who spent forty-five years "at the focal point of major policy-making and administration," view the position, task and achievements of a manager?[32] What was the philosophy that enabled him in his own view to offer successful competition to Henry Ford? The issue between them was the conflict between manager and entrepreneur, a conflict which pinpointed a decisive moment in economic history. For this important landmark to be put into its proper perspective, it is useful to compare Sloan's statements with those contained in Henry Ford's autobiography.[33]

The objection may be raised that the characteristics distinguishing the two men are not so much an expression of difference between two economic theories, as of psychological differences between two personalities. But to consider this a satisfactory explanation is to overrate the psychological forces which contribute to the chance of success in given situations.

In purely chronological terms, Ford and Sloan were almost contemporary; the former having been born in 1863 and the latter in 1875. Nevertheless, looked at *cum grano salis,* Ford can be considered to be the last of the great American entrepreneurs, and Sloan as the first of the great self-made managers. No two books could be more different than these two autobiographies. Ford's central theme is his invention and his theories regarding his enterprise. Sloan has only one theme: the development of the General Motors organization.[34]

[30] The following titles have been used as a basis for this section of the chapter: Adolf A. Berle, Jr. and Gardiner C. Means, *The Modern Corporation and Private Property* (New York, 1932); Adolf A. Berle, Jr., *The 20th Century Capitalist Revolution* (New York, 1954); Edward S. Mason, *The Corporation in Modern Society* (Cambridge, Mass., 1960); Helge Pross, *Manager und Aktionäre in Deutschland: Studien zum Verhältnis von Eigentum und Verfügungsgewalt,* (Frankfurt-am-Main, 1965).

[31] Alfred P. Sloan, Jr., *My Years with General Motors* (New York, 1964).

[32] *Ibid.,* p. vii.

[33] Henry Ford, *My Life and Work* (London, 1924).

[34] In the Foreword to the German edition of Ford's book (the edition consulted by this author), the translators write that his careless style is indicative of a self-educated person. Sloan, however, had his "editorial staff" and his book is written in the smooth, synthetic style associated with *Fortune* magazine, to whose staff Sloan's editorial helpers belonged.

Obsessed by the idea to which he owed his success, Ford recommends it as a means of realizing an ideal existence. Sloan, on the other hand, describes the continuous development of an organization. Ford used chapter headings like: "Money—Master or Servant," "Why Be Poor?" " Why Charity?" Sloan's chapters bear such titles as: "Co-Ordination by Committee," "Concept of the Organization," "The Development of Financial Controls," or " The Management: How it Works."

As a sort of statement of his faith, Ford writes, "The place to begin manufacturing is with the article. The factory, the organization, the selling and financial plans will shape themselves to the article."[35] Sloan on the other hand refers to his accomplishments as having created "an organization which could adapt itself to the great changes in the market."

Ford sees a business enterprise only in terms of the entrepreneur's function. He firmly believes that "whoever possesses the greatest amount of working strength and thinking power will inevitably be successful." He had little respect for organization and its departments: "Where responsibility is broken up . . . and divided into many departments, each department under its own titular head, it is difficult to find any one who really feels responsible."[36] Sloan presents himself as a "management specialist," and expounds the General Motors doctrine, according to which business policy, while it may originate anywhere, has to be evaluated and approved by committees before being administered by individuals.

The firm of General Motors was created by William C. Durant. Sloan describes Ford and Durant as personalities possessing unusual powers of imagination, daring and foresight. Durant's great weakness, he says, was that "he could create, but he could not administer." Important decisions had to wait until he was free, and were often made impulsively. And he was "constantly involved in extensive and complicated financial negotiations."[37]

Durant, more of a capitalist than Ford, created an industrial empire by the expedient of buying up subsidiary companies. The "impulsive decisions" which underlay his actions did, however, lead the business into financial difficulties. This resulted, first of all, in a 1918 takeover of almost 25 percent of General Motors' stock by the Du Pont company. Ultimately, shareholders and those banking interests which had supplied

---

[35] Ford, *op. cit.*, pp. 16–17.
[36] *Ibid.*, p. 94.
[37] Sloan, *op. cit.*, pp. 4 and 25.

credit demanded Durant's resignation, which occurred in 1920. Sloan's "history of the organization" begins with that year.

Ford, who was less in favor of buying businesses than Durant, was, however, in danger of being asked to resign by shareholders and banks because of his "adventurous" business methods. Sloan concludes from this that it was necessary to develop a thoroughly organized administrative system and, at the same time, to establish a permanent business policy which would inspire confidence both inside and outside the company. However, Ford sees in the attack on his business policy criticism of the entrepreneur and his daring. Thus he writes, "I do not want stockholders in the ordinary sense of the term," or "we have no place for the nonworking stockholders."[38] In 1919 he borrowed $70 million on notes, in order to buy up all Ford company shares, and to be able to act as a free, independent entrepreneur—an action which brought him to the edge of bankruptcy.[39]

Sloan sees his own merit especially in having established, after Durant's resignation, organizational methods and business policies designed to prevent friction all around. Ford notes, in contrast, "I pity the poor fellow who is so soft and flabby that he must always have 'an atmosphere of good feeling' around him before he can do his work."[40]

Ford and Durant experienced their business success at a time when, as Sloan puts it, "Most of the hundreds of automobile companies organized in that period made only sample cars and then expired."[41] Sloan's administrative skills proved themselves in a company whose growth, between August 1, 1917, and December 31, 1962, he could describe as follows: ". . . the number of employees increased from 25,000 to over 600,000 and the number of shareholders from less than 3,000 to more than one million. . . . Dollar sales rose . . . from 270 million in 1918 to $14.6 billion in 1962, and total assets grew from $134 million to $9.2 billion."[42]

After Durant's resignation, it was Sloan's particular concern that the former had "expanded General Motors between 1918 and 1920 without an explicit policy of management with which to control the various parts of the organization."[43] The "Organization Study," which Sloan prepared for General Motors, represented his attempt to organize the company

[38] Ford, *op. cit.*, p. 162.
[39] *Ibid.*, p. 169.
[40] *Ibid.*, p. 265.
[41] Sloan, *op. cit.*, p. 19.
[42] *Ibid.*, p. 213.
[43] *Ibid.*, p. 26.

on efficient lines. He says he wrote it, "as a possible solution for the specific problems created by the expansion of the corporation after World War I."[44] From this time on, Sloan became involved in creating and coordinating committees, and with evolving a general business policy.

In following the organizational problems Sloan experienced, one cannot help recalling a statement made by Kenneth Boulding, that the problems of coordination facing large corporations are similar to those experienced by socialist states.[45] This analogy comes to mind especially because one essential problem, with which Sloan waged endless battle, was how to develop a healthy balance between centralization and decentralization. In a corporation consisting of dozens of large companies, manufacturing hundreds of finished products, it was only natural that directors concern themselves above all with their own specific area of interest. Sloan soon discovered that their internal competition for capital appropriations wrought havoc in General Motors' entire financial structure. It was not enough merely to create an executive committee and a financial committee to make decisions. First of all, a committee had to be set up to work out a system of general business policy before any subsequent decisions could be made by relevant committees.

Despite the establishment of a capital appropriation committee and publication of a manual dealing with appropriation procedure, Sloan found that "the division managers failed to stay within their authorized limits on inventory or capital expenditures."[46] Speaking of having acquired the technique of control in the areas of capital appropriation, cash, inventory and production, Sloan goes on: "the general question remained: How could we exercise permanent control over the whole corporation in a way consistent with the decentralized scheme of organization? We never ceased to attack this paradox."[47]

Sloan was also faced with the task of developing a principle of coordination that would not jeopardize the gains of decentralization. He noted in his "Organization Study" that while it was necessary to strengthen the feeling of belonging to the organization as a whole, at the same time each production procedure had to be calculated on the basis of profit and loss.[48] Retrospectively, Sloan had to admit that centralization and

---

[44] *Ibid.*, p. 47.

[45] Kenneth, E. Boulding, *The Organizational Revolution* (New York, 1953), p. 35.

[46] Sloan, *op. cit.*, p. 30.

[47] *Ibid.*, pp. 139–140.

[48] Sloan found such calculations required statistics, which would serve as a useful control in gauging the relation between capital invested in, and net return, of each operating division. Not long before Ford had announced that statistics could not be used in building automobiles—that is why he had stopped using them in his business.

decentralization could not help but be contradictory. In the first part of his study he had recommended maximum decentralization of divisional operations; in the second section he had advocated limitations on the responsibility of divisional heads. Practically, the problem could be solved only in the organization's day-to-day operations.

Sloan's study did not try to solve all the problems inherent in his company's development; but it was, according to him, "the first written statement of the broad principles of financial control in General Motors." In a certain sense, no doubt, it provided a sign that the automobile industry had passed from the age of inventor-entrepreneur to that of organization by management. Perhaps it was also symptomatic that the four members of the Executive Committee entrusted with the guidance of the corporation "had never before had the responsibility of producing an automobile."[49]

Another problem of economic importance solved by Sloan was, in his words, "a matter of statistical controls versus salesmanship." This situation came to a head in 1924, when a recession occurred in the economy right after the boom year of 1923. General Motors' salesmen and general managers were so impressed by that boom, they failed to notice the downward sales trend and to curtail production accordingly. This helped Sloan to conclude that programming and planning were essential to operating in the automobile industry. "It is a matter of respecting figures on the future as a guide," states Sloan. "The essential elements are the forecast and the correction, each equally critical."[50]

An essential part of the new planning system was the analysis of the relation between growth of national income and automobile sales as well as the maintenance of production at an even rate, independent of seasonal fluctuations. Production and market planning led to techniques for influencing and expanding the market, and to the concept of changing the model annually.

Sloan's extensive organizational system was another means of controlling the market. The corporation took over the wholesale trade, establishing a stable sales organization. Sales licenses were only issued after districts had been analyzed, so that the number of dealers in one area should not exceed its potential. The founding of the Motors Holding Corporation (later the Motors Holding Division) provided an additional source of income for the corporation; it extended the necessary capital to dealers

[49] Sloan, pp. 50 and 55.
[50] *Ibid.*, pp. 135 and 136.

and consequently influenced their business practices. Of even greater importance was consumer financing. The credit financing through which two-thirds of all cars were sold, could not be handled by dealers. General Motors' Acceptance Corporation was established to finance purchases of dealers as well as consumers. At the same time, the General Exchange Insurance Corporation, a subsidiary company, was responsible for insuring vehicles purchased under GMAC against theft and damage through accident.

If, as Sloan expresses it, the primary goal of the corporation is profit and not the production of automobiles, then a long-term, return-on-investment goal, independent of the latter, had to be included in planning objectives. To this end, the "standard volume" concept was introduced, which consisted, among other things, of fixing a given rate of return on capital over a number of years. As soon as profit fell below the projected goal, necessary costing revisions had to be undertaken.

Sloan was aware of the fact that growing fixed costs meant considerable increases in car prices as soon as production output was lowered, and that the price decreases doubled losses in a bad market. In order not to fall below a set amount of capital return, prices were fixed on the basis of a standard volume of production considerably lower than the volume in a good year. The favorable financial result to which Sloan points with pride, was achieved because on a long-term basis the average production volume was above the standard volume.

Much that is taken for granted now, is described by Sloan as it was developed. His book sets forth his belief in organization and planning. A highly complex organization cannot be abandoned to the vagaries of the commodity or capital market. Sloan gives the following figures: "The total capital employed in the business has grown since 1917 from about $100 million to about $6.9 billion. . . . of this almost $5.4 billion came from reinvestment of earnings."[51] Only about $800 million came from the capital market. The real source of capital was the consumer who paid the controlled price.

Programming, planning, market organization, controlled prices, manipulated demand, self-financing—all these are a far cry from the market conceived by Adam Smith. But had not Smith warned that directors of stock corporations, who only manage other people's money, could not be expected to administer this money with the same careful attention as partners would pay to their own funds in a private partnership? Sloan

[51] *Ibid.,* p. 216.

mentions that when he became president of General Motors, he decided to "make any personal sacrifice for the cause."[52] Even if such "sacrifices" were not made without material compensation, no reader of his book can doubt that the man's entire life was in fact devoted to General Motors. There is no mention anywhere in these memoirs of any personal interest; Sloan the man is completely swallowed up by everything pertaining to the company's progress. Adam Smith had not realized what role man would be required to play one day in economic history: the ability to identify with an organization. It was a role unknown to his time.

The classical theory of political economy held that in pursuing his immediate interests, the individual furthers the interest of all, that is, the national income. Or, as Adam Smith expressed it, the individual is driven by an invisible force to achieve a goal he had not intended. In the "organization," however, the influence of the invisible force is constantly being limited. Hence "organization" is not merely an institution replacing an enterprise, it is also a new productive force.

"Organization" is the new productive force of the twentieth century but it is also a bureaucracy and is burdened with its problems. The economy's large-scale enterprises have their *faux-frais,* their irrational costs. These not only include expenditures for managerial prestige which explain the administrative palaces which have sprung up in place of citadels and castles; they also include those incalculable complex administrative expenditures which used to be considered governmental bureaucracy's great disadvantage in comparison with the financial structure of a business enterprise. One hundred and fifty years after Karl Ludwig von Haller wrote on the theory of the natural state, another professor from Bern, Hans Zbinden, again advises against the formation of large organizations, against centralization and against the "exaggeration of purely rational considerations," but this time in the business rather than the political sphere. Professor Zbinden finds that

The growth of large corporations is, however, also accompanied by changes which not only reduce the advantages, but can become positive *dangers* and *obstacles.* Above all, there are *self-inflating administrative expenditures* which occur in any oversized administration and organization as a result of increased waste of energy, of friction over authority and coordination, of complexity and many other factors. Then there are such matters as "bureaucratic sand in the machinery," the flood of paperwork; in short, numerous consequences which tend to paralyze fresh initiative or independent thought and action. Difficulties are

[52] *Ibid.,* p. 98.

magnified by the growth in manpower, above all in finding and holding on to a rapidly increasing number of qualified personnel.[53]

In fact, all the "laws" which had been considered peculiar to governmental administration are now to be found in industrial bureaucracy. In an article entitled "Parkinson in Industry," Hans Walter shows how it is precisely their monopoly which permits large corporations to build up an administrative organization. More and more persons and departments become involved in dividing up and then coordinating individual tasks and procedures. Printed forms and copies are produced in large quantities; receipts for goods received and delivered, order confirmations, stock receipts, payroll slips, sales invoices all have to be sent to the business office, the stockroom, the purchase and sales department, the bookkeeping and accounting department, the financial administration, the auditing department, the management and head office. As Walter says: "The same procedure is often unnecessarily duplicated by several departments. No department is prepared to renounce its authority. If at any time a department is not fully occupied, it develops its activity all the more intensely in an effort to emphasize the esteem in which it is held."

Specific individuals and department members see organizing, establishing of norms and overall planning as their special task. In this way the working process only becomes more involved. The effort outweighs the usefulness of the operation. Walter remarks, "The employees themselves find it difficult to judge what purpose is served by their work."

Particular problems arise when the head office and the company's plants and other establishments are in different locations. Frequently the various divisions of a company try to establish an administration resembling that of the central office in its completeness, leading to duplication of work.[54]

The Employee Society

As industry becomes more affected by administration and organization, the number of its employees has to increase in proportion to productive work. Rudolf Hilferding describes this new class in society as

that social class . . . which of late has come to be sloppily classified as the "new middle class." This term refers to those employed by trade and industry,

---

[53] Excerpted from an article by Hans Zbinden, *Neue Zürcher Zeitung*, August 27, 1965.
[54] Cited from an article by Hans Walter in *Frankfurter Allgemeine Zeitung*, November 28, 1958.

whose number has increased to an extraordinary degree as a result of the growth and organizational structure of large corporations. Hierarchical nuances make of these employees the actual directors of production. This class is growing faster than the proletariat. The progress achieved by a greater integration of capital, means there is a relative, and in some instances and places even an absolute, decrease in the labor force. But this must not occur in the case of technical personnel, whose number increases, although not at the same rate as the size of the enterprise. The development of shares at first works in similar fashion. It separates management from ownership, and makes the former the special function of higher paid salaried workers and employees.[55]

Twenty-six years later, Peter Drucker referred to the industrial state as "The Employee Society," in which even the "boss" is an employee. Drucker sees the emergence of this employee society as a highly significant social change. It is a system in which "everybody is related to people through his relationship to a strictly impersonal, strictly objective, strictly abstract thing, the 'organization,' the 'corporation,' the 'government agency,' etc." The thoughts, action, ethics and conduct of society are increasingly determined by this system.[56]

But if the "boss" is also an employee, the problem of succession in office arises—something which Otto Heinrich von der Gablentz had already taken up in the twenties.[57] There is no doubt that the matter of succession to the most important posts in industry, and the way in which successors are chosen, are of great importance to the whole fabric of society.

Experience has shown that in large industrial corporations, the successors of those holding important positions are co-opted. The inevitable result is that those who are chosen correspond to the preconceived image of the selectors. Advancement within the industrial hierarchy is, therefore, related to constant adjustment to the methodology of the existing system, as well as to its prevailing philosophy. This is all the more applicable when—as is the case at least in large American industrial corporations—advancement occurs within a given company.

The type of professional person who develops as a result of organizational needs and élite selection is referred to as "the organization man" by William Whyte, Jr.[58] Some of the fundamental characteristics determining this type of élite selection are seen by Karl Mannheim in the

[55] Rudolf Hilferding, *Das Finanzkapital* (Vienna, 1927).

[56] Peter F. Drucker, "The Employee Society," *The American Journal of Sociology*, LVIII, 4 (January 1953), p. 358.

[57] Gablentz, "Industriebureaukratie," *op. cit.*

[58] William H. Whyte, Jr., *The Organization Man* (New York, 1956).

following way: "The bureaucratic type of élite selection favours methodical workers who have a flair for meeting every situation in terms of prescriptions previously laid down. Their perspective must be limited to rules and regulations; individuals who show free-ranging interests and propensities for improvisation are passed over in promotion."[59]

It is the manager's task in organized industry to see that each man has his defined area of responsibility and that he remains within its boundaries. The manager sets up the organization. He has to manipulate human machinery and that requires the study of "human relations." A handbook issued by General Electric for training managers states: "You can always get anybody to do what you wish"; and as a guide on promotion the book advises: "Never say anything controversial."

Anything controversial or contradictory is seen as a hindrance or destructive factor in the smooth running of an organization; it is a subjective element which does not belong in an objective, regulated setup. Management personnel adapt to regulated procedure by identifying with the organization they feel they embody. The principle of regulation evolved by the "head office" controls the entire company.

Bureaucracy grows within a company by means of the administrative activity it engenders. This consists of distribution and specialization of work procedure on the one hand, and subsequent necessary coordination on the other. Hans Moetteli adds to this:

Modern accounting has become management's backbone. . . . The intuitive method of running a business is outdated. . . . Large corporations have their specialists in merchandising and administration. They are in close touch with technical specialists, they can provide every consumer with statistics on management and sales procedures. . . and ensure that all expenditure of human and technical resources is worthwhile.[60]

The growth in the whole bureaucratic process is reflected in the increase in sheer numbers of white collar as against blue collar personnel in all industries.[61]

[59] Karl Mannheim, "The Problem of Democratization as a General Cultural Phenomenon," in *Essays on the Sociology of Culture* (London, 1956), p. 202.

[60] Hans Moetteli, "Rechnungswesen und Industrie," *Rechnungsführung in Unternehmung und Staatsverwaltung; Festgabe für Otto Juri* (Zürich, 1946).

[61] In the United States, the number of white collar workers between 1947 and 1965 increased by 9.6 million, while blue collar workers decreased by 4 million. In 1965 the former showed an increase of 8 million over the latter. *Manpower Report of the President*, U. S. Department of Labor (March, 1966), p. 165.

Swedish industrial figures show an increase of 78 percent in number of blue collar workers between 1915 and 1948, against an increase of 367 percent in the number of white collar employees. Whereas industry had about twelve to thirteen workers for every employee in 1915, after 1950 it was only two or three.

However, organizational discipline has also been extended to the field of actual production. Control of the entire operational procedure is facilitated by routine. The need to control all operational procedures so that they mesh leads to an ever greater emphasis on routine. As the gap increases between the offices where decisions are made and the plants where production takes place, the need arises for a system in which individuals become interchangeable parts with uniform, circumscribed functions. According to Hilferding, higher administrative positions become

influential and well-endowed positions, to which any employee can conceivably aspire. In this way every single employee is interested in his own career and advancement—an interest which develops under any hierarchical system and which overpowers the individuals' feelings of mutual loyalty. . . . On the other hand, an ever greater division and specialization of work develops among these highly qualified employees in large corporations. A portion of this work, possessing a routine character, is performed by less qualified personnel.[62]

In the offices where decisions are made, the loss of self-identification caused by job division is compensated by identification with the organization. Precisely the opposite is true for those working on the assembly line; there employees feel themselves to be controlled by the administration. The administration means "them" in the offices, upstairs, from whom the worker feels himself separated by a whole world.[63]

Between the "upstairs" offices and the workers exist the numberless departments concerned with management, bookkeeping, cost-accounting, purchase, sales, statistics and personnel. In those departments the individual may try to feel part of the organization, but it is only a weak ray from a faraway sun which gives him little warmth. It is more likely that he will participate in "departmental politics," through which he can gain more authority and prestige and thereby increase his self-esteem. However, bureaucratic structure is changing as a result of new data-processing technology. As the administrative system becomes more mechanized, it hires more unqualified semiskilled employees. Certain nuances in status do indeed exist among them, but they do not have the chance of achieving an actual career. The employee is no longer clearly marked with the symbols of prestige; he has no "rising expectations," and consequently suffers a loss of status.[64] The dividing line between manual

---

[62] Hilferding, *op. cit.*

[63] A great deal of literature is available on today's worker. *See* especially, Heinrich Popitz *et al., Das Gesellschaftsbild des Arbeiters* (Tübingen, 1957).

[64] *See* Urs Jaeggi and Herbert Wiedemann, *Der Angestellte in der Industriegesellschaft* (Stuttgart, 1966).

and nonmanual labor tends to disappear, and with it the basis for a white-collar ideology. Among the employees themselves a growing polarization occurs. At the top are those entrusted with programming, planning and other administrative functions; below them is the army of automatically working assistants, performing mechanical work or checking operations. We perceive here something that applies to industry as a whole[65]—the division of personnel into "the powerless" and "the powerful."[66]

[65] For a further discussion of this phenomenon, *see* Friedrich Pollock, *Automation* (Frankfurt, 1964). English edition, *Automation: A Study of its Economic and Social Consequences,* tr. W. O. Henderson and W. H. Chalonet (New York, 1957).

[66] Jaeggi and Wiedemann, *op. cit.*

7

THE DEMYSTIFICATION
OF POLITICS

Liberalism Capitulates

Commenting on his book *The Limits of State Action*, Wilhelm von Humboldt wrote on June 1, 1792: "I have tried to oppose the mania for governing and to tighten the limits of state action everywhere. Yes, I even went so far as to insist that such action be limited exclusively to ensuring the security of the individual."[1] Schiller, who reprinted a chapter of the book in *Die neue Thalia*, wrote to the publisher Göschen, "Books of such content and written in this spirit are necessary for our times." The French Revolution had favored the development of an individualistic trend of thought, directed against the oppressive and arrogant bureaucracy of the Prussian state as well as the paternalism of Joseph II of Austria. However, it was not effective enough to make Göschen publish Humboldt's entire work. The book finally appeared in 1851 and in reviewing it Rudolf Haym said:

Surely, it is sound and appropriate to contrast the principle of freedom with the practice of absolutism; to oppose the concept of autonomy to the system of bureaucratic and governmental protection; to prefer action by the people to that of sovereigns and officials, and to demand the right of free association over the state's omnipotent interference and autocratic function. But this application of good principles can go too far. The theory was originally proposed as a critique of a bad form of government and a bad governmental practice.[2]

In the half-century between the composition of Humboldt's book and its publication, state and bourgeoisie had become reconciled. Humboldt's principles appeared superfluous when seen in the light of "reformed" state and "reformed" practice. Bureaucracy was no longer considered

---

[1] The book was *Ideen zu einem Versuch die Grenzen der Wirksamkeit des Staates zu bestimmen*, ed. Alexander von Gleichen Russwurm (Berlin, n.d.). The editor quotes Haym in his Introduction. English edition, *The Limits of State Action*, ed. and tr. J. W. Burrow (Cambridge, England, 1969).

[2] *Ibid.*

a hostile power but a rather a useful institution, in which younger sons of the bourgeoisie could find positions, just as the nobility's sons had once obtained them in the hierarchy of the church. Humboldt's philosophy, defining the limits of state effectiveness, could be filed away. The financial ledger-book not the bureaucracy was decisive in the daily practice of the economy. The impartiality of the free market had replaced the arbitrariness of governmental bureaucracy. Representatives of the liberal party filled important official positions.

However correct it is to maintain that liberalism developed along with and among the middle class, expressing its political and economic interests, John Hallowell rightly emphasized that liberalism had originally been more than a convenient rationale for capitalism.[3] On the contrary, it derived from the individualistic Weltanschauung, the struggle for the liberation of the individual, which began with the Renaissance and Reformation and ended with the demand contained in Kant's and Fichte's philosophy that each individual be considered an end in himself.

Johannes Scherr, an enthusiastic liberal historian himself, felt that the late eighteenth century—the era when Humboldt tried to oppose the mania for governing—was ready for an intellectual renewal of the world. He states:

The great shift of ideas which in this epoch involved religious, political and social attitudes as well as agricultural, industrial, commercial, scientific, pedagogical and esthetic concepts, thrust the regenerated bourgeoisie to the head of civilization. . . . It burst open all the laces and clasps of the autocratic strait jacket, ploughed furrows everywhere, and scattered those seeds which in our days have grown slowly into a vigorous manifestation of free, popular self-determination and self-government.[4]

However, the liberal ideology, opposing personal freedom to governmental power, which did not want the individual to be subservient to the state's aims, faded in the liberal parties' practice whose main interest lay in laissez-faire and free trade. Things came to the point where free trade became synonymous with the word liberalism, as Guido de Ruggiero points out in his study.[5] However, free trade and freedom only have one common syllable. As Karl Polanyi sees it, "Laissez-faire was not a method to achieve a thing, it was the thing to be achieved." Or,

---

[3] John H. Hallowell, *The Decline of Liberalism as an Ideology* (London, 1946). *See* especially Chap. I, pp. 1–20.
[4] Johannes Scherr, *Blücher; Seine Zeit und sein Leben* (Leipzig, 1865), I, pp. 205–206.
[5] Guido de Ruggiero, *Geschichte des Liberalismus in Europa* (München, 1930). English edition, *The History of European Liberalism*, tr. R. G. Collingwood (London, 1927).

speaking of the way in which the system was made possible, "The road to the free market was opened and kept open by an enormous increase in continuous, centrally organized and controlled interventionism."[6]

If the liberal party's victory entailed new tasks for the state, it also effected a simultaneous extensive transformation of society. With that clearsightedness often peculiar to representatives of the conservative opposition, Julius Stahl, a conservative professor of constitutional law at the University of Berlin in the middle of the nineteenth century, expounded and criticized the aims of the Liberal party.[7] Liberalism, as Stahl saw it, held that "Men of means should administer legislation and justice, they should be the ones to raise their voices in the press. The poor should obey and be silent." Stahl criticized this view:

The preference given to the wealthy over the poor ought, theoretically, to offend our natural feelings more than anything else could, even the advantage of birth. This inequality, and only this, has the great excuse that it is inorganic. Because the rich have their special privileges, they do not constitute a separate grouping or organized institution within society, as seems to be the case with landowners, the clergy or guilds. Men of property have not prevented society from being a mere aggregate, a mass of isolated individuals.

Stahl maintained that the Liberal party, "has succeeded, to a high degree, in effecting the dismembering of society. To achieve this aim, the Liberal party used the government itself . . . as its accomplice and instrument. Nor did the consequences fail to materialize. . . . The people thus left to their own devices and isolated, degenerate *en masse;* and this is the main source of the proletariat." This new sector of the population accepted Schiller's judgment that Humboldt's principles of free association and activity by the people (instead of official decision-making) were absolutely "necessary for our times."

The Victory of the State

The Commune

The new mass-produced class—the proletariat—was, however, not quite so "isolated" as Stahl had supposed. Thrown together in factories

[6] Karl Polanyi, *The Great Transformation* (Boston, 1957), pp. 139 and 140.

[7] These statements were included in lectures given by Prof. Stahl at the University of Berlin between 1850–1851 and 1856–1857. The lectures are contained in Friedrich Julius Stahl, *Die gegenwärtigen Parteien in Staat und Kirche* (Berlin, 1868).

and tenements, sitting together in crowded bars, the uprooted proletarians were brought into close contact with one another. In the factories it was their common interest to resist exploitation; in their homes their everyday needs produced a communal feeling and prepared the soil in which their new faith in a better world could flourish.

To this class it seemed like an awaited signal when the "normal course of evolution" was interrupted by an event which, although it was only of short duration and hardly altered anything in existing conditions, created a myth and contrasted the existing with an alternative system. For the followers of the current regime, the event had the qualities of a nightmare threatening the possible disruption of their whole governmental and administrative structure. Almost half a century later, this myth was to become the leading idea for a great revolution—at first seeming to transform the nightmare into reality, but soon tending to resolve itself in a different direction. The myth-making event was the Paris Commune.

The Commune, proclaimed in Paris on the morning of March 18, 1871, came to a quick and bloody end on May 28 of that year. The war and the Prussian occupation of the city, the surrender of *Napoléon le petit* and the conclusion of an ignominious armistice by the new republican regime, had all resulted in building up deep ressentiment in Paris. At the same time, organizations and revolutionary ideas, dating back to the 1848 uprising and suppressed for twenty years, resurfaced. The combination of suffering endured, national ressentiment and political agitation created revolutionary ferment in the city. A further cause for ressentiment lay in the fact that under the pseudo-Napoleonic dictatorship Paris had not had the same type of communal administration as other cities; rather, it had been administered by a commission. Now the people demanded an autonomous administration. The Paris national guard, which had been reestablished, soon became the symbol of those who guaranteed a new independence. National guard units were formed in all city districts, officers were elected and a guard central committee established, to prepare the defense of the institution against all attacks by administrative bureaucratic authorities. Solicitation lists were circulated for the purchase of cannon, which proudly bore the name of the district which had paid for them. An attempt by the government on March 18 to take the cannon away from the increasingly restive city unleashed a strong popular uprising with which large segments of the regular army—

originally brought in to help the government—fraternized. Paris declared itself a free commune and the government fled to Versailles.

What was the Paris Commune and how did it manage to be effective in the world of political ideas, despite its short existence? The French sociologist Henri Lefèbvre has tried to answer the question with the aid of the abundant available literature and documentation. His essential thesis is that the Commune did not result from a coup d'état. No organization existed for its preparation and none to direct it. Political groups participating in it had greatly differing attitudes—Jacobins with centralist concepts and followers of the old revolutionary Blanqui; antiauthoritarian and federalist-oriented disciples of Proudhon; and a relatively weak group of the International Working Men's Association controlled by Marx in London.[8]

Surprised by the spontaneity and force of the popular uprising defending the city's newly created autonomous power, the National Guard's central committee, which was in control, tried to legalize matters by municipal elections. In this way it lost the chance of gaining control over the Versailles government.

Lefèbvre writes of the group who constituted the central committee that they were taken unawares by the responsibility they suddenly had to assume. Legalists though they were, including noteworthy personalities but no man of genius, they nevertheless kept Paris going and proved that a large modern city can survive without the state.

One of the most distinguished historians of the Paris Commune, Lissagaray, described how public services functioned without any state control, but were skillfully and efficiently administered by amateurs. For instance, the post office council not only continued postal operations, it established new salary and advancement regulations, and abolished the prevailing system run by patronage and incompetence.

Its leaders proudly pointed to the spontaneous nature of the Commune. One of the leaders, Felix Pyat, wrote in the paper *La Commune:*

Your revolution of March 18 has a special character. . . . Its original greatness is due to its being . . . quite collective, communal . . . it is a revolution . . . anonymous, unanimous, and for the first time without a leader. . . . no surprise attack, no attempt at assassination, no coup d'état were involved. . . . It is a creation as massive and powerful as its creator, the people. It is a spontaneous natural force, neither falsified nor forced . . . a power which owes nothing to

[8] Henri Lefèbvre, *La Proclamation de la commune* (Paris, 1965).

the influence of a name, the authority of fame, the prestige of a leader or party artifice.[9]

The concept of communal autonomous administration ruled the city. A manifesto issued by the Commune stated that each commune in France was to be autonomous, to determine its budget, fix its taxes, elect its city council and all officials, organize its judicial, police, educational and defense systems, and delegate its representatives to the central administration.[10]

In all short-lived institutions of the Commune Lefèbvre found the federative principle: the greatest possible autonomy of the constituency and the direct election of delegates subject to recall. In no instance was there an attempt at establishing a permanent apparatus over the movement; there was no trace nor hint of any governmental machinery.

When Thiers' republican government suppressed the Paris Commune with relentless cruelty—abruptly revealing the fragility of the much-praised nineteenth century humanism and progressive spirit—it did so because it feared the basic deep-seated rejection of governmental bureaucracy that had come to the surface.

Speaking before the National Assembly at Versailles on March 21, Thiers said: "If Paris accepts a system which permits no form of government, then we must intervene."

Lefèbvre writes that it was the state, together with Thiers, which defeated the Commune.[11] He recalls Thiers' remark: "Paris will be subject to state power as if it were a hamlet of one hundred inhabitants." In this man's eyes, the state represented reality, the law and the highest good all at once. Their preservation justified and legitimized any action. The real raison d'être of the Commune, however, was to decrease the state's power.

Given the realities of its time, the Commune had no chance of surviving. Although it had developed in the wake of a change in regimes, it had not come about as a result of a revolutionary situation. Indeed, the Paris Commune was not a completely isolated event. Ten thousand workers of Schneider's metalworks in Creuzot had previously proclaimed *la commune industrielle* in the course of a general strike, calling for autonomous administration of the works by a workers' council. Because

[9] Felix Pyat, *La Commune,* March 24, 1871.
[10] The Manifesto appeared in *Le Cri du Peuple,* March 27, 1871.
[11] Lefèbvre, *op. cit.*

of the Paris Commune, similar movements developed in various cities, but they were far weaker than in Paris and did not last long. Anticentralist tendencies in rural districts were often merely final outgrowths of resistance by local notables against the centralization of the administration.

In fact, the Commune's importance was due more to the hopes it raised and the myth it created than to its direct effect on France. These hopes were based on more than economic cooperative concepts alone. From its beginning, the Commune manifested a tendency which went far beyond the principle of communal self-government. Edmond Lepelletier, who participated actively, writes in his detailed (but unfinished) history of the Commune: "An idea germinated in the blood-soaked fields of Paris: Paris was to be free and autonomous, it was to practice the dictatorship of example, to serve as model for cities, provinces, states and kingdoms. Paris as a focal point of democracy and the center of social progress was, first of all, to become the capital of the united states of Europe and then to be the Rome of a universal federation of nations."[12]

Lefèbvre summarizes the Commune's aims as influenced by Proudhon: a decentralized and federative plan to turn society into a free association of free associations. It was immaterial whether this plan was realizable under existing conditions; it was nonetheless vital and stimulating. It indicated a possibility. The events in Paris were to serve as an example of such an alternative.[13]

Marx's Political Testament

A few days after the suppression of the Commune, on May 30, 1871, Karl Marx addressed the General Council of the First International Working Men's Association on France's civil war.[14] Maximilian Rubel says of this address: "The Paris Commune of 1871 inspired Marx to formulate a number of thoughts which can rightly be defined as his political testament and the high point in his sociological writing."[15]

Marx sketches the Paris events in bold strokes and analyzes the Commune's political structure:

[12] Edmond Lepelletier, "Histoire de la Commune de 1871," *Mercure de France,* (1911), pp. 13–14.
[13] Lefèbvre, *op. cit.*
[14] Karl Marx, "Address of the General Council of the International Working Men's Association on the Civil War in France, 1871," in *The Civil War in France* (New York, 1962), pp. 57, 58–59, and 60.
[15] Maximilian Rubel, *Karl Marx: essai de biographie intellectuelle* (Paris, 1971), pp. 397–398.

The Commune was formed of the municipal councillors, chosen by universal suffrage in the various wards of the town, responsible and revocable at short terms. The majority of its members were naturally working men, or acknowledged representatives of the working class. The Commune was to be a working, not a parliamentary body, executive and legislative at the same time. Instead of continuing to be the agent of the Central Government, the police was at once stripped of its political attributes, and turned into the responsible and at all times revocable agent of the Commune. So were the officials of all other branches of the administration. . . .

The judicial functionaries were to be divested of that sham independence which had but served to mask their abject subserviency to all succeeding governments to which, in turn, they had taken, and broken, the oaths of allegiance. Like the rest of public servants, magistrates and judges were to be elective, responsible and revocable. . . . In a rough sketch of national organization which the Commune had no time to develop, it states clearly that the Commune was to be the political form of even the smallest country hamlet, and that in the rural districts the standing army was to be replaced by a national militia, with an extremely short term of service. The rural communes of every district were to administer their common affairs by an assembly of delegates in the central town, and these district assemblies were again to send deputies to the National Delegation in Paris. . . . The few but important functions which still would remain for a central government were . . . to be discharged by Communal and therefore strictly responsible agents. The unity of the nation was not to be broken, but, on the contrary, to be organized by the communal constitution, and to become a reality by the destruction of the state power which claimed to be the embodiment of that unity independent of, and superior to, the nation itself. . . . While the merely repressive organs of the old governmental power were to be amputated, its legitimate functions were to be . . . restored to the responsible agents of society. . . . Its [the Commune's] true secret was this. It was essentially a *working class government* . . . the political form at last discovered under which to work out the economical emancipation of labour.

However one decides to judge the reality contained in this "discovery," what was involved for Marx was the emergence of the method by which could come about "the lifting of the proletariat into a ruling position, the struggle for democracy," of which he had spoken in the Communist Manifesto. As Rubel puts it, "Marx, apparently without being aware of it, projected into his vision of the Commune all the images and concepts of the socialist community he had harbored for so long but had never expressed so openly."[16]

Up to the time of the Paris Commune, Marx, who declined to invent

[16] Rubel, *op. cit.*

future types of societies, had been limited to the experiences gained from the 1789 Revolution. The Jacobin example had not satisfied him. He had already complained that all upheavals complete rather than destroy the machinery of state.[17] Now the Commune provided Marxian theory with the opportunity of taking the missing link from reality itself.

While Marx devoted his attention in the following years to the rapidly growing German labor movement, he tried to fit this last piece of his theory into the program of the Social Democratic party. This attempt found its fundamental expression in 1875.[18] But, however much the Paris Commune served the rising socialist movement as an example of an alternative system, reality was forcing the movement in a different direction. The working class expected its organizations to influence the state in the interests of improving its social and economic condition. To an ever greater extent the goals of the labor movement's organizations were to influence, and co-operate with, the state. The German Marxist, Otto Rühle, writes: "The proletariat adopts Marx's theory only in a form that corresponds to its own nature. . . . In this way the proletariat achieves a Marxism more akin to the intellect adopting it than to the one which created it. It develops a type of Marxism in which the momentum of real events prevails over that of human creativity."[19]

Although the history of the Commune inspired generations of young people in the socialist movement and became part of the socialist saga, in a practical sense it remained only a ritualistic glorification of martyrs. The final link of Marxist theory fell increasingly into oblivion until the beginning of the Russian Revolution, when Lenin referred to it in 1917.[20]

Organization of the Masses

The Party

The ideas manifested by the Paris Commune became the common property—in varied interpretations—of nineteenth century European workers' parties. In its various forms, the nineteenth century labor move-

---

[17] Karl Marx, "Der Achzehnte Brumaire des Louis-Bonaparte," *Die Revolution* (New York, 1852). Reprinted in Karl Marx-Friedrich Engels, *Werke* (Frankfurt, 1966), IV. English edition, *The Eighteenth Brumaire of Louis Bonaparte* (Moscow, 1967).

[18] Karl Marx, *Kritik des Sozialdemokratischen Programms von Gotha* (Berlin, 1946). English edition, *The Socialist Programme*, tr. Eden and Cedar Paul (Glasgow, 1919).

[19] Otto Rühle, *Mut zur Utopie: Baupläne für eine neue Gesellschaft*, ed. Henry Jacoby (Reinbeck-bei-Hamburg, 1971).

[20] Vladimir Il'ich Lenin, *Staat und Revolution: Die Staatstheorie des Marxismus und die Aufgaben des Proletariats in der Revolution* (Wien, 1929). English edition, *State and Revolution* (New York, 1932).

ment was not only influenced by its belief in a social system without exploitation or poverty; it also expressed its intention of determining its own destiny. The masses, beginning to be politically conscious, were ready to become involved in social organization, to change it in such a way that they themselves would determine social conditions at their own level.

Organizations developed, such as the Working Men's Associations, trade unions and cooperatives, which embodied this intention. They were the material expression of the spirit of social self-determination. It was the workers who organized themselves; members passed the message on to one another by the spoken or written word; they organized meetings, sought new members, delivered newspapers and collected the necessary funds. Looking back on that period Alfred Weber writes: "The party system, the way in which public opinion was formed and leaders were elected, was, briefly, quite unorganized—as was everything still connected with and embedded in the existing traditional organization of society with its neighborhood relationships."[21]

The labor movement developed from neighborhood relationships. One turned to one's neighbor in factories, tenements, or bars to get him to go along, to become a party member and make the bond tighter. Indeed, neighborhood association was no longer that of the past based on small districts; now fate threw men together in large industrial towns. The new relationships acquired through party membership gave this mass of humanity some structure again. At the end of the nineteenth century, writing on socialism and social movements, Werner Sombart could say: "If we want to characterize modern times, perhaps it is possible to do so with the following words: above all else it possesses a vitality unlike any other period of which I can think. A current of life is being infused into modern society which no earlier era knew, enabling individual members of society to contact one another much faster than before."[22]

In 1890 Paul Göhre, a young theology student, spent three months working in a factory. He says of this experience:

The fact is, the so-called working class of Chemnitz and its environs, whom I came to know, with very few exceptions is closely connected in some way with the Social Democratic party. They more or less exist in an atmosphere of the party's ideas. . . . The average worker with whom I had contact is drawn—consciously or instinctively—towards a united, active mass organization

[21] Alfred Weber, *Die Krise des modernen Staatsgedanken in Europa* (Berlin, 1925).
[22] Werner Sombart, *Sozialismus und soziale Bewegung im 19. Jahrhundert* (Jena, 1897). English edition, *Socialism and the Social Movement in the 19th Century*, tr. Anson P. Atterbury (London and New York, 1898).

93

to which he can belong. He yearns for vast progress, for the advance of the entire fourth estate ... and he knows, sees, feels that this elementary urging and yearning, this striving and wanting has not been satisfied by anyone until now but the Social Democratic party. It does so without restraint and self-interest, in an energetic and far-reaching manner.[23]

But soon the enthusiastic observer was replaced by the skeptic. Moisei Ostrogorski's book on democracy and political parties appeared in French in 1903.[24] His views were based mainly on American experience and not directly concerned with socialist parties, but rather with popular parties as a general political tool. He noted that under the democratic system, large parties are integrated into the state. The usefulness to public life of this amalgamation of state and parties was doubtful. The original release of power generated by united human beings was being replaced, to an ever larger extent, by machinery resulting from the party's drive to become part of the state. The permanent organization this required became an end in itself, subordinating everything else: principles, convictions, personalities, laws of social morality and even private ethics. The Labour Party in England developed, he held, in the same manner as bourgeois parties. The mass of affiliated workers was passive in the face of the party machine and gladly followed its leader. The more a party grew, the less it was able to encourage the enthusiasm of its membership; hence, even in the Labour party, the organizational apparatus became of primary concern.

Ostrogorski suggested, therefore, that since the party system tends to turn into an undemocratic machine it be replaced by temporary associations, formed only to achieve immediate objectives, and which can then be disbanded.

A few years after the publication of Ostrogorski's book, another investigation took place into the nature of political parties.[25] But this time the German Social Democratic party was the focal issue. Robert Michels' study first appeared in 1910, dedicated to Max Weber, to whom the development of twentieth century thought appeared as a "demystification

[23] Paul Göhre, *Drei Monate Fabrikarbeiter und Handwerksbursche: eine praktische Studie* (Leipzig, 1891).

[24] Moisei Iakovlevich Ostrogorski, *La democratie et l'organisation des partis politiques* (Paris 1912), 2 vols., pp. 618, 642 and 271. The work was first published in English, in a translation based on the French manuscript, *Democracy and the Organisations of Political Parties*, tr. F. Clarke (London, 1902).

[25] Robert Michels, *Zur Soziologie des Parteiwesens in der modernen Demokratie: Untersuchungen über die oligarchischen Tendenzen des Gruppenlebens* (Leipzig, 1925). The book was first issued in 1910. The following discussion of democracy and political parties is based on Michels' book unless otherwise indicated. English edition, *Political Parties: A Sociological Study of the Oligarchical Tendencies of Modern Democracy*, tr. Eden and Cedar Paul (New York, 1915).

of the world." Robert Michels contributed to this demystification by contrasting existing party structure with its ideal model. He noted that with increasing organization, democracy diminishes and bureaucracy grows. Original enthusiasm and spontaneity are no longer sufficient to support the organization. In the end the majority of members are glad that some few can be found who are willing to take care of organizational business.

As the organization expands, not only do administrative functions increase, but they become more difficult to manage, and supervision becomes fictitious. The principle of distribution of labor becomes more urgent. A strictly defined bureaucracy develops. Michels saw that as people lose interest in the political realm on account of their professional involvement and the cares of daily life, the leaders are led to concern themselves with the technique of politics in all its detail. There is an increase in specialization, compounded by routine. Distribution of work produces specialists, but specialization means authority. Party representatives become party officials. An appointment turns into an official position, the official position acquires permanency. Party officials' independence increases in proportion to their indispensability. The most talented elements among the membership are spurred on to join the bureaucracy. In its isolation, he concluded, leadership develops a tendency to fill any gaps which may exist by means of co-optation.

Michels mentions two elements fundamental to the socialist point of view:

As party bureaucracy grows stronger, two elements belonging to the fundamentals of any socialist concept must, of necessity be impaired: understanding of the larger goals and the cultural objectives of socialism; and understanding of its international diversity. Mechanics becomes the main issue. The ability to understand correctly the peculiarities and conditions necessary for its existence . . . decreases at the same rate at which development of the national organization is completed.

According to Michels, organizational growth prevents the struggle for higher principles. Great differences of opinion within democratic parties are resolved less and less as matters of high principle or through the considerations of theory alone. The policy of glossing over is inevitably used by a bureaucratically controlled organization.

The party, which was supposed to have been the means to a higher end, has become an end in itself out of internal necessity. It is an unchangeable social law that any collective body evolved from the distribution of labor must, as soon as it is consolidated, develop a self-interest, an interest in and with itself.

In the political debates following the Russian October revolution, adherents of the new communist parties rejected Robert Michels' pessimistic theory of the unavoidable autonomy of bureaucratic machines. They held that the bureaucratic expansion within Social Democratic parties derived solely from the latters' political opportunism.[26] In his critique, written twenty years after the Communist Party was founded, Sebastian Franck comments that basic characteristics of proletarian organization do not differ from those of the bourgeois system.[27] Here, too, the function of performance turns into that of control, and the leadership possesses the sum of applied experience using it to control the entire organization independently of its base. Franck notes that the distinguishing mark of both organizations is their substitution of the party machine for human beings. The party machine appears much more powerful in the Comintern's organization, which is far more modern than the Second International. It is not by accident that the word "apparatus" has become part of the party jargon. In this apparatus the individual remains a mere cog, without force of his own, because that force, as represented by individual thought, interferes with the smooth functioning of the total process. Franck saw that rationalized structure brings administrative officials and managers to the fore whose replacement or mutual substitution in no way affects the operation of the apparatus. Whoever is best able to adapt himself to the machine is carried to the top. The "manager types" of a reformist, unionist, Communist or fascist organization, or of a bourgeois business enterprise naturally differ from one another according to the kind of "business" they represent; but in each case the type is a standard, completely mediocre one, never a creative person. Franck noted that Rosa Luxemburg, Karl Liebknecht and Franz Mehring were already outsiders in the old Social Democratic party. They developed, so to speak, in the breaches of the organization while there was still enough room for their development. The Comintern's structure—rationalized and without breaches—made it impossible for such independent spirits to develop.

After World War II, political parties in those nations having a parlia-

---

[26] One left-communist movement did recognize the inevitability of bureaucratization; it disapproved of the party as a system of bourgeois organization, contrasting it with proletarian councils. These ideas were expressed in the writing of men like Otto Rühle, Anton Pannekoek and Herman Gorter. When this period of political unrest ended, the movement disappeared, leaving some numerically unimportant sects.

[27] Sebastian Franck, *Zur Kritik der politischen Moral: Kritik des politischen Verhaltens* (Offenbach, 1947). The basic arguments that follow were developed by Franck.

mentary system became "people's parties," came to resemble each other increasingly. Conservative parties, such as in England, and socialist labor parties as well, turned into "people's parties"; that is, into parties representing neither a distinct social class nor its ideology. They are, rather, coalitions of groups representing specific interests, who substitute administrative principles for a basic political attitude. The parties' values tend to be more alike, and essentially it is by their administrative methods that they promise to outdo each other.

Herbert Tingsten, the Swedish sociologist, has seen one of democracy's basic problems in the fact that conflicting ideologies have been replaced by competing bureaucracies.[28] In countries where parties alternate, changes in voting behavior bring about a change in government, but not necessarily one of policy.

The relationship between social forces and political parties has been reversed. The former have changed from creating political policies to consuming them; whereas the policy they are to consume is worked out and made palatable by party bureaucrats.[29] The parties no longer reflect their members' political leanings, but inform the public of what they consider to be the correct policy position. This is frequently tied to loss in membership. Administrative machinery has practically become the party itself, and new members are acquired far less on the basis of their ideology than of their desire to participate in administrative activity in or connected with the party.

A random survey conducted in the Federal Republic of Germany by Erich Reigrotzki, makes it clear that membership in political parties plays a minor role.[30] Answering the question, "would you be willing to join a party?" only six percent of those questioned said "yes" and three percent said "they already were members." Reigrotzki adds that a party membership of three percent of the adult population is probably fairly accurate according to all available material. In the period from 1945–1953, three quarters of the Federal Republic's adult population had not attended any party or election meetings. These figures probably have remained unchanged in the following years.

Administrations of political parties consider themselves to be an increasingly integrated part of that structure possessing control over the public and hence in all good conscience demand governmental financial support. As the Parliamentary Secretary of the German FDP (*Freie De-*

[28] Herbert Tingsten, *The Problem of Democracy* (Totowa, N. J., 1965), p. 197.
[29] Franck, *op. cit.*
[30] Erich Reigrotzki, *Soziale Verflechtungen in der Bundesrepublik* (Tübingen, 1956).

mokratische Partei, the liberal business party) says: "Not only are political parties, like other organizations, assured of a constitutionally secure position vis à vis the state; they are themselves state executive bodies and function as such."[31]

At one time, people sharing political convictions subsidized their own political activity; now it is becoming customary to tax the general public and utilize funds, as the above-mentioned Parliamentary Secretary phrases it, "to provide the individual citizen with detailed information regarding their (the parties') aims, and decisions to be made and taken in the legislative and governmental sphere."[32]

Walter Lippmann, journalist and political scientist, anxiously asks how—in the absence of ideological differences between parties (as shown by coalition governments)—the party system we have inherited from the nineteenth century can survive. After all, he maintains, parties were formed as an expression of doctrines and political attitudes which have lost their importance. We are, therefore, not only facing the problem of whether our political values can be maintained if the party system dies out, but whether we ought not "prepare ourselves for political innovations as radical as the technological revolution in which we live."[33]

Labor Unions

Labor unions, even more than workers' parties, resulted from direct, spontaneous activity by members. They were a creation of the workers themselves. Labor unions developed to defend workers' interests despite prohibitions on associations of this sort. In England, in 1800, a law was passed prohibiting all conspiracies, meetings or associations of paid workers for purposes of improving wage conditions, on pain of penal servitude. But, Otto Rühle points out, as if in defiance of that law, the movement for freedom of association grew in size and strength.[34] A wealth of underground activity was carried on. Rühle quotes Lujo Brentano, to whom old English workers recounted how, in their youth, they buried books and minutes of labor association meetings in the Bolton moors of Lancashire because of police surveillance. New members had to take a strong oath to be admitted. The organizations resembled secret, dicta-

[31] Excerpted from an article by the Parliamentary Secretary of the *FDP, Die Welt,* September 5, 1964.

[32] *Ibid.*

[33] Walter Lippmann, *Herald Tribune,* Paris, December 7, 1966, p. 4.

[34] Otto Rühle, *Illustrierte Kultur- und Sittengeschichte des Proletariats* (Berlin, 1930).

tor-controlled associations with strict discipline and surprise attack tactics, and they were not afraid of using force.

Conditions were less romantic at the time of the actual founding of German labor unions, towards the end of the nineteenth century. But essentially a network of organizational functionaries formed the basis of the organization. Reminiscences by German metal workers of the early period of their union's organization provide the picture:[35]

In 1888 we again had a general *Metallarbeiterkongress* (Metal Workers' Congress), whose main issue was the organizational problem. It was agreed to appoint several officials to organize the Metal Workers, of which I was one. . . . I became very active: published appeals in the "Metallarbeiter-Zeitung," and gave instructions in that paper on how to form associations, and sent sample statutes to well-known colleagues. . . . The organizational system had become essentially established by the time of the general Metal Workers' Congress in Weimar in the spring of 1890. . . . In addition to cultivating collegial relationship with affiliated trade associations, it was the organizing officials' task to see to a systematic regulation of strikes, and to institute a fair distribution of relief funds raised by collection to striking or locked-out workers. The numerous strikes and lock-outs . . . required, by the standards of those times, vast sums for relief, propaganda and other matters. There were no permanent funds, everything had to be raised by collection. The molders' known feeling of solidarity proved itself once again. . . . However, the organizational system soon became too limited for the many unions with their growing membership, and the social movement spreading among metal workers. . . . Hardly had the German Metal Workers' Congress . . . concluded in Frankfurt on June 4, 1891, when doubt was expressed on all sides whether it was possible to carry out what had been decided. . . . The Congress had given the Union a constitution, guaranteeing its members considerable support, and without realizing how much work was to be done, it had immediately appointed three salaried officials (according to conditions and attitudes then prevailing, it was a good salary) to head the Union. That was daring . . . some skeptics even maintained it was reckless.

If the appointment of three salaried administrative officials still seemed "reckless" in 1891, thirty-four years later Robert Michels was able to comment that the number of paid officials was increasing rapidly in unions as well as in socialist parties.[36] In 1897, German union officials numbered 104; in 1904 that number had risen to 677. By the time Michels

[35] "25 Jahre Metallarbeiter-Zeitung," *Metallarbeiter-Zeitung*, September 12, 1908; reproduced in Fritz Opel and Dieter Schneider, *Fünfundsiebzig Jahre Industriegewerkschaft* (Frankfurt-am-Main, 1966).
[36] Michels, *Zur Soziologie des Parteiwesens, op. cit.* Most of the following discussion is drawn from Michels' work.

wrote, the type of person involved in union functions had also changed. Characteristics required in managing an organization still financially weak and largely concerned with disseminating ideas and leading strikes, were different from those required in organizing a union well-endowed with relief funds. That unions had outgrown their infancy was shown by Michels' analysis of the complexity of their functions and the technological orientation of their structure. In fact, most union managers prominently revealed a businesslike seriousness, because they felt direct responsibility and high pressure, and were engaged in dull, predominantly administrative and technical work. In Michels' description, that seriousness often intermingled with incomprehension of larger problems. Apart from their competence as men of vision and experience in professional matters, they were separated from members by the ramparts and moats of statutes which they enforced and by means of which they controlled members. The art of administration became their special subject. The German Metal Workers' Association's statutes were contained in forty-seven printed pages of thirty-nine sections, many of which again contained ten to twelve paragraphs.

Prior to Michels' sociological comments, Rosa Luxemburg noted similarities in politics. However, her recognition that she was dealing with a "natural historical product" contradicts her political activity, which was oriented toward promoting the people's initiative and democratizing society. In a polemic which she published in 1906 she says:

The rapid growth in Germany's trade union movement over the last fifteen years . . . resulted in unions making themselves independent, in the specialization . . . of their administration and, finally, in the rise of a regular class of union officials. All these phenomena represent a completely explicable and natural historical product. . . . Even if they are inseparable from certain inconveniences, they are, doubtless, a historically necessary evil. . . . Their professional specialization as union leaders . . . makes it only too easy for union officials to turn to bureaucracy and acquire a certain narrowness in outlook, as manifested in a number of tendencies. . . . Overestimation of the organization is one such tendency, which starts out by being the means to an end but gradually becomes transformed into an end in itself—into the greatest good. . . . Collegial direction by local commissions, with its undoubted shortcomings, has been replaced by that of businesslike union officials. In this way initiative and ability to form judgments have, so to speak, become part of professional specialization whereas the masses are required to submit to the passive virtue of discipline.[37]

[37] Rosa Luxemburg, *Massenstreik, Partei und Gewerkschaften* (Hamburg, 1906). English edition, *Mass Strike, the Political Party and the Trade Unions with the Junius Pamphlet* (New York, 1971).

Vital stages in this development are shown in a more recent historic-sociological study of the German Metal Workers' Association (now known as the *DMV, Deutscher Metallarbeiter-Verband*) by Fritz Opel:

The *DMV*, like all trade union federations, developed as a democratic organiza-tion, whose policy was determined by its membership—either by direct vote, or by elected representatives—and enforced by eligible union officials, responsible to that membership. . . . However, the *DMV* underwent certain changes, as happens in all organizations in a modern, hierarchically structured social system practising distribution of labor . . . changes which can be defined in terms of "bureaucracy" and "control by apparatus" . . .

When the general meeting of 1899 decided to introduce unemployment insur-ance, it was said right away that it would increase the union's administrative functions which could then no longer be executed by honorary officials on a part-time basis. The chairman, Mr. Schlicke, therefore recommended in behalf of the executive committee . . . the appointment of salaried district officials.

Their appointment affected the growth of a permanent union bureau-cracy in three ways: it increased the executive committee's power, since officials were its employees; it enhanced the stature of the apparatus in size and importance once its officials acquired new duties, such as the institution of wage agreements; and by interposing a new layer of authority, it lessened membership's direct influence on the union's man-agement.

A further result of the increase in functionaries was the delegation of union employees . . . to general meetings, which soon came to be known as "employee parliaments." . . . In 1914 the union had 149 offices with a staff of 639 employ-ees, 544 occupying administrative positions. As the executive committee's power increased, so did its tendency to limit democratic procedures which had enabled the membership to voice their opinions directly. It also became increasingly sensitive toward any criticism, which was mostly interpreted as personal interfer-ence even when it was relevant. . . . The professional functionary believes that he knows better what is needed than a mere member, since that is his profession. He is not necessarily against democratic procedures, but he often finds them an interfering element in the speedy and proper execution of business.[38]

The opinions of professional functionaries were not always accepted; nor was the "passive virtue of discipline" opposed by Rosa Luxemburg always practiced by members. Union history reveals many examples of tensions, indeed of dramatic disagreements between organization man-

[38] Fritz Opel, *Der Deutsche Metallarbeiter-Verband während des Ersten Weltkrieges und der Revolution* (Hannover, 1962).

agement and membership; important strikes were carried out against the wish and without the sanction of union management. In Germany, towards the end of World War I, tension between workers suffering from the hardships of war, and union officials concerned about the organization's existence, led to an open break; members in Berlin and other large cities returned to the old shop steward system, calling them "revolutionary spokesmen," so that strike actions could be engaged in without and against the official machine. Shortly after the war ended, the union's internal relationship again became "normalized."

In the second half of the twentieth century, unions in democratic industrial nations became involved in the organizational network surrounding society, within which the democratic process is largely carried on in the interests of its constituent groups. The unions have become part of a changed world, in which bureaucracy has developed not only out of the laws inherent in mass organizations, but where members' interests must also be extensively represented by interbureaucratic negotiations. Such interests can no longer be looked after merely in a business or within a specific industry's frame of reference, since they have, to a large extent, become subject to state control. Decisive negotiations must be undertaken with governmental departments. Even direct wage agreements are no longer negotiated with obstinate businessmen but with bureaucrats hired by employers' groups. The real problem of wages is generally only one of the subjects of such negotiations. When the American Steelworkers Union (formerly known as the Steel Workers Organizing Committee) arrived at its first wage settlement, the printed text hardly amounted to a page; in 1965 the agreement ran to 142 printed pages. After settlement was reached, a further month was needed for unanimous agreement on the exact wording, and it took another three months to make corrections and minor changes.

Wage agreements are also being concluded for longer periods of time. Figures given by Frank Marquart indicate that in 1948, only 25 percent of all American wage agreements were long-term, whereas by 1957 they had already increased to 81 percent.[39] However, long-term agreements necessitate ongoing negotiations during their lifetime; this being the only way to avoid interpretation and practices which would conflict with their overall spirit.

But even the unions' internal administration requires an expanding and ever more complex organization. In 1967, unions belonging to the German *Gewerkschaftsverband* (federation of unions) had funds amounting

[39] Frank Marquart, "New Problems for the Unions," *Dissent*, VI, no. 4 (Autumn 1959), p. 378.

to 1300 million Marks. To administer these funds, a trust company was established, and union funds have been invested in many sectors of the economy. For a long time, it has been American union practice to invest such funds in an industry whose workers it represents, thus frequently helping it to become more stable. An item in *The New York Times,* June 1, 1959, deals with this issue:

Alex Rose, President of the United Hatters, Cap and Millinery Workers' Industrial Union, reported yesterday that the Union has spent more than $6 million to help the headwear industry recover from the recession. . . . In addition to the loans and investments, the Union spent more than $3,500,000 to block rent increases to millinery manufacturers in New York which would have forced relocations and dispersal of the industry. It purchased two buildings in the garment district and is renting the space to millinery makers "at moderate rentals."

There can be no doubt that what we are dealing with here are actions far removed from the spontaneous self-help out of which unions developed. This type of intervention requires a powerful administrative organization which, like all regularly functioning bureaucratic organizations, needs an ongoing, predictable budget.

In his observations on American unions, Frank Marquart comments that only a few decades ago, a new worker was soon approached by the shop steward to join the union and pay his dues. Today the new worker finds out about his union through the "union shop and the check-off" which, in spite of its advantages, decreases contact between workers and their shop steward and contributes to union members' inactivity and indifference.[40]

The difference between union procedures of the past and present can also be demonstrated by the following example. The German Building Workers' union *Bau* lost many membership dues because of great fluctuations in the numbers of those who joined it. If a member paid no dues for a period of eight weeks, the union automatically lost a membership according to its by-laws. In other words, whoever did not meet his obligation toward the union was no longer considered worthy of being part of its membership. In 1960 this particular regulation was altered in the by-laws; any member wishing to leave the union had to notify the executive committee half a year in advance. This regulation enables the committee to obtain dues by billing delinquent members as long as adequate notice has not been given, or up to the expiration of the membership.

[40] Marquart, *op. cit.,* p. 384.

A computerized billing system prevents indifferent members from stopping payments and thereby leaving the union.

It has frequently been said that because unions have become large administrative organizations their membership has grown increasingly inactive in terms of union affairs. But this inactivity can be considered just as much a cause for the expansion of bureaucracy. C. Wright Mills discovered in his investigation of American unions that many workers look on their unions in the same way that the middle class views insurance policies. They do not want to be personally involved, but as long as no sacrifice is required, they are willing to benefit from their membership. Like the insured, or like stockholders, they make no use of their right to vote or to take part in the organization's management, but that does not indicate their unwillingness to belong.[41]

A similar attitude on the part of union membership was found in a study undertaken in France in 1965 by André Andrieux and Jean Lignon. They found that about 80 percent of those belonging to unions—who, incidentally, made up only 30 percent of the total labor force—were completely inactive members.[42]

On the other hand, Marquart's survey points out to what extent the modern collective bargaining system and more efficient production methods preclude spontaneous action and direct participation. Management control is made easier by setting out a procedure to be followed when grievances arise in the factory. When the Autoworkers' Union was first founded, a certain amount of real economic democracy existed which is in the process of disappearing. Workers were then able to make important decisions at work regarding production norms or rest periods. Such direct, collective participation by the workers is difficult to maintain in a highly efficient and mechanized industry.

Old-time union members like to recall how workers used to flock to union meetings. For instance, if serious complaints developed in a shop department, members hurried to the union hall at the close of the shift to discuss these matters with the shop stewards and local officers. It was some time before they gave this up and got used to following the prescribed grievance procedure which put an end to spontaneity. Unions have become increasingly centralized, now that collective initiative has been replaced by a more efficient system for reaching agreements. All important labor policy is settled by executives.[43]

[41] C. Wright Mills, *The New Men of Power: America's Labor Leaders* (New York, 1948), p. 37.
[42] André Andrieux and Jean Lignon, "Gewandelte Vorstellung vom Wesen der Demokratie," *Gewerkschaftliche Monatshefte*, February, 1966.
[43] Marquart, *op. cit.*, pp. 383–384.

In his paper *A New Philosophy for Labor,* Gus Tyler writes that the conference table has replaced pickets, and negotiations have taken the place of mass action. Instead of workers participating in face-to-face meetings, they are now represented by labor mediators. All of this is far more "civilized" than the earlier fights, but it does mean that the idealism is lost, on the part of the executive as well as the membership. This is especially true when the generation which rose to leadership after a hard struggle is succeeded by a second generation no longer knowing anything about the union's early history.[44]

The unions' example also shows that no simplified value judgment can be applied to bureaucratic procedure. It is not only that bureaucratic negotiating, as described by Tyler, is more "civilized" and better suited to the circumstances of rational production than is spontaneous discussion alone; it is also the case that the administration often understands workers' interests better than they do themselves, and is better able to bring their demands into line with overall union or company interests.

To this end, writes Andreas Villiger, governments and public opinion have been requesting unions more frequently to restrict their wage policy, since this seems desirable to maintain a stable economy without inflation. Every pressure thus exerted on the unions will tend to limit further their internal democratic processes. If an agreement is reached, company owners and the public are justified in demanding that unions observe the contractual terms. Observance of the contract then comes before intra-union democracy. The distinction between "responsible" and "democratic" union policy is deliberately ignored by many who criticize the union bosses.[45]

Under certain circumstances the bureaucratic leadership is not only more farsighted, but also less biased than the membership. American union managements have time and again come out against memberships' prevailing prejudices against equal rights for blacks in their sector of industry; however, they have just as often faithfully represented their members' biases.

But even the members' inactivity is far less clear-cut than would appear at first glance. As C. Wright Mills found in his study, the test of union loyalty does not lie in the number of meetings attended, or regular voting. The real test comes during public discussions and crises: whether members will support strikes, whether they join or cross the picket line.

[44] Gus Tyler, *A New Philosophy for Labor* (New York, 1959), p. 8.
[45] Andreas Villiger, *Aufbau und Verfassung der britischen und amerikanischen Gewerkschaften—Wachstum und Strukturentwicklung der Gewerkschaftsbewegung: Probleme der innerverbandlichen Demokratie* (Berlin, 1966).

Experience has shown that this solidarity, although it will vary greatly from one period to another and from one union to another, comprises from half to three quarters of all the people in the unions.[46]

Perhaps even more noteworthy, because of its importance in the tension-laden relationship between democracy and bureaucracy, is a "third category" in the union's structure, pointed out by Mark van de Vall. He notes that in addition to the specialized and hence powerful leadership, and to the uninterested, passive membership, there is a third category, namely that of active members. Because they have a dual relationship within the organization—transmitting criticism from membership to leadership, and instructions from leadership to membership—they act as a democratic nucleus.[47]

In past and present, these active elements of the labor force doubtlessly functioned as shop stewards of sorts. Although they themselves held no official position, they not only provided an important base for union organization, but as the nucleus of spontaneous movements they represented an element of direct social and democratic participation.[48]

The relationship between democracy and increased bureaucracy in the unions entails another problem of special significance. After all, what was at issue in the unions' development and growth was not only a larger slice of the universal cake for one section of society, but intervention by democratic forces, possessed of a sense of mission, in the authoritarian-paternalistic industrial system.

The complaint about the dying out of the unions' democratic spirit has been countered by the argument that it is their task to protect and improve the living standard of their members, and not to provide them with an "exercise in self-government."[49]

American industrial sociologists have maintained that unions, which usually came into being "as a protest against managerial decisions," would lose their moral position if they proved to be undemocratic.[50]

[46] Mills, *op. cit.*, p. 37.

[47] Mark van de Vall, *Die Gewerkschaften im Wohlfartstaat* (Köln and Opladen, 1966).

[48] It may also happen that individuals become part of union leadership who, according to their nature and previous history, belong to this group and who try, within the framework of what is still possible, to act as political rather than bureaucratic leaders. If one considers Walter Reuther (late President of the Autoworkers Union) or Otto Brenner (late Chairman of the German IG-Metall) as examples of such leadership, it is significant that they represented unions whose democratic militant history is not too far distant, and that their approach was shaped by their early experience in small, nonbureaucratic parties such as the American Socialist party and the German Socialist Workers' Party (S.A.P.).

[49] V. L. Allen, *Power in Trade Unions: A Study of their Organization in Great Britain* (London, New York and Toronto, 1954), p. 15.

[50] Joel Seidman *et al.*, *The Worker Views His Union* (Chicago, 1958), p. 185.

In a chapter devoted to the missionary spirit in American unionism, Richard A. Lester writes that organized labor had its own folklore, songs, traditions and martyrs. Union members called themselves "brothers," they had their ethics, which meant that they did not "scab" on one another or cross other unions' picket lines, and that they were willing to make sacrifices for the common cause. Their personal loyalty and devotion, their unpaid, voluntary work at the local level all contributed to the unions' vitality and moral tone. If these were to be preserved, the democratic tradition of American unionism had to be defended against the centralizing encroachment of an efficient administration.[51]

The centralization of some union functions and the fact that others have come under governmental control has shifted the focus away from the microsocial level—that of the individual worker—according to Dutch sociologist Mark van de Vall. For instance, unemployment insurance has been taken over by the state social security program, individual grievances are now the concern of industrial welfare, and collective bargaining has replaced negotiations within the plant.[52]

The missionary democratic spirit could only find expression as long as thousands participated in union activity, thus acquiring a meaningful, satisfying existence. In a survey conducted by Van de Vall (mentioned in his work Die Gewerkschaften im Wohlfahrtsstaat), union members were asked why they had become inactive. A typical answer was: I feel so powerless. Van de Vall also found that there was a close relationship between the feeling of frustration and the occasional wildcat strikes against the organization. Prior to World War II wildcat strikes in Holland were much rarer than union-organized strikes. This relationship has been reversed since the war.[53] Information on England shows that there, too, many postwar wildcat strikes took place not only against employers, but especially against "their own Government and their own Party."[54] If many of these strikes did not appear to be very rational, one must conclude that there is a dialectical connection between apathy and defiance.

Even if unions acquire many of the attributes of other large and established organizations, their members' discontent remains.[55] That fact

---

[51] Richard A. Lester, As Unions Mature: An Analysis of the Evolution of American Unionism (Princeton, 1958), p. 51.

[52] Mark van de Vall, "The Workers' Councils in Western Europe: Aims and Results," in Proceedings of Seventeenth Annual Meeting of Industrial Relations Research Association (Chicago, 1965), p. 283.

[53] Ibid., p. 289.

[54] Ian Mirkado, "Trade Unions in a Full Employment Economy," in New Fabian Essays, ed. R. H. S. Crossman (London, 1953), p. 144.

[55] Lester, op. cit., p. 60.

contains an important truth. For the increase in automated production also affects the industrial worker's position. As Marx anticipated, the labor involved in this type of production "no longer appears as enclosed in the process of production; man relates himself to the process of production as supervisor and regulator." Hence industrial work frequently becomes administrative activity and, as Marx went on to say, "what applies to the machine applies equally to men working together and to the development of human functions, and to the development of human intercourse."[56]

Man's greater activity as "supervisor and regulator" of the production process has not only led to an increase in the number of employees over that of industrial workers, it is in the process of changing the industrial worker's position. In those large corporations where, with growing automation, the circulating capital necessary to pay wages appears to be a marginal supplement to the much greater fixed capital, labor is as interested as management in permanent working conditions with opportunities for advancement. Serge Mallet has spoken of the civil service mentality among workers, because labor has been influenced by the concepts of pension systems and industrial careers.[57] Galbraith has shown that by substituting automated for manual processes, the worker's tendency to identify with the company can be increased. While this identification is beneficial to the company, in that production and price planning are facilitated, it introduces a process which must eventually lead to a decrease in union power.[58]

Cooperatives

Nowhere has the attempt to use direct neighborly contact and self-help been so emphasized or used as a motivating idea as in the growth of the cooperative movement. This movement developed to provide the individual with a feeling of security in large cities and in industrial society. The well-known story of the twenty-eight weavers of Rochdale, England, who pooled their meager resources to purchase the goods they needed, is the outstanding example in the history of the English cooperative movement as described by Sidney and Beatrice Webb. Perhaps as a result of its genuine working class origins, the cooperative movement in Great Britain matured before the theory on which it was based was fully worked

[56] Karl Marx, *Grundrisse der Kritik der politischen Ökonomie* (Berlin, 1953), p. 592. English edition, *The Grundrisse*, ed. and tr. Davis S. McLellan (New York, 1971).
[57] Serge Mallet, *La Nouvelle classe ouvrière* (Paris, 1963).
[58] John Kenneth Galbraith, *The New Industrial State* (Boston, 1967), p. 152.

out. Its immediate aim was to free the worker from the credit system developed by the small shopkeepers and the employers' "truck shop." Its final and actual aim, however, was to free workers from wage slavery. To use the words of its founders: production, distribution, education and government were to be so constituted as to form a "self-supporting home colony."

The Rochdale pioneers' main discovery and practical accomplishment lay in the organization of a consumer-oriented economy. From the beginning, the economy was to be based on production of goods for consumption instead of exchange; and it was to be administered by those who had produced the goods, not as producers but as consumers.

The cooperatives' success was due to the changeover from merely buying goods wholesale for their members to the actual production of goods for consumption. Their business increased yearly, and created a genuine and successful alternative to the capitalist system, which was based on production and distribution for private profit.[59]

English cooperatives remained true to their original objectives for a longer period than did other organizations. This may explain the fact that their importance and efficiency diminished to an ever greater degree in the latter half of the twentieth century.[60] But where efficient sales organization was based on self-service stores and its own mass-produced goods, a conflict arose between the original cooperative concept and modern organizational theories. This is illustrated by Eric Descoeudres, in an article which appeared in a Swiss cooperative newspaper in 1965.[61] He writes that if one wishes to understand today's problem, one must remember that the cooperative societies' aim when they were established was to serve. Their final objective was to serve all consumers, but the latter had to become members of the cooperative to enjoy its benefits. Consequently, anyone could become a member.

The general costs were limited as far as possible, according to Descoeudres. Members voluntarily took on administrative duties; advertising expenses were avoided, the stores were fitted out as little as possible. Hence members were entitled to a considerable refund, but they had to undertake the financial effort of subscribing their share toward the business. This sum represented a small, hard-earned amount of capital

[59] Sidney and Beatrice Webb, *The Consumers' Co-operative Movement* (London, 1921), pp. 1, 2 and 4.

[60] Between 1956 and 1966, membership investments decreased from one-third to one-quarter of the year's returns.

[61] Excerpted from an article by Eric Descoeudres, "Les coopératives et la protection des consommateurs," *Coopération*, no. 46, November 13, 1965.

at a time when wages were low, and it was proof of loyalty and patience since it would not be refunded until the end of the year. Meantime one had to make do with a more limited choice and less efficient service than was to be found at the local grocer's.

It is no longer feasible today to expect the consumer to make a special effort and buy into a consumer cooperative on account of a profit which he can only expect to receive after twelve months have elapsed. Descoeudres points out that today's business policy has to be consumer-oriented, one which will guarantee him special benefits.

Cooperative members have the right to attend meetings, to elect delegates or be elected to the cooperative councils. That is no small matter; on the contrary, the opportunity thus given consumers to play an active role in the economy and exert some democratic influence is of great importance. But only a small minority of consumers seems to be aware of the benefits.

Descoeudres concludes that it is becoming customary for any purchaser to benefit from the same discount as members. Of course the cooperative is still an organization based on an association of consumers. But the relationship between the organization and the consumer membership is transformed to the benefit of the organization which assumes an ever greater importance, and which is forced in the relentless competitive struggle to mistake its own development for the consumers' interests. Advertising becomes more important than providing the consumer with information, and propaganda acquires more significance than education. The virtues of the cooperatives are forgotten or falsified.

PART THREE

THE RULE OF BUREAUCRACY

BUREAUCRATIC GOVERNMENT— THE RUSSIAN EXAMPLE

Special Characteristics of Russian History

In the introduction to his work on Russian History, Valentin Gitermann writes that with few exceptions bourgeois as well as Marxist historians categorically deny the existence of any "special characteristics" in the unfolding of Russian history.[1] However, the Russian political opposition frequently directed attention to these "special characteristics." Gitermann describes how Nikita Muravev, who participated in the Decembrist rising of 1825, tried to point out their origins in a dialogue written for propaganda purposes:

Question: What type of government did Russia have before it achieved autocracy?

Answer: There were always *Veche,* assemblies of the people.

Question: When and for what reason did the *Veche* cease to function?

Answer: This happened when the Tatars invaded and converted our ancestors, who submitted to their tyrannical rule without offering any resistance.

Question: Why did not this abuse cease with the end of Tatar rule?

Answer: The tradition of slavery and the oriental concepts by which they had imposed their rule inflicted still greater suffering on Russia. The people who had borne the Batu yoke suffered equally patiently under the rule of the princes who imitated the tyrants in all they did.

Gitermann notes that Tatar rule, which put an end to the old Russia with its conquest of Kiev in 1240, opened a new, singular era in Russian history. The Tatars immediately established a systematically functioning administration in the conquered country. Tatar officials took the census

[1] Valentin Gitermann, *Geschichte Russlands,* 3 vols. (Hamburg, 1949).

and registered the population. Special officials collected taxes, and other functionaries took care of drafting Russian recruits. However, there was one measure of national importance in Russia's development which the Tatars did not undertake until the fourteenth century. It was then that they allowed a Muscovite grand duke, aided by his own staff, to administer the payment of tribute to the Tatar treasury. This was a decisive step toward making Moscow a central and dominating power.

This power, the Muscovite state, soon managed to suppress other independent cities. Thus, in particular, Novgorod, already a trade center in the twelfth century, possessing a far-reaching autonomous administration with independent subadministrations for every street and city district, was subjected to the rule of Ivan III in 1471. The independent republic of Novgorod-the-Great came to an end. The merchants were deported and contacts ceased with the West.

Ivan ordered that the *veche* bell, which had been used to assemble the people, be rung no more; the office of *posadnik*, the elected mayor, was discontinued. More than 7,000 inhabitants were deported from Novgorod to Moscow in 1478. In 1570, Ivan IV (the Terrible) destroyed what remained of the city's independence. Terror reigned in the city for five weeks and more than 60,000 inhabitants were killed. The city's population decreased by 80 percent.

This intervention prevented the formation of an independent business or guild bourgeoisie. Gitermann maintains that the Muscovite tsar was first and foremost interested in his treasury's needs. The tsar was the biggest merchant in the entire country. After he had completely exhausted his subjects' tax-paying capacities he was forced to tax trade with the help of an army of officials and agents. Sigmund von Herberstein, whom Gitermann quotes, was a German Imperial Ambassador to Moscow during that period. His commentary on Moscow affairs was published in 1549. It described how anyone importing any goods into Moscow was required to inform the customs officials immediately and give an exact description of the merchandise. After they had been assessed, goods were not allowed to be sold until they had been shown to the tsar.

The urban tradesmen had no guild privileges. They remained economically weak, because the peasants were forced by their financial obligations—they had to pay property and body taxes—to take on additional craft work during the long winter months. Rural cottage industry provided competition for the urban craftsmen, and no professional differentiation existed between peasants and the middle class.

When Peter the Great returned from his trip to Western Europe, he established city councils modelled on those of the West. Their main purpose, according to Erik Amburger, was to improve the revenue system; in no way were they intended to promote a municipal community.[2] As Amburger sees it, "The functions of self-government were hardly able to develop under this system, in fact they were strangled at birth by the governmental bureaucracy."[3]

The relationship between the aristocracy and the government was also different from that of the West. The central executive frequently changed the status of the nobility, and eventually the hereditary aristocracy became indistinguishable from the aristocracy created by official appointment. Amburger points out that the nobility had no provincial parliamentary organization or representation. It was not until a decree of 1766 that for technical administrative reasons the aristocracy became a corporation within each provincial government with an elected leader, the Marshall of the Nobility (*Adelsmarschall*).

Between the years 1462 and 1584, political feudalism was broken up and finally destroyed. Ivan the Terrible decimated the higher aristocracy which opposed the centralization of authority and expropriated their land. The remaining nobles were moved to new residences and integrated with the newly titled civil servants. Peter the Great tried to organize the entire population into a system serving the state. Social status and property rights depended on the individual's position in government service. Peter's table of ranks mixed the old aristocracy, consisting of princes and Boyars, with officials of diverse origin.[4] The new aristocracy differed greatly from a nobility produced by feudalism. Its members were given land and serfs, and were freed from paying taxes in exchange for performing certain functions in local administration.[5] As a result the nobles

---

[2] Erik Amburger, *Geschichte der Behördenorganisation Russlands von Peter dem Grossen bis 1917* (Leiden, 1966).

[3] Johann Georg Korb, who spent fifteen months in 1698–1699 at the court of Peter the Great as secretary to the German Imperial Ambassador, noted in his diary: "The cities' official positions are not held by mayors or the most respected citizens; rather a *diak* is appointed by the tsar to administer justice. This man, together with the clerks assigned to him, make up the *prikaz* or chancery, which deals with all judicial matters." *See* Johann Georg Korb, *Diarium Itineris Moscoviam* (Vienna, 1700). Most easily consulted in the German version, *Tagebuch der Reise nach Russland* (Graz, 1968).

[4] Due to the purely mechanical effects of the table of ranks, the number of Russian nobles increased to such an extent that in the nineteenth century steps had to be taken to make the acquisition of title more difficult. *See* especially Amburger on this point.

[5] James Mavor wrote that the peasants were apparently considered to belong to the state, and were temporarily entrusted to the landowners. *See* James Mavor, *An Economic History of Russia,* 2 vols. (New York, 1965), I, p. 91. In 1762, Peter III put an end to the nobility's official functions, and later on their duties in local governments were also curtailed.

tended to be more interested in maintaining their privileges and their ownership of land and serfs than in performing their administrative duties.[6] This became quite obvious when, at the beginning of the nineteenth century, Count Mikhail Mikhailovich Speransky tried to induce the tsar to modernize and reform the administration. He found that the nobility was not capable of supplying the requisite number of educated and honest officials.[7]

As the aristocracy lost interest in participating in public administration, the government was forced to depend increasingly on professional civil servants, so that social and official status became synonymous.[8] However, this was not what the aristocracy wanted. When N. M. Karamzin presented his famous Memoir on ancient and modern Russia to Tsar Alexander in 1811, he acted as self-appointed spokesman of the aristocracy and severely criticized the way in which the government was filling official positions. Karamzin felt that changes in official personnel should not mean the exclusion of the hereditary nobility, nor should it affect their basic rights. Noble rank should not depend on official status, but official status should be bestowed on those of noble birth. He claimed that ministerial departments had replaced the collegial system. Those positions which had once been filled by "eminent officials" were now occupied by unimportant directors, department heads and file clerks who functioned as they pleased under the protection of a minister. Karamzin wondered whether the Minister of the Interior, who controlled practically the whole of Russia, was capable of reading and properly assimilating the endless flood of papers which passed through his office. Did he understand all the problems connected with so many subjects? Committees mushroomed. Of course, the government had finally understood the extreme complexity of the Ministry of the Interior, but what had it done? It had created a further ministry, whose structure was no less complicated and unintelligible.

[6] *See* Gitermann, *op. cit. See also* Richard Pipes, *Karamzin's Memoir on Ancient and Modern Russia: A Translation and Analysis* (Cambridge, Mass., 1959); and B. H. Sumner, *Survey of Russian History* (London, 1944).

[7] Amburger, *op. cit.*

[8] When Alexander Pushkin died in a duel in 1837, the literary journal which had published a deeply moving obituary received a ministerial reprimand. The paper was asked why it had used a mourning-border and mentioned the death of a man who belonged to no office, nor held any rank in the government. But once Pushkin was recognized as a national poet he was considered part of the system. Mayakovsky describes an event which took place in 1913: "Prior to a reading I was to give in one of the southern towns, an 'official' came up to me and said, 'remember, you are not permitted to make any disparaging remarks about the government, or to comment on matters such as Pushkin!' "

Karamzin mentioned further that a decree on ministerial responsibilities detailing the ministries' functions had been issued. This was intended to explain, beyond any doubt, the competence, purpose, working procedures and responsibilities of each ministry. But it did nothing of the sort. After a minimal statement on the principal issues, the decree contained nothing but bureaucratic trivia: how the ministerial departments were to correspond with one another, or how files were to be transmitted.

Everything remained the same, Karamzin complained. New titles and different methods were invented whose end results were the same. The reforms which were carried out led no one to believe that future reforms would be any more successful.[9]

One Essential Fact

The early centralization of power and quite rudimentary development of political feudalism and an urban bourgeoisie, together with the rise of a politically powerful administrative machine, all contributed to the special characteristics of Russian history. Historians like Gitermann and Sumner, who particularly emphasized these characteristics, may have been led to do so by events taking place after 1917.[10] Hence it may be appropriate to consider a Russian author's views of the prerevolutionary era and thus gain insight into the evolution of Russian history.

Maxim Kovalevsky, a former professor of Public Law at the University of Moscow, belonged to the underground "Liberation" society founded by liberal intellectuals in 1903.[11] In the introduction to the work in which he endeavored to present the West with a history and analysis of Russia's political institutions, he wrote that those who consulted his book would note *one* essential fact: the reforms of Peter the Great, Catherine II, and Alexander I and II transformed Russia from an oriental, despotic state into a European one by grafting the bureaucratic institutions of the ab-

---

[9] Pipes, *op. cit.*, pp. 201, 149–150, 153–154 and 155.

[10] However, Herder had already noted in his history of European nations: "From the very beginning it [Russia] developed quite differently from the Western nations of Europe . . ." J. G. von Herder, *Ideen zur Philosophie der Geschichte der Menschheit*, 2 vols. (Berlin, 1952), I, 613, n. English edition, *Outlines of a Philosophy of the History of Man*, tr. John Godfrey (London, 1800).

[11] Maxim Kovalevsky, *Institutions politiques de la Russie: naissance et développement de ses institutions des commencements de l'histoire de Russie jusqu'à nos jours* (Paris, 1905). English edition, *Russian Political Institutions: The Growth and Development of these Institutions from the Beginnings of Russian History to the Present Time* (Chicago, 1902).

solute monarchy onto the existing Russian structure of the seventeenth and eighteenth centuries. However, in actual fact, oriental despotism changed only in outward form, and to the despotic head were added the hundred arms of a centralized bureaucracy.

The first three tsars, Ivan III, Basil III and Ivan the Terrible established an autocratic regime simply by eliminating what remained of any primitive democratic institutions, according to Kovalevsky. Their marriages opened the country to byzantine influences, and they were successful in limiting the Boyars' power. Prior to the end of the seventeenth century, the *Sobors* (Estates-General or General Council) were summoned for the last time; already under Ivan the Terrible they had consisted only of administrative officials and members of the army.

The Boyars who presided over administrative departments in the grand duchy of Moscow, the heart of the empire, employed *diaki* or clerks to execute their functions. A considerable number of these clerks were soon admitted to the lower nobility. As the empire expanded, the feudal lords entrusted with administrative duties were compelled to pass these on to their clerical assistants with greater frequency. Newly established departments became partially independent. These departments were the responsibility of single individuals, who then appointed their own assistants. Each office had its own budget and, as Kovalevsky states, the right to levy certain taxes to meet expenditures. The functions of these various departments were by no means strictly separated. For example, several departments were concerned with financial and military administration quite independently of one another. Newly acquired territories were given a special administration, independent of the country's existing arrangements. A maze of departments was thus created: offices to supply victuals to the court; offices in charge of administering villages which were direct possessions of the crown; offices concerned with the manufacture of silver tableware, the supervision of religious ceremonies in memory of deceased tsars and grand dukes, or with the granting of permits to enter or leave the country; finally endless offices involved in administering the army.

Kovalevsky points out that just as in the West the changeover from the feudal to the permanent army system was decisive in the expansion of bureaucracy, the transformation was unavoidable once the feudal armies failed in their wars against Poland, Sweden and other neighboring states. But the financing of a permanent army depended on continuous tax revenues. In the sixteenth century, direct taxation produced only an insignificant amount, mostly paid in the form of grain;

in the seventeenth century it was converted to a tax which every family had to pay in species. The simultaneous increase in indirect taxation gave a considerable impetus to the growth of administrative functions.

Travelers visiting Russia in those times unanimously report on the boundless arrogance of department heads and the degrading slavishness of the underlings.[12] Although Peter the Great's reforms were modelled on the bureaucratic institutions of Western regimes, they were unable to change the moral conditions engendered by oriental despotism over the centuries. These reforms were aimed particularly at making the administration more efficient. The clerks appointed by feudal administrators, whose main interest was their own enrichment, were replaced by officials directly responsible to the crown.[13] The confusion of departments was minimized by consolidation.

At the same time it became necessary to institute a central control over these various departments. Kovalevsky describes how the Boyars' Council (the *Duma*) was disbanded once the Boyars lost their power. Peter therefore established a regular assembly of important office holders, who were joined by the heads of the most important departments. This institution, known as the Senate, controlled public affairs, the administrative bodies and courts, and also passed judgment on political offenses. However, the outcome was that administrative heads supervised their own actions. To help in this supervision, Peter adopted a Swedish idea; he appointed public prosecutors who investigated all complaints by private individuals against officials or judges, and who were entitled to undertake investigations on their own initiative. It soon became obvious, however, that these prosecutors misused their office to extort money from the plaintiffs. This necessitated supervision of the supervisors, and the appointment of a high official with Senate rank.

Peter the Great's successors partially changed and partially restored

---

[12] Johann Georg Korb (*op. cit.*) noted in his diary: "The entire Russian population is more enslaved than free, since everyone, whatever his rank, lives without any respect for his person and under the yoke of the most oppressive slavery . . . The people . . . roughly reject any vestige of freedom. They are tame under their oppression, they do not even resist the yoke. They declare themselves slaves of their tsar of their own accord. He has a right to their wealth, to their bodies, to their lives. Even the Turks have a no more degrading and despicable veneration of the scepter of their Ottomen."

[13] Alexander Herzen mentioned in his Memoirs that one of the saddest outcomes of Peter's revolution was the formation of a class of civil servants. It was an artificially created, hungry and uncultivated class, with no function except to "serve," and which knew of nothing save official documents. This class formed a type of civilian priesthood, which held its services in offices and police departments, and sucked the people's blood with thousands of bloody, dirty mouths. *See* Alexander Ivanovich Herzen, *The Memoirs of Alexander Herzen*, tr. J. D. Duff, Parts I and II (New York, 1967).

his reforms. But none of the reforms prevented the accumulation of thousands of incomplete measures and unfinished procedures—many of them dating back several decades—which Catherine II discovered in the Senate. Senate instructions to lower administrative departments had to be repeated two or three times before they were carried out. The system of departmental supervision soon degenerated into one of espionage, enabling criminal elements to divert attention from themselves by denouncing others.

Under Catherine's regime, a certain type of aristocratic self-government was permitted in the provinces, but which, according to Kovalevsky, was put under the control of official governors by her successors. Under Nicholas I these aristocratic representatives were only allowed to convene with the permission of the governors, whose orders they had to execute. But because of the nobility existed by exploiting the serfs, they had created a situation whereby the people supported them in their demands for greater personal freedom and control of public affairs.

The limited autonomous government which Catherine had permitted the cities—albeit with strict dependence on the provincial governors—also soon came to an end because of bureaucratic intervention. The governors had the leading members of the urban representative assemblies arrested and exiled, so that within a short period there were no more respected personalities left willing to act as mayor.

Speransky, adviser to Alexander I, developed plans for radical reform of the central administration. But Speransky was soon exiled and only a few changes in bureaucratic institutions remained of the reform which was to have limited bureaucratic power. Such changes did indeed take place constantly. A secret secretariat was established in 1812, whose third section soon acted as the centralized organization of the secret police. This was later transferred to a special department in the Ministry of the Interior. Western newspapers demonstrated their ignorance of Russian affairs when they praised such acts as examples of the tsar's good intentions; in fact these reforms represented nothing but name changes.

Nor did the introduction of local autonomous administrative bodies in the nineteenth century entail any fundamental change. Kovalevsky notes that at the beginning of the twentieth century the rights of these self-governing bodies were restricted to precautionary measures against fire, preservation of order on market days, and maintenance of public sanitation and roads. But even in these areas they were not allowed to enforce any regulations without authorization from the provincial governor, who only gave his permission after checking with a special department created for that purpose in 1890.

The main points of Kovalevsky's thesis can be summarized as follows: the political power of feudalism was destroyed early on. Attempts to expand the cities' self-government met with no success. The lack of autonomous powers enabled bureaucratic administration, patterned on the Western European model, to gain control. The bureaucracy thoroughly exploited the situation, but without being able to organize an efficient administration. Their constant mismanagement led to the "great reforms" which were all enacted without changing anything fundamental in the regime's characteristics. Thus an enormous and expensive bureaucratic apparatus grew up in Russia, able to exercise its power without any control or opposition. Anyone was subject to exile via administrative appointment and no one was allowed freedom of movement. Peasants and workers who wanted to move from one province to another required a passport. It was forbidden to change one's religious denomination, and books and newspapers were strictly censored. Censorship not only applied to political writers but also to novelists and poets.[14] It was forbidden to sign collective petitions or to participate in meetings.

In the preface to his book, published shortly before the Russian Revolution of 1905, Kovalevsky noted that European ideas were beginning to have an increasing influence in Russia and that only the bureaucracy stood to lose anything from their introduction.

Capitalism in the Bureaucratic Hothouse

The "one essential fact" in Russian history which Kovalevsky tried to demonstrate was that in opposition to the autocratically controlled state bureaucracy, feudal forces had only played a temporary and peripheral role. The feudal upper class constantly remained under the political pressure of the state. Hence it was no coincidence, as Nicholas Berdyaev maintained, that anarchists like Bakunin, Kropotkin and Tolstoy all belonged to the Russian aristocracy.[15]

---

[14] One final measure undertaken by Catherine II, who was commended in the West by Diderot and Voltaire, was to turn the census into an independent governmental institution.

[15] As did Alexander Herzen, who was influenced by Proudhon. *See* Nicolas Berdyaev, *The Russian Idea*, tr. R. M. French (London, 1947), p. 142ff.

If Kovalevsky then expressed the hope that the introduction of European ideas would have an adverse influence on bureaucracy, he was anticipating the maturation of a liberally inclined bourgeoisie. This would have required the broad expansion of a capitalist market economy, which did not exist. Although the bureaucracy had undertaken to cultivate Russian capitalism artificially, the middle class could not mature completely in this hothouse atmosphere. Berdyaev has pointed out that the word "bourgeois" connoted disapproval in Russian, whether used as noun or adjective, at a time when in Western usage it referred to a social class demanding respect. Whereas conservative as well as revolutionary anarchist utopias had existed in Russia, liberal bourgeois ideology had not exerted any influence.[16] The Marquis de Custine had already noted in his book in 1839 that the merchants, who constituted a middle class, were so few in number that they were unable to influence the government, especially since most of them were also foreigners.[17]

In the West, the mercantilist bureaucracy was satisfied on the whole merely to supervise and administer the developing industries, but in Russia they were largely controlled by the administration. As James Mavor points out, Peter the Great's enthusiastic energy and his desire that Russia become one of the great industrial nations of the West caused him to establish a vast artificial structure, whose maintenance required permanent governmental support.[18] Government aid and state control of the factory system were the responsibility of the Manufactures Collegium, which had been founded on Peter's orders.

Mavor mentions that compulsion was not lacking in factory administration. Just as serfs were forced to work in factories, merchants were also forced to participate in industrial enterprises. Factory service became a public duty as were military and civil administrative services. In the interests of the treasury it was necessary to secure a monopoly of production, which of course helped to discourage private initiative. Governmental authority and insistent inspection frightened private capital away.

The fact that industrial development was based on military-political

---

[16] *Ibid.*

[17] Adolphe Louis Léonard, Marquis de Custine, *La Russie en 1839, par le marquis de Custine* (Paris, 1843). English edition, *Russia, Translated from the French of the Marquis de Custine* (New York, 1854).

[18] Peter had factories established, which were later transferred to private merchants, but he had neither free workers nor free capital at his disposal. Bureaucratic control was further strengthened because entire districts had to supply workers for the factories, and mines, and for the transportation system involved in the distribution of raw materials. Mavor also concludes that in spite of any formal transfers, the properties involved were still considered state property; if the conditions of transfer were not met, the entirety reverted back to state ownership. Mavor, *An Economic History*, pp. 122, 124–129.

organization prevented the accumulation of private capital. The comparatively rapid industrialization which occurred at the end of the nineteenth and beginning of the twentieth century was in large measure due to the investment of foreign capital. Russian business enterprise grew slowly. At the beginning of World War I large sectors of the Russian economy belonged to the state, or else were regulated and controlled by it. In his history of the Russian Revolution, Trotsky writes that the Russian state consumed a far greater portion of its national wealth than did Western nations.[19] This not only condemned the masses to greater poverty, it also undermined the foundations of the monied class. But since the state needed the latter's support, it taxed and controlled their enterprises. Once they had come under bureaucratic influence, the privileged classes were unable to fend sufficiently for themselves so that the Russian state tended to a large extent to assume the characteristics of despotic Asian states. Prior to 1917, Russian socialists frequently discussed the possibility that if it came to power through a revolution, their party might be overwhelmed by the restoration of an Asian type of despotic government—a concern soon forgotten in the practical problems of revolution.[20]

Splendor and Misery of Revolutionary Self-Government

In 1917 the tsarist regime, already weakened by the war, was finally crushed by the hammerlike blows of a revolution undertaken by a population weary of deprivation. Bolshevik leaders, Lenin in particular, who had come to power by a coup d'état in the course of the Revolution, had oriented their political theories toward the special social conditions existing in Russia. The way in which their party developed was influenced by several factors. There was no strong bourgeois class with a liberal tradition which could have taken up the legacy of the former regime. The working class, even though relatively concentrated in a few areas, was numerically limited and surrounded by a sea of small-holders.[21]

[19] Leon Trotsky, *Geschichte der Russischen Revolution: Februar Revolution* (Berlin, 1931). English edition, *History of the Russian Revolution* (New York, 1932).

[20] For more details, see Karl A. Wittfogel, *Oriental Despotism: A Comparative Study of Total Power* (New Haven, 1959), pp. 6–7, and 391–392.

[21] In 1913, less than 3 million workers, or only 1.8 percent of the population, were employed in industry and mining. More than one fourth of all industrial workers was concentrated in the districts of Moscow and Vladimir. *See* Frank Lorimer, *The Population of the Soviet Union* (Geneva, 1946), pp. 21–23.

Thus the party which came to be established was essentially different from the socialist parties of Western capitalist countries in that it was based on concepts of jacobinism and dictatorship.[22]

The Revolution brought the entire administrative machine to a standstill and released spontaneous forces to an extent which had hardly been anticipated. The hopes for the future called forth by the downfall of the despotic regime and the widespread trend toward self-sufficiency generated high enthusiasm in those individuals and groups unexpectedly called upon to participate in the making of history. This enthusiasm led Bolshevik leaders to think in terms of completely new ways of organizing society, or at least to identify themselves with this belief. The workers' and soldiers' soviets which sprang up everywhere in the country and which took charge of social planning obviously replaced the dead bureaucratic state machinery.

In his book *State and Revolution* written a few weeks prior to the Bolshevik seizure of power in 1917, Lenin recalled the conclusions Marx had drawn from the experience of the Paris Commune, saying that the Russian soviets would create a state of this type.[24] He predicted that the principle of self-government would be carried so far that in the future any cook could govern the state. Since *everyone* was to participate in the government, *everyone* would become a temporary "bureaucrat," and thus *no one* would be a real bureaucrat. He thus predicted that bureaucracy would die out. In his "Theses on Bourgeois Democracy and Proletarian Dictatorship," Lenin wrote that the elimination of governmental power was the aim of all socialists, including, and especially, Marx. Unless this aim were realized, real democracy, that is, equality and freedom, could not be achieved. But according to Lenin, the only practical way of reaching this goal was through soviet or proletarian democracy, because the latter immediately began the withering-away of the state by involving working class organizations in continuous and total participation in governmental administration.

But, in fact, incalculable difficulties arose in establishing a system that would at least function minimally in a situation of civil war. Ultimately,

[22] The concept which distinguished Russian socialism from that practiced elsewhere was explored by Rosa Luxemburg in her dialogue with Lenin in *Die Neue Zeit*. For this article and her other relevant writings, see *Die Russische Revolution 1918*, ed. Ossip K. Flechtheim (Frankfurt, 1963), English edition, *The Russian Revolution and Leninism or Marxism* (Ann Arbor, Mich., 1961).

[23] *See* Leon Trotsky, *Die Russische Revolution 1905* (Berlin, 1923). English edition, *The Revolution of 1905* (New York, 1931).

[24] Vladimir Il'ich Lenin, *Staat und Revolution: die Staatstheorie des Marxismus und die Aufgabe des Proletariats in der Revolution* (Wien, 1929). English edition, *State and Revolution* (New York, 1932).

the difficulties led to the suppression of all spontaneous self-government. Writing of that heroic period of the Revolution, L. Kritzmann describes the process which contributed to a rapid growth of bureaucracy.[25] It was exceedingly difficult to provide for a country in which production depended on innumerable small businesses, and whose normally inadequate transportation system was barely able to function. The already famine-struck land was subjected to a growing number of new and stricter regulations to assure the delivery and distribution of agricultural products.

For a short period the workers did control the country, but the reserve of competent persons was much too small and the general level of education too low to stem the rising tide of bureaucratic power. Cadres of thousands of workers were sent to the provinces and into the countryside to take control and assume administrative functions. Instead of being able to criticize governmental policy or the violation of democratic rights, they suddenly found themselves appointed as presidents of collective farms, as directors of state farms, or organizers of asiatic tribes. In this way the political energy of the working class was exhausted.[26]

At the same time, in view of the declining economy, the Bolshevik leadership lost patience with manifestations of local willfulness. Praise of self-government was replaced by the demand for discipline and subordination. Bukharin had been one of the first, in April 1918, to warn against "bureaucratic centralization," and the danger of the "enslavement of the working class."[27] But shortly after he argued that the nationalization of unions and the political nationalization of all proletarian mass organizations resulted from the internal logic of the process of change itself. He held that the smallest nuclei of the workers' apparatus had to become the basic transmission units of a universal process of organization systematically planned and controlled by the collective judgment of the working class. The latter would find its material embodiment in the highest and all-encompassing organization, its governmental machine.[28]

[25] Lev Kritzmann, *Die heroische Periode der Grossen russischen Revolution: ein Versuch der Analyse des sogenannten "Kriegskommunismus"* (Berlin and Wien, 1929).

[26] *See* André Stawar, *Libres essais marxistes,* tr. from Polish, Jerzy Warszawski (Paris, 1963), p. 187.

[27] The magazine which he edited together with Radek and others stated that once the policy concerning workers was only concerned with reconstituting discipline, governmental structure would tend toward bureaucratic centralization and the establishment of all sorts of commissars. This would end by destroying the independence of local soviets. *Kommunist* (April-May, 1918).

[28] Nikolai Bukharin, *Ökonomie der Transformationsperiode,* tr. Frieda Rubiner (Hamburg, 1922).

125

Trotsky, for his part, maintained that the problem was not due to the bad characteristics of bureaucracy but to the fact that the many good ones were not properly assimilated. In his pamphlet on the role of unions (1920), he not only opposed union management of enterprises, but defended the policy of union nationalization.[29] Although Lenin was against the expansion of control by the workers, he stressed the necessity of maintaining the unions as independent organs of the workers. He wrote that the Russian state was such that the working class had to be in a position to protect itself against the government. Lenin found that invisible hands were suddenly controlling the state. In his lengthy pamphlet *What Is To Be Done?*, published in English in 1929, he complained that the party leaders who had started the Revolution and who had been dispersed during the civil war would be replaced by an anonymous class of functionaries.

In 1917 approximately a million people were employed in the administrative offices of European Russia; by 1921 this number had already increased to almost two and one-half million. Of course many bureaucratic functions had been assumed by those active in the Revolution, but most official positions had remained under, or had been returned to, the old bureaucracy. In one of his last public statements, a report he submitted to the Central Committee before its Ninth Congress, Lenin declared that although the Communists had now obtained the most important governmental positions, they were actually still being controlled by the old bureaucratic machine. He said that just as conquering nations had in the past frequently been assimilated into the culture of the conquered country, the Communists appeared to be undergoing a similar experience—although the culture they were being devoured by was a miserable one. Lenin stressed the same theme speaking at the Fourth World Congress of the Communist International (November-December, 1922). He declared that the Communist take-over of the old Russian governmental apparatus was in reality a misfortune. Deep down below the surface there existed hundreds of thousands of old-time officials inherited from the tsarist regime and from bourgeois society. Shortly before he was removed from the political stage by a stroke, Lenin characterized the new government as being largely a remnant of the old one with just a slightly repainted surface.

The bureaucratic restoration was effected much more rapidly and brutally once freedom of political expression came under greater control.

[29] Trotsky opposed the demand for control by the workers to the prospect of the promotion of talented workers in the administrative hierarchy.

Already in 1921 Alexandra Kollontai had complained to the Bolshevik party on behalf of the "Workers' Opposition," that if bureaucracy had been revived in the life of the country this was in no small measure because of the party's fear of criticism, its chasing of heretics and its restrictions on initiative and discussion.[30]

In March 1921 the sailors rioted at Kronstadt, demanding political and economic freedom and new secret elections of the soviets. The suppression of this revolt led to further limitations on freedom of expression and to the renewed tightening of bureaucratic control. At first all the remaining socialist parties were excluded from any participation in political life. Subsequently, all opposition within the Communist Party was labelled criminal and met with police methods. To all practical purposes this destroyed the independence of the unions, since all their activities came under the control of the party's Central Committee. The unions no longer had the right to have their say at work. They were only able to influence working conditions for a short period under the New Economic Policy.[31] This last expression of independence was denied them once the first Five Year Plan was put into effect in October 1928. The workers' freedom of movement was also restricted and unions became part of the state administration. Nothing remained of self-government and control by the workers, or of the type of state represented by the Paris Commune.

It is important to recognize the causes contributing to the defeat of the principles of self-government after its auspicious beginnings. Many people had heralded this type of administration as the beginning of an era of new interpersonal relationships. An understanding of why it failed will provide greater insight into the bureaucratic problem as a whole, especially since Russian bureaucracy evolved in such an extreme manner.

It was no coincidence that once the tasrist regime collapsed its power was finally acquired by that party which most clearly embodied the Russian bureaucratic principle. This principle was expressed in the concept of a strictly centralized and hierarchic party organization; in the idea that the party represented the objectives of a working class, solely interested in unionization; and finally in the evaluation of the role of a party's

[30] Her statement is taken from: Frits Kool and Erwin Oberlander, eds., *Arbeiterdemokratie und Parteidiktatur* (Olten, 1967).

[31] The New Economic Policy (N.E.P.) mainly consisted of abandoning the forced requisition of agricultural products, the legalization of private trade and granting of concessions to private industrial entrepreneurs. It was introduced after the Kronstadt uprising, which had been an expression of the masses' dissatisfaction at the deprivations they underwent in the period of the so-called War Communism.

subjective will in the historical process. In criticizing Lenin's concepts, Rosa Luxemburg wrote in 1904: "And Lenin has perhaps characterized his point of view more clearly than any one of his opponents could do, in defining his 'revolutionary Social Democrat' as a 'Jacobin indissolubly joined to the organization of the class-conscious proletariat.' In actual fact, however, Social Democracy is not joined to the organization of the working class; it is itself the proletariat."[32] This statement defined the two decisive and conflicting attitudes of the socialist movement. Rosa Luxemburg does admit that the conditions necessary for a socialist movement, as she saw it, were lacking in Russia. She then continues:

But in our opinion it is wrong to believe that the party majority rule by the enlightened workers, which is not yet feasible, could be "provisionally" replaced by the absolute power of a Central Committee, nor that the missing open control by the workers of the party's organizations be replaced by the Central Committee exercising reverse regulation over the revolutionary proletariat. He [Lenin] reveals a much too mechanistic concept of the social democratic organization . . . when he praises the pedagogical importance of the factory, which accustoms the proletariat to "discipline and organization" from the time they leave home. The "discipline" to which Lenin refers is by no means impressed on the proletariat by the factory alone. It is also acquired in the army barracks, and from modern bureaucracy generally; in short, from the entire mechanism of the centralized bourgeois state.

It is precisely the absolute authority of the Central Committee and the strict statutory delineation of the party that Lenin sees as the effective dam to stem the current of opportunism. . . . As Lenin puts it, "Bureaucracy versus Democracy, that is the organizational principle of revolutionary Social Democracy in opposition to the methods of opportunist organization."[33]

Thus it is not surprising that after a brief period of postrevolutionary enthusiasm, spontaneous self-governing organizations had to come into conflict with a party trained on centralist principles. Rosa Luxemburg was able to note as early as 1918:

In place of the representative bodies elected by general plebiscite, Lenin and Trotsky have proclaimed the soviets as the only true representatives of the proletariat. However, as the country's political activities are progressively suppressed, the soviets, too, must grow weaker. But unless general elections are held, unless there is freedom of the press and of assembly, as well as freedom of expression, life dies out in every public institution. What is left is a sham existence, in which only bureaucracy remains as the active element.[34]

[32] Luxemburg, *Die Russische Revolution.*
[33] *Ibid.*
[34] *Ibid.*

When the Bolshevik party finally came to power it forced out all other parties represented in the soviets. Contrary to all of Marx' theories, the Bolsheviks expected to establish a socialist system in a country whose conditions of productivity were completely undeveloped, because they were convinced that the party, in its role as the organized repository of the spirit of history, was able to dictate the course of historical events. This assumption—to which we will return—in itself reflects bureaucratic thinking.

Rosa Luxemburg recognized this subjective trait in Lenin's theory early on. In her 1904 article she wrote:

This anxious effort by part of Russia's Social Democratic movement to protect the promising and vigorous Russian labor movement from making blunders by placing it under the guardianship of an omniscient and ubiquitous Central Committee, seems to us, moreover, to contain the same subjectivism which has already played more than one trick on Russian Socialist thinking . . . The ego having been crushed and flattened by Russian absolutism, obtains its revenge by establishing itself on the throne of its revolutionary, ideal world and proclaims itself an omnipotent committee of conspirators in the name of a nonexistent "Will of the People."[35]

At the beginning of the Russian Revolution, influenced by revolutionary events and in an effort to demonstrate that he had Marx on his side in his position on the soviets, Lenin welcomed the development of a state on the lines of the Paris Commune. Only four years later, in his foreword to a book on the Commune by the historian, Thalès, written in 1921, Trotsky referred to the Communards' policies as an attempt to bypass the proletarian revolution by means of petty-bourgeois reform, namely communal autonomous administration. He maintained that the Commune showed the heroism of the masses, but it also showed their inability to find their way; their leaders clung to the movement's tail and there were no experienced organizers who could have been given complete authority. In contrast he pointed to Petrograd in 1917 where the party had quite definitely assumed full power.[36]

After this the Commune no longer served as an example to the new state; on the contrary, the Commune had to fail because it lacked the example of the Bolshevik party. The actors participating in the Commune drama were destroyed because they tried to withstand the current of history, but they left a wonderful myth behind. In order to remain at the wheel, which it had seized with such a firm hand, the Russian party

[35] Ibid.
[36] C. Talès, La Commune de 1871 (Paris, 1921); preface by Leon Trotsky.

tried to move with the current of Russian history. It preserved the name it had given to the ship of state, and the flag it had attached to the mast. However, the party did not keep to the same direction in which it had set out. The actors who performed in this historical drama suffered the same fate as had their French confrères; but what remained was the wreckage of a myth.

Of course Lenin tried at the last minute to alter the direction in which the state was drifting. He spoke of "invisible hands" which had begun to control the wheel. He hoped to halt the renewed bureaucratizing of Russian society by speaking out against the nationalization of unions; and finally, as late as May 1923, he reversed his negative views, expressed two years earlier, on the importance of consumer societies as a democratic organization. But it was too late.

Otto Rühle, the former Social Democratic representative of the Imperial Diet, and cofounder of the German Communist Party, concluded as early as September 1920 that the Bolsheviks

Changed over to socialism with a magnificently daring leap. At least they persuaded themselves that it was sufficient for socialists to obtain political power in order to develop a socialist era. They thought they could achieve by overt action what had to evolve slowly, as a product of organic development.

They saw revolution and socialism first and foremost as political matters. How could such excellent Marxists ever forget that these are primarily economic matters? The indispensable prerequisites for a socialist economy, and for socialism as a whole, are highly developed capitalist production, developed technology, a trained labor force and the highest possible productive output. Where did such conditions obtain in Russia? The rapid progress of revolution in the world would supply what is missing. The Bolsheviks did all they could to bring this revolution about. But it did not take place. Thus a vacuum was created. What they had was political socialism without an economic basis; a theoretical design; a bureaucratic arrangement; a collection of paper decrees; a few inflammatory phrases; and, above all, a dreadful disappointment.[37]

Restoration of Bureaucratic Rule—The Party as a Means of Control

Lenin recognized that the restoration of the old bureaucracy was a possibility to be reckoned with; but because of his belief in the role of the party as the embodiment of the popular political will, he

[37] Excerpted from an article by Otto Rühle, *Die Aktion* (Berlin, September, 1920).

held the view that such a restoration could be prevented as long as power remained in the hands of the old, reliable cadre leaders of the party. However, power was taken away from these cadres and they were finally physically destroyed.

The ideological concepts of the revolution were maintained during this process and the party continued to exist as an organization. This was possible because Lenin's concept of leadership justified the use of bureaucratic regulations and policies, and because the party itself was transformed into a bureaucratic instrument. It also was the source of recruits for the bureaucracy. Political power was concentrated in the hands of the party's general secretary. The Eleventh Party Congress, held in March–April 1922, already included a resolution pointing out that the party's organizations were in the process of being overwhelmed by the large administrative machine serving them. This machine, according to the resolution, had expanded gradually and had begun to absorb an excessive number of the party's members.

According to Merle Fainsod, one out of twenty-five members held full-time administrative positions in the party.[38] Once the local party secretaries were directly subordinated to the central organization, from whom they not only received their orders but on whom they also depended for their promotion, their hierarchy became a special group in society. This development was paralleled by a growing reverence for the state which replaced socialist concepts.

André Stawar has pointed out that when Lenin spoke of the bureaucratic degeneration of the workers' state and of the dangers of bureaucratic restoration, he was not referring to administrative deficiencies, to the snail's pace at which state business was accomplished, or to procedural delays. What he had in mind was the growth of an administrative machine which would try to govern rather than to administer and which would have a claim on material as well as political privileges.[39]

Such "purely" formal bureaucratic deficiencies did indeed begin to reappear in the new regime. However, what enables one to speak of restoration, in spite of all the differences between the old and new regimes, is the extent to which direct bureaucratic control characterized them both.[40]

[38] Merle Fainsod, *How Russia is Ruled* (Cambridge, Mass., 1962), p. 156.

[39] Stawar, *Libres essais marxistes, op. cit.*

[40] However, policies and methods were also directly transmitted and perpetuated by tsarist officials. There were still administrative offices in 1932, almost half of whose staff was made up of former tsarist functionaries. *See* Barrington Moore, Jr., *Soviet Politics—The Dilemma of Power: The Role of Ideas in Social Change* (Cambridge, Mass., 1959), p. 163.

Under this "direct control," every official acted as direct representative of state authority, even if he belonged to a lower echelon. With all power concentrated at the top, the provincial official acted as a satrap who demanded obedience just because he represented that power and its historic mission.[41]

It has rightly been pointed out that although it enjoyed a certain prestige of fear, the Russian bureaucracy was never regarded as highly as the Prussian bureaucracy.[42] This prestige was always concentrated in the topmost authorities of the state, and it was always hoped that the latter would be able to control the lower and local officials. These authorities—Catherine as well as Stalin—only too frequently lent themselves to criticism of the bureaucracy, a fact which helped deflect criticism from governmental policy and enabled it to be carried out.

Russian history offers many examples of such criticisms followed by great administrative changes which resulted in the elimination of entire administrative sections.[43] But in Catherine's reign and under Stalin, as well as after Khrushchev's great decentralization, administrative affairs went on as usual.

Although bureaucracy usually bowed before the highest authority in the state and although it received terrible blows in return, in the end the latter generally accommodated itself to the tenacity of the former. The bureaucracy's esprit de corps and its method of optimistic reportage proved themselves to be an effective armor.

[41] In connection with this point, Raymond Aron asks how an omnipotent bureaucracy could achieve obedience if it merely represented itself as a bureaucracy? It has to appeal to something higher or to some historic mission in order to justify all the efforts and privations it demands. In this respect, the deification of the head of the bureaucracy appears as a natural process even though it may be connected with special historical circumstances. See Raymond Aron, "Social Structure and the Ruling Class," in *Political Sociology*, ed. L. A. Coser (New York, 1967), p. 83.

[42] B. H. Sumner, *A Short History of Russia* (New York, 1943), p. 64.

[43] During the Great Purge of 1937–1938, almost 100 percent of the higher Ukrainian officials serving in 1937 were replaced at the end of 1938 by persons hitherto unknown to the public. See John A. Armstrong, *The Soviet Bureaucratic Elite: A Case Study of the Ukrainian Apparatus* (New York, 1959), p. 6.

However, the sacrifice of individual bureaucrats is by no means a specifically Communist or Russian manifestation. It is part of the method used by the bureaucratic system. Etienne Balazs, the sinologist, comes to the following conclusions regarding the ruling class of Chinese scholar-officials: "The first thing that strikes one about this social stratum is the precarious position of its members individually, contrasted with their continuous existence as a social class. Even the highest officials were, as individuals, at the mercy of the absolute and despotic state, and were liable to disappear suddenly from view. Any one of them might be minister one day, and consigned to a dungeon the next; yet within the same state that had condemned him as an individual, the body of officials as a whole continued, undisturbed, to play its part. The twenty-four official histories, a massive monument to the reign of the bureaucracy, contain innumerable examples of capital punishment meted out to officials . . ." See Etienne Balazs, *Chinese Civilization and Bureaucracy: Variations on a Theme*, tr. H. M. Wright, ed. Arthur F. Wright (New Haven and London, 1966), p. 6.

The essential similarities between the tsarist and soviet systems described by Sumner include the enormous centralization of power and decision-making, the wide scope of state action, the massive bureaucracy, the extreme importance of the army, the drastic use of force, and the overriding role of the head of state.[44] But centralization of power and thorough-going state action are without question much more clearly evident in the new Russia than they were under the tsars. This is not only because the technical methods of exercising power and control have improved greatly over those of the past, but also because the individual has become so much more dependent on administrative action. People's work, their living quarters and their recreation are all regulated and organized according to governmental standards. Whereas in the past the economy was under bureaucratic influence, under the new system it is directly controlled by the government. While censorship formerly protected the arts against the enemies of the state, its new and positive duty is to justify the state. Sumner observed that bureaucracy's special place in Russian history as a social class with its own ideology is most obvious in its separation from the liberal, educated minority; this analysis can also be applied to the soviet system. Contemporary Russian literature has delineated this sharp division of the two groups by its attacks on the bureaucracy. The government has emphasized the split by administrative actions taken against writers.

The Expansion of the Administration and its Methods

The bureaucratic restoration was marked by the continued subordination of all social relationships to administrative regulations. Revolution and restoration found their expression in two decrees dealing with the workers' position in society. One, which introduced worker control, was issued on November 27, 1917. The other was the labor penal code which came into effect on August 1, 1933, and which listed detention and deportation as punishments for strikes.

The transformation of justice into an administrative prerogative was finalized on October 27, 1934. All institutions of detention which had till then been under the control of the Justice Commissariats of the republics, were now put under the jurisdiction of the Commissariat for Internal Affairs.

[44] Sumner, *op. cit.,* pp. 84–85.

The total authority of bureaucracy was assured, however, once it gained control over the entire economy.[45]

The maintenance and expansion of governmental machinery required that the economic basis of the country be strengthened, but this could only be achieved by rapid industrialization. The necessary capital accumulation was paid for by an amount of human suffering which probably exceeded that of early capitalism in the West. For in Russia accumulation was helped along by organized pressure from the state. The bureaucracy was more interested in furthering this accumulation than it was in the welfare of the workers.[46] However, a number of contradictions developed between the administrative control of the economy and the demands created by production.

Agricultural production was the first to come into conflict with bureaucratic regulations, which could only be enforced by desperate means. Because of its faith in the power of the administrative systems, the bureaucracy tended to forget the inherent laws of nature with which agricultural work had to deal. Stalin's October 1948 project to transform the natural environment, as well as Khrushchev's orders to increase the cultivation of corn were examples of this faith.

In fact, the spirit of absolute bureaucratic government has nowhere been better illustrated than in its quixotic tilting at agriculture. Failure in production was met with changes in the administrative machine, or by changes in personnel. At best, governmental directions were issued to alter methods of cultivation or of crop rotation. The rational idea of subjecting agriculture to planned, calculated organization, was transformed into the irrational attempt to force the always precarious relationship between human labor and nature into a Procrustean bed. Differences in soil and climate and the undependability of the weather were disregarded; rather it was required that orders be obeyed to the letter. In the end, this insistence on the letter of the law threatened the very existence of the system.

Khrushchev had to come to terms with this threat. In a dramatic speech made on March 9, 1962, he examined the transformation of a rational

---

[45] It has often been said that bureaucratic rule resulted from centralized economic administration; however, bureaucratic control was established before the economy could be centralized.

[46] At the beginning of this century, the Polish revolutionary Jan Waclaw Machajski (1866–1926), who regarded the class of intellectual workers as the exploiters of the future, argued that in a backward country like Russia worship of industrialization meant greater exploitation of the workers. *See* V. F. Calverton, *The Making of Society* (New York, 1937); and Max Nomad, "White Collars and Horny Hands," *Modern Quarterly* (Autumn, 1932).

idea into an irrational performance. He suggested taking the example of a sow who has a litter of twelve piglets, in a collective which has no feed for them. What are they to do? They could decide to slaughter the piglets, which is what the individual farmer used to do. Khrushchev asked the audience to picture the situation in which such a kolkhoz chairman finds himself. He cannot allow the piglets to be slaughtered because they have already been included in the statistical reports. The district party committee will be less critical of him if the piglets die of their own accord. However, Khrushchev's own policy remained within the limits set by the system. Between 1953 and 1962 he changed the structure of the agricultural administration five times.

But it was not only by structural administrative changes that the government tried to cope with agricultural failures. Problems involving mere technical matters became power issues in the governmental machine. For instance, infighting occurred over growing winter as against summer wheat, grass as against corn.[47]

The concept "administrative method" signifies among other things that the way in which social matters are dealt with is decided by the interests of relevant agencies, and that those who are entrusted with putting the decisions into practice are bound by the regulations of those agencies. Thus administrative strategy becomes the most important issue. Naturally conflicts do arise between administrative strategies and those who are supposed to enforce them.

A factory director complained in the *Literaturnaya Gazeta* of December 1, 1955, that directors were paralyzed by the current planning and administrative organization. But factory directors have always sought to extricate themselves from administrative bonds by contrived methods. A former Soviet factory manager cites an example: "We always had our stories straight, and had the necessary papers to prove whatever we wanted to. If we were accused of falsifying the gross output or some other plan, or of pirating workers from other enterprises, or of procuring raw materials illegally, I could always count on every member of my team to deny it."[48]

Premier Kosygin once spoke of the "way in which the methods of planning and controlling the national economy had been underestimated

---

[47] Sidney I. Ploss, *Conflict and Decision-Making in Soviet Russia: A Case Study of Agricultural Policy 1953–1963* (Princeton, 1965), pp. 59–112.

[48] Gregory Ryapolov, "I was a Soviet Manager," *Harvard Business Review*, XLIV, 1 (January-February, 1966), p. 118.

135

until now." Obviously he mentioned this because the attempt to solve economic problems by administrative methods caused difficulties which came into conflict with the dynamics inherent in modern industry.[49]

In 1957 Khrushchev criticized the ministerial system because it created unnecessary administrative layers between enterprises and the central ministries and thus delayed decisions.[50] He pointed out that the ministries wanted to become as independent as possible, so as to meet their goals. This prevented rational cooperation between enterprises of the same region who came under the jurisdiction of different ministries. Identical functions were duplicated again and again. Finally it became necessary to undertake massive decentralization measures; numerous ministries were eliminated and enterprises were subordinated to regional administrations. This soon engendered complaints that these regional administrations were weighted with administrative officials, who were not willing to delegate sufficient authority to the enterprises.[51] Regional independence was established at the expense of general national interest. The various republics maintained organizations to coordinate regional administration.

After Khrushchev lost power, the regional administrations were abolished and central administrative ministries for various economic sectors were reintroduced.[52] Those ministries which had been dissolved were reconstituted and the bureaucrats whom Khrushchev had dismissed were reinstated. A journalist, who visited one such ministry, wrote that when one glanced at the personnel register of the new ministry, and when one walked along the different floors and read the new nameplates on the doors, one realized that they were all well-known people.[53]

[49] Excerpted from *Pravda*, September 28, 1965.

[50] In the ministerial system, planned economic development was characterized by what were in principle strictly vertically organized official departments. The Presidium of the Council of Ministers stood at the head of the organization as its chief planning agency. Directly below it was the *Gosplan*, for long-range planning, the State Planning Committee for short-range planning, as well as various other committees responsible for special economic problems with general implications such as price policy, wage policy, or statistics. In addition to the classic ministries, there were forty-two branch ministries. Authority trickled down from the branch ministries either directly, through the all-union ministries, or indirectly, through the republic ministries to the specific planning organizations of the republics, and to other official intermediate levels until it finally reached the production sectors. *See* Fainsod, *How Russia is Ruled*, pp. 327–353.

[51] Fainsod, *op. cit.*

[52] Khrushchev's accusers came to exactly the same conclusion as was reached by contemporary research regarding Catherine II's reforms. Erik Amburger writes: "Her government is marked by the destruction of the central agencies in favor of decentralization. This leads to hopeless disorder and confusion and a constant picking at details, and to the unmethodical formation of small specialized agencies . . ." Erik Amburger, *Geschichte der Behördenorganisation.*

[53] The account appeared in *Izvestiya*, April 16, 1966.

136

Policy and Concepts

In his analysis of the Smolensk administration, Merle Fainsod deals with the regime of Rumyantsev, first secretary of the Western *Oblast* (regional administrative unit). He describes how Rumyantsev modelled himself after Stalin: his portraits and photographs could be seen everywhere, and even factories were named for him and his second secretary. He ruled with an iron hand and brooked no contradiction.

The relations existing between oblast party membership and the central administration were marked by both rewards and punishments. The central directives constituted pressure, they were "suspicious and capricious."[54] The central executive which manifested itself in great detail on paper was not actually very efficient. The regional administration knew how to "build barricades against intervention by the central authorities." Its main weapon was the "family circle"; that is, the occupation of key positions in the district by officials dependent on one another, who managed to suppress or control that criticism without which the central administration is unable to function effectively. Even when it came to electing delegates to oblast congresses, the Party secretariat handed down detailed instructions for procedure.

This type of regional government suffered of necessity from corruption and other adverse administrative symptoms. However, there were also "periodic campaigns to root them out." Rumyantsev himself finally fell victim to one such campaign. In spite of the losses incurred by corruption and embezzlement, the regional government accomplished its main task. It projected central power into the districts, and while it often functioned haltingly and inefficiently, on the whole it enforced the central authority's directives. This was achieved under constant tension and pressure, and the awareness on the part of the regional administration that it would be considered expendable once it could no longer produce results.[55] As the Smolensk example shows, the subordinated bureaucracy enacts central directives as the arbitrary representative of governmental power. In the process of identifying with the latter, differences between position and person are effaced. The importance of an official position increases the individual's importance the longer he occupies that position. A novel, which appeared in the Leningrad journal *Neva* in January 1963, describes

---

[54] Merle Fainsod, *Smolensk under Soviet Rule* (Cambridge, Mass., 1958), pp. 59–60 and 77.
[55] *Ibid.*, pp. 85, 93, 94, 107–108.

this as follows: "It was no longer a question of his serving the Soviet system; the Soviet system had to serve *him*."[56]

In the hierarchical ladder each one wants to be considered as a representative of the whole and to see himself included in the veneration of the state. The insecure position which the functionary occupies—since he is subject to dismissal at any time—and the impotence he feels vis-à-vis the upper hierarchy, are compensated for by his augmented authority.

Valery Tarsis describes the pressure created by the longing for compensation in his novel *The Bluebottle*. The hero of the book, a writer, is forced to work as an official in a housing department. His position is explained to him by his superior:

Krasnobryukov explained to me: "You are the lowest form of life: you make the preliminary check on applicants. As a senior inspector, Rosalia Grib checks on you. Both of you are controlled by our lawyer. Then all of you are checked by me and my two assistants. I am controlled," he ticked them off on his fingers, "by the District Soviet inspector—one, by the District Party Committee inspector—two, by the deputy chairman of the District Soviet, Ivan Solovey—three, by the Chairman himself, Mosolkin—four, and then by innumerable officials of the Moscow Housing Administration, the Moscow City Soviet, the State Control Commission, and a commission of the Supreme Soviet . . . and so on without end."[57]

The hero feels that his main function is to cause harm. But the hero in the novel, like the author himself, is a rebel against state doctrine. Ideology serves the purpose of all the others, for they seek refuge in the certainty of the doctrine. Or, as Alfred Meyer once put it: "Orthodoxy is an armour plate, or corset, for insecure authoritarians."[58]

If suffering and harm have to be inflicted it is done to benefit the state. A story which appeared in 1963 in the journal *Novy Mir* included this statement: "If this is necessary for the sake of the state how could I be dissatisfied with it!"[59] If there is opposition to activity designed to "serve the cause" or which is "necessary for the sake of the state," then it must have developed out of sheer evil.

Another Russian story, by Anatoly Rybakov, which appeared in *Novy*

---

[56] This novel has also been published in English. *See* Fyodor Abramov, *The Dodgers*, tr. David Floyd (London, 1963), p. 109.

[57] Valery Tarsis, *The Bluebottle* (New York, 1963), tr. Thomas Jones and David Alger, p. 119.

[58] Alfred G. Meyer, "The Functions of Ideology in the Soviet Political System: A Speculative Essay Designed to Provoke Discussion," *Soviet Studies*, XVII, 3 (January, 1966), p. 282.

[59] Significantly the story by Alexander Solzhenitsyn was entitled *To Serve the Cause*.

138

Mir in 1964 under the title "Summer in Sosnyaki," deals with a man named Angelyuk, a minor clerk, a pillar of the regime:

In our technological age Angelyuk could handle only one tool—the paper punch. In a period of the greatest enthusiasm and greatest self-sacrifice he did not see one good person. All around him there were only parasites, saboteurs, sycophants, aliens, double-dealers, enemies of the people, kulaks, slaves of kulaks, appeasers, idlers, the politically irresponsible, the politically unstable, the aggrieved, the dissemblers, the masked and the foreign secret agents. Angelyuk saw through them all, he exposed them, pulled them into the open, smoked them out of their holes, he burned them out and exterminated them.[60]

But because bureaucracy identifies with the thing it wants to serve, it becomes that very thing. What Marx criticized in Hegel's "Philosophy of Right," namely, that it superordinates bureaucracy as the knowing spirit, over civil society, has in fact become a reality.[61] This is due to the fact that much that is seen as irrational from the outside appears as rational to the administration. What appears as illogical policy is explained by the internal dynamics of the bureaucracy, which first of all considers all problems in the light of its own interests. The vehement and strongly emphasized resistance to the publication of Kafka's works in Russia can only be understood in these terms. Actually one might have thought that a writer as abstract as Kafka, who describes a dream world, would not have appeared dangerous to the defenders of Russian governmental institutions. But Kafka's dramatic development of the inexorably logical situations which originate in an imaginary, all-pervasive self-justifying bureaucratic administration seemed to Russian bureaucrats to expose real conditions. Just as in Kafka's novel *The Castle*, K. is accused of having witnessed the distribution of the files, "Something that nobody was allowed to watch except the people most closely involved," the Russian bureaucracy felt that Kafka had not only witnessed something forbidden but had also revealed it.[62]

Fainsod has shown how each department tries to manipulate its environment in such a way that it is able to meet the demands made on it, and tries at the same time to receive as much political support as

[60] The two stories mentioned are cited by Barbara Bode, "Sowjetliteratur 1964," *Ost-Europa*, XVI, 1 (January, 1966), pp. 30, 35 and 39.

[61] Karl Marx, *Critique of Hegel's 'Philosophy of Right'*, ed. Joseph O'Malley, tr. Annette Jolin and Joseph O'Malley (Cambridge, England, 1970), p. 74.

[62] Franz Kafka, *The Castle* (New York, 1962), p. 363.

possible from higher authorities.[63] Hence many efforts are made primarily for the sake of the department before they concern themselves with the subject at issue. Khrushchev referred to this situation at the Twenty-First Party Congress when he spoke of officials who could be described as "busy loafers."

Bureaucratic manipulation of the environment does not, however, eliminate the issues which contribute to social conflict. They often reappear as bureaucratic conflicts, perhaps as conflicts between territorial party secretaries and ministerial department sections. But Fainsod was able to show, by using the Smolensk archives as an example, that governmental methods are purposely based on overlapping and duplicated functions. While there is a distinct demarcation between the upper and lower levels within each hierarchy, it is precisely by means of an extensive undelineated area of competence—especially among party officials and the general administration—that political decisions are implemented. One section of the administration always keeps an eye on another section.[64]

Administrative reforms are a constant phenomenon of the Russian governmental system, but in spite of all the fluctuations between the utmost centralization (with the attendant danger of excessive departmental power), and decentralization (with the danger of exaggerated regionalism), duplication of activity was never eliminated.

On the other hand, it has been correctly pointed out that in spite of all the administrative duplication, departments and organizations are part of an all-encompassing hierarchical structure.[65] In fact, it can be said that however respective functions were distributed within the administrative machine, it always operated as a totality. Even when the pendulum of administrative reforms swung in favor of decentralization,

---

[63] Merle Fainsod deals with this problem in both of his works quoted in this chapter.

[64] *See* Fainsod, *Smolensk under Soviet Rule*, pp. 93–95. *See* also Gitermann, *Geschichte Russlands*, who says the same about the administrative reforms of Alexander II: "The significance of the *zemstvos* was also further diminished by the fact that they were not given authority over a single administrative department. In fact the result was overlapping of functions with departments of the central administration."

Such strategy is apparently inherent in bureaucratic types of government. Wilhelm Ensslin describes the byzantine imperial administration: "a system of mutual control was established: such a system, it was true, might produce disputes between rival authorities through overlapping of their spheres of duty or from questions of precedence, but this the Government was content to accept, in order to increase its own powers of supervision." Wilhelm Ensslin, "The Emperor and the Imperial Administration," in *Byzantium: An Introduction to East Roman Civilization*, eds. Norman H. Baynes and H. St. L. B. Moss (Oxford, 1948), pp. 281–282.

[65] For a discussion of this problem see Carl J. Friedrich and Zbigniew K. Brzezinski, *Totalitarian Dictatorship and Autocracy* (Cambridge, Mass., 1956), esp. pp. 177–190.

this did not change anything in the principle of central administration. For decentralization in no way indicated the establishment of autonomous administrative bodies; it was always used as a technical way of organizing the administration, and never as a means of changing the distribution of power. All institutions connected with the economic as well as social life remained subordinated to the same centralized system. Thus what James Mavor wrote in 1914 still holds true: "The State has assumed control of everything, and it is therefore held responsible for everything. The burden of life which falls upon it thus tends to become intolerable, and the deficiencies of the overburdened Government tend to become intolerable also. The course of Russian history abounds in examples."[66]

Since the bureaucratic apparatus not only administers but also governs, power remains the motivating force in its relationship with the world surrounding it, regardless of the real purpose of its specific function. It is the nature of all bureaucratic authorities to use a policy of manipulation and repression, which may vary in its intensity and the way in which it is applied. In the same way faith in the state continues to serve as the principle which molds the world according to bureaucratic concepts. This bears out Marx' statement that "Bureaucracy asserts itself to be the final end of the state."[67]

The conclusion Merle Fainsod arrived at in his analysis of the regional administration of Smolensk may be used to refer to the system as a whole. In spite of great human sacrifice, in spite of the fact that it operated under constant tension and pressure, the bureaucratic regime managed to transform the country into a powerful industrial nation.[68]

Under the political and ideological banner of Stalinism, industrialization came about as in the land of Philemon and Baucis:

> Nightly rose a wailing sorrow,
> Sacrifice of human blood;
> Trim canal was seen the morrow,
> Where had ebbed the fiery flood.[69]

As industry developed, bureaucracy acquired a progressively technical orientation and structure which began to render its operation repetitive and automatic. Creative personalities, however, managed to break

---

[66] Mavor, *An Economic History*, I, p. 76.

[67] Marx, *op. cit.*, p. 46.

[68] Fainsod, *Smolensk*, pp. 107–108.

[69] Goethe, *Faust, Part Two*, tr. and introduction Philip Wayne (London, 1962), Act V, p. 254.

through the bureaucratic barriers time and again. The procedure may have occurred in a fashion similar to what transpired in the bureaucratic apparatus of Kafka's *Castle*: "Suddenly in a flash the decision comes in some unforeseen place, which, moreover, can't be found any longer later on—a decision that settles the matter, if in most cases justly, yet all the same arbitrarily. It's as if the administrative apparatus were unable any longer to bear the tension . . . and had hit on the decision by itself, without the assistance of the officials.[70] Yet the fact that some social interests rather than others were represented and expressed by certain official departments, does not mean that one can speak of the existence of independent institutions and pluralistic forces in society.

However, it is not inconceivable that the existing social organization could promote local self-government in spite of its bureaucratic structure. It was pointed out in the *Bulletin of the Executive Committee of the Moscow City Soviet*, 1965, no. 5, that whereas in previous years "questions of administration of housing were decided at times by the *ispolkom* and the close circles of members of the ispolkom and chiefs of housing agencies, now it has become customary to see at sessions of the ispolkom deputies, representatives of social organizations and activists."[71] It must be added, however, that most of these organizations do not function very effectively so that it requires some deeper conviction to accept the claims of Soviet writers that they herald the growth of Communist self-government of the future. On the other hand there can be little doubt that public participation in local administration has been steadily expanded over the past decade and that fundamental local matters such as housing allocation and maintenance, expansion of kindergartens and nurseries, allocation of places in boarding schools, health, trade and social services, are being increasingly controlled by these grass-roots organizations.[72]

Apart from short revolutionary periods, Russian history has provided no real example from which one might conclude that independent institutions have been so to speak "called into being." Socialist theoreticians like Plekhanov and Lenin, too, from time to time expressed their misgivings that there would be a bureaucratic or Asiatic restoration after the

---

[70] Kafka, *op. cit.*, pp. 88–89.

[71] Quoted by L. G. Churchward, "Soviet Local Government Today," *Soviet Studies*, XVII, 4 (April, 1966), p. 445, n. 54.

[72] *Ibid.*, p. 445. The Party Program for the year 1961 announced that governmental bodies would gradually become organs of public self-government. Local councils were to have the final say in all matters of local importance.

142

fall of the Tsar—which would be equivalent to establishing a type of oriental despotism. Their concerns did not, however, take into consideration the motivating forces inherent in industrial society which have nothing in common with the "stationary condition" of the peasant economy of the old oriental societies.[73] But whether changes in culture and achievement, which are part of industrial development, can also lead to changes in the prevailing system of government, is a question which cannot yet be answered.

Official criticism of the way in which bureaucratic administration functions is hardly likely to be the point of departure for any change in the system since it never comes to grips with its real nature. The new literary movement, however, which does voice such criticism appears to be the expression of a real social opposition.

[73] *See* Wittfogel, *Oriental Despotism,* especially pp. 391–400.

PART FOUR

BUREAUCRACY: THE PROBLEM
OF AN ADMINISTERED WORLD

THE BUREAUCRATIC SYSTEM
AND ITS EFFECTIVENESS

Max Weber and the Dilemma of Bureaucracy

Once capitalism transformed the traditional way of life, factors such as the effectiveness of competition, freedom of movement and the absence of any system of social security compelled the state to assume responsibility for the protection and welfare of the individual. Because each man was responsible for himself, and because that individualism became a social principle, the state remained as almost the only regulatory authority. Specific official agencies dealt with problems according to regulations prescribed by those at the top.

Max Weber was the first to consider bureaucracy as *the* problem of industrial society and to make it the basic subject of sociological analysis. He laid the foundation for all future discussion of this problem by means of a series of precise formulations—although in doing so he also generalized on the basis of specific German phenomena. In his writings he made students of sociology and politics aware of the fact that the bureaucratization of society, although undesirable, was inevitable. It was undesirable because it stood in the way of true democracy and the development of self-responsible, socially active citizens, and because it led to their "passive" democratization, that is, to their "levelling." It was inevitable, because it was a phenomenon characteristic of *mass* democracy, in contrast to the democratic self-government of small homogeneous units. Mass democracy which does away with feudal, patrimonial and—at least in intent—plutocratic privileges in the administration, must of necessity substitute paid professional labor for the part-time voluntary administration performed by people of rank. That does not only apply to the state. It is not by chance that popular democratic parties have completely broken with the traditional system of rule by notables, based on personal relationship and personal esteem, within their own party organizations.

They have instead placed themselves under the bureaucratic control of party officials, and professional party and trade union secretaries.

However, it must always be remembered that the term "democratization" can be misleading. The *demos*, in the sense of an unstructured mass, never "governs" larger associations, but is governed. What changes is the way in which executive leaders are chosen and the amount of influence exerted by the *demos,* or rather by the social circles drawn from its midst, upon the content and direction of administrative functions through "public opinion."

The development of bureaucracy is not only linked to that of mass society, it also has its roots in the efforts of industrial society to establish an efficient structure, to realize technical objectivity and to integrate man into a mechanized system. The decisive factor in the advance of bureaucratic organization has always been its purely *technical* superiority over any other system. A fully developed bureaucratic system compares with other types of organizations as does a machine when compared with nontechnical methods of production. Precision, speed, clarity, familiarity with files, continuity, discretion, conformity, strict subordination, decrease in friction, and in material and personal costs—all of these are increased to their optimum value in a strictly bureaucratic administration, especially in its monocratic form. Trained individual officials function far more efficiently than do collegiate, honorary or voluntary administrators. Large modern capitalist enterprises are usually themselves superior examples of strict bureaucratic organization. Above all, however, bureaucracy offers the greatest opportunity for the specialization of administrative functions.

What may be seen as a special characteristic of the modern entrepreneur is that he classifies himself as the "first executive" of his business, just as the ruler of a specifically modern bureaucratic state once defined himself as its "first servant."

The notion that there is an internal difference between bureaucratic office methods of the state and those used by private enterprises belongs to the European continent. Americans are unaware of such a difference.[1]

The capitalist economic system, with its computability, brought bureaucratic control to its fullest development. Max Weber notes that the more "dehumanized" bureaucracy becomes, the better it is able to evolve

---

[1] Max Weber, *Wirtschaft und Gesellschaft* (Tübingen, 1922), Chapter. XI. English edition: *Economy and Society: An Outline of Interpretive Sociology,* ed. Guenther Roth and Claus Wittich, tr. Ephraim Fischoff *et al.* (New York, 1968).

those features esteemed by capitalism. Its techniques become all the more refined as it eliminates from its official business love, hatred and all those purely personal, irrational and emotional elements which defy calculation.[2]

Max Weber sees the process of bureaucratization as one of "disenchantment," that is to say, the belief has become dominant that with increasing intellectualization and rationalization all things can be controlled by means of calculation.[3]

But as Weber recognizes and stresses the relationship between bureaucracy and the computational system of the capitalist industrialized society, he emphasizes and even overemphasizes its rational character. There is little indication of the popular attitude regarding the bureaucratic bumbler and red tape in Weber's interpretation. He endows bureaucratic administration with such attributes as precision, stability, strict discipline and reliability, which all make for calculability of results, benefitting executives as well as clients. Weber claims that bureaucracy is superior in the efficiency and scope of its functions, and in its technical ability to perform all sorts of administrative duties. He describes it as the most rational means of exercising control over human beings.[4]

The invention of a machine of such precision as a means of control excludes the possibility of any other system. The complexity of industrial society does not permit any but bureaucratic administration, since the material destiny of the masses is tied to the continuous functioning of the bureaucratic apparatus. Weber points out that one has a choice between "bureaucracy" and "dilettantism" in the matter of administration. The former's superiority lies in its technical expertise. The power position of a fully developed bureaucracy is always a strong one— regardless of who is in control. The "political master" always finds himself to be the "dilettante" when he comes face to face with the bureaucratic "expert." Every bureaucracy tries to increase the advantage of its professional administrators by *keeping secret* its expertise and its intentions. The tendency of bureaucratic administration is to exclude the public.[5]

The relationship between the bureaucracy and those ruling society,

---

[2] Max Weber, *Schriften zur theoretischen Soziologie, zur Soziologie der Politik und Verfassung*, ed. Max Graf zu Solms (Frankfurt-am-Main, 1947).

[3] Max Weber, "Wissenschaft als Beruf," in *Gesammelte Aufsaetze zur Wissenschaftslehre* (Tübingen, 1922). English edition: "Science as a Vocation," in *From Max Weber: Essays in Sociology*, ed. and tr. H. H. Gerth and C. Wright Mills (New York, 1958), pp. 129–156.

[4] Weber, *Wirtschaft, op. cit.*, Chapter III.

[5] *Ibid.*, Chapter XI.

that is, the extent to which the former shares the power, can vary greatly. Hence it is necessary "in each individual historical case to analyze the particular directions in which bureaucratization has developed."[6]

Weber realized that the bureaucratic machine could arrogate an ever greater amount of control: "The Russian tsar of the ancien régime was seldom able to insist on the permanent enactment of any measure which displeased and was contrary to the interests of his bureaucracy."[7]

Whatever happens to be the real distribution of power, the main problem is that "Once it is fully established, bureaucracy is one of those social structures which are hardest to destroy." The individual bureaucrat cannot break away from the apparatus to which he has been harnessed. The professional bureaucrat, in contrast to the part-time "honorary administrator," is chained to his work through his entire economic and ideological existence. He is, above all, linked to all the other functionaries who are part of this mechanism by a common interest, which is to promote its perpetuation.[8]

Yet in spite of all of Weber's admiration for the precision of bureaucratic administration, and the well-founded reasons he gave for its permanence, he continued to stress the necessity for opposition to the growth of bureaucracy in society. In his discussion with the *Katheder* (or state) socialists in 1909, in the *Verein für Sozialpolitik* (Society for Social Policy), Weber presented the dilemma as follows. On the one hand, he pointed out that no machine in the world was as efficient as this human machine (bureaucracy). From the technical-functional point of view it was unsurpassable. On the other hand, he asked what there was to substitute for this machinery, in order to keep a remnant of humanity free from that splintering of the soul, from autocratic imposition of the bureaucratic way of life. As the state increasingly assumes the role of an entrepreneur, it also assumes the point of view of an employer, instead of becoming, contrariwise, the implementing mechanism of socio-political policies.[9]

Weber was not even afraid of asking whether the corrupt officialdom of some countries was not preferable to cold "efficiency." After his trip to America in 1904 he repeatedly referred to the viewpoint expressed by American workers, that corrupt politicians who can be removed from office were preferable to a permanent, specialized bureaucracy. But he found that such concepts in their turn led to a dilemma. While democracy

---

[6] *Ibid.*

[7] *Ibid.*

[8] *Ibid.*

[9] Marianne Weber, *Max Weber: Ein Lebensbild* (Tübingen, 1926), III, Chap. 12, p. 421.

had to oppose bureaucracy, which tended to promote a mandarin caste, the political "spoils system" with its corruption, its waste of public revenues, and its lack of administrative technology was becoming more unsatisfactory and coming into conflict with democratic tendencies. Paradoxically, then, exponents of democratic procedures found themselves advocating a bureaucratic structure which politically they rejected.

As a historian, Weber knew that all genuine democratic movements advocated "minimization of domination," but he realized that their current attitude toward bureaucracy had to be ambivalent. For the only way to ensure "equality before the law" and legal guarantees against arbitrariness was by means of the formal, rational "objectivity" of the administration as contrasted with dependence on the personal discretion and grace of the old patrimonial system. But the masses postulate substantive justice directed toward concrete circumstances and persons; the "ethos" which consequently guides them on individual problems inevitably conflicts with the formalism and cold, rule-bound "efficiency" of bureaucratic administration. Hence it must reject, on emotional grounds, what reason demands. In particular, the disinherited masses are not served by formal "equality before the law" or the calculable justice and administration demanded by bourgeois interests. They naturally require that justice and administration serve to equalize their economic and social chances with those of the propertied classes. This can only come about if justice and administration assume a character that is informal because it is "ethical."[10]

The attempt on the part of democratic movements to break out of this bureaucratic closed sphere always ends by leading back into it, since "mass" formations in turn require bureaucratic organization. The bureaucratic organization of all genuine mass parties offers the most obvious example of how sheer quantity can influence the bureaucratization of social structures. Such parties are the German Social Democratic party and the two "historic" American parties.

Weber saw no way of avoiding bureaucratic influence on the ideology of either free enterprise or socialism. He considered official administrative activity as separated from the private sphere of life, and as a condition which had developed over a long period of time. This condition is found in public as well as private enterprise, and in the latter it even affects the director himself.[11]

[10] Weber, *Wirtschaft*, Chap. XI.
[11] *Ibid.*

Weber anticipated that socialism would only complete what had already begun to happen in the political sphere, when the feudal authorities lost their political power to a paid officialdom. It was his feeling, after the Russian October Revolution, that what was developing was not a workers' dictatorship, but a dictatorship by the bureaucracy. "Since the advance of bureaucracy is irresistible, the question of future forms of political organization must be formulated as follows: How can the remnants of any kind of 'individualistic' freedom of movement be salvaged in the face of the overpowering tendency toward bureaucratization? For it is ultimately a gross self-deception to believe that we can exist at all today without this great achievement of the era of 'human rights.' "[12]

The Bureaucratic Mind

Max Weber recognized that bureaucracy is part of the larger problem of the internal structure of modern society. The mind of bureaucracy and the reaction of those who are governed by it form a closed sphere within which the atmosphere of the administered world is generated. But in reality that closed sphere is already being formed by the conditions leading to the development of bureaucracy. They are the conditions which, as Karl Marx put it, separate within each individual the citizen from the member of civil society. Thus the individual reflects a *universal law:*

Civil society and the state are separated. Consequently the citizen of the state and the member of civil society are also separated. The individual must thus undertake an essential schism within himself. As *actual* citizen he finds himself in a two-fold organization: (a) the *bureaucratic,* which is an external formal determination of the otherworldly state of the executive power, which does not touch him and his independent actuality; (b) the *social,* the organization of civil society, within which he stands outside the state as a *private man,* for civil society does not touch upon the political state as such. The former [the bureaucratic] is an organization of the state to which he continually contributes the *material.* The latter [the social] is a *civil organization* whose material is not the state. In the former the state relates to him as formal opposition; in the latter he himself relates to the state as material opposition. Thus, in order to behave as *actual citizen* of the state . . . he must abandon his civil actuality, abstract from it . . . because the only existence that he finds for his state-citizenship is his pure,

[12] Max Weber, *Gesammelte politische Schriften* (München, 1921).

152

bare *individuality*, for the existence of the state as executive is complete without him, and his existence in civil society is complete without the state.[13]

The division, or schism, by which the citizen belongs to the "two-fold organization," provides the basis for bureaucracy according to Marx. The way in which citizen is separated from state, or member from organization, or producer from production is both the cause and result of the growth of bureaucracy in the world. As a continuous process it has modernized and given currency to the concept of alienation in the second half of the twentieth century. For alienation is the natural result of separation.

But there is also the separation of the individual from an office, "that kind of man-made irreality—indeed, that strange construction of a human mind which finally becomes slave to its own fictions," so that as an official he regretfully undertakes that which he would scorn to do as a human being.[14]

The bureaucratic mind permeates and controls all spheres of life to an ever greater extent as everything in the world becomes subject to administrative agencies. Having criticized Hegel for not providing any content for bureaucracy in his "Philosophy of Right," Marx pointed out the origin and orientation of the bureaucratic mind:

The mind of the bureaucracy is the formal mind of the state. It therefore makes the formal mind of the state, or the *real* mindlessness of the state, a categorical imperative. The bureaucracy asserts itself to the final end of the state. Because the bureaucracy makes its formal aims its content, it comes into conflict everywhere with the real aims. Hence it is obliged to present what is formal for the content and the content for what is formal. The aims of the state are transformed into aims of bureaus, or the aims of bureaus into the aims of the state. The bureaucracy is a circle from which no one can escape. Its hierarchy is a *hierarchy of knowledge*. The highest point entrusts the understanding of particulars to the lower echelons, whereas these, on the other hand, credit the highest with an understanding in regard to the universal . . .

[13] Karl Marx, *Critique of Hegel's 'Philosophy of Right,'* ed. Joseph O'Malley, tr. Annette Jolin and Joseph O'Malley (Cambridge, England, 1970), pp. 77–78.

[14] Ernst H. Kantorowicz has dealt with the medieval fiction of the king's two bodies, which marked the inception of this "invention." A law report by Elizabethan jurists, cited by Kantorowicz, stated: " 'The king has two Capacities, for he has two Bodies, the one whereof is a Body natural . . . subject to Passions and Death . . . the other is a Body politic . . .' However, the seemingly ludicrous and in many respects awkward, concept . . ." says Kantorowicz, "provided an important heuristic fiction which served the lawyers at a certain time 'to harmonize modern with ancient law,' or to bring into agreement the personal with the more impersonal concepts of government." Ernst H. Kantorowicz, *The King's Two Bodies: A Study in Medieval Political Theology* (Princeton, 1957), pp. 5 and 13.

153

Accordingly *authority* is the principle of its knowledge and being, and the deification of authority is its *mentality*. But at the very heart of the bureaucracy this *spiritualism* turns into a *crass materialism*, the materialism of passive obedience, of trust in authority. . . . As far as the individual bureaucrat is concerned, the end of the state becomes his private end: a *pursuit of higher posts*, the *building of a career*. In the first place, he considers real life to be purely *material*, for the *spirit of this life has its separate existence* in the bureaucracy. Thus the bureaucrat must make life as materialistic as possible. Secondly, real life is material for the bureaucrat, i.e., in so far as it becomes an object of bureaucratic action, because his spirit is prescribed for him, his end lies outside of him, his existence is the existence of the bureau. The state, then, exists only as various bureau-minds whose connexion consists of subordination and dumb obedience.

While the bureaucracy is on one hand this crass materialism, it manifests its crass spiritualism in its *will to do everything*, i.e., in its making the will the *causa prima*, for it is pure *active* existence which receives its content from without; thus it can manifest its existence only through forming and restricting this content. The bureaucrat has the world as a mere object of his action.[15]

Thus Marx considers the two basic characteristics of the bureaucratic mind to be the deification of authority, and consideration of the world as a mere object of bureaucratic action.

As has already been noted, anything of a controversial nature is regarded as disruptive in those places where everything is subject to "impartial" regulation. With the increasing transfer of social functions to official agencies, and the officialization of all independent associations, a negative attitude develops toward the expression of *differing* opinions. Obviously this is true where bureaucracy exercises dictatorial power; in fact, it is common knowledge in such institutions that the only correct point of view is the one publicly expressed by the bureaucracy. Elsewhere the techniques used are "defamation generally, . . . simple opposition leading to furtive ostracism . . . [and] the even more common outlawing of opposition per se."[16]

Once man is the universal object of administrative activity, he is expected to adapt his ideas accordingly and not express his own point of view. He is also expected to leave the matter of opposition to those competent to express it. When the authorities require an expression of opinion, they themselves ask for it. Such opinions are thus not instances of active social participation, but merely echoes of induced attitudes whose success

[15] Marx, *op. cit.,* pp. 46–48.
[16] Ulrich Sonnemann, *Die Einführung des Ungehorsams in Deutschland* (Hamburg, 1964).

is gauged by questionnaires. In its dealings with the world, the nondespotic bureaucracy does take into consideration the viewpoint of the objects it manipulates. But because of the increasing number of individuals who "build a career" in the bureaucratic system (or would like to do so), there must be a corresponding growth in the number of people who ought to keep silent.

Those who have grown accustomed to being the object of bureaucratic attention voluntarily relinquish the right to express their opposition. Indifference to social processes becomes a universal phenomenon. The expression "nothing can be done anyway" is typical of the attitude. Anything and everything is left up to those in authority, but certainly not because one trusts them. On the contrary, mistrust exists everywhere as does the ultimate feeling that the state is an alien power. There is latent ressentiment against all forms of bureaucracy—not only against that of the state. It is a type of ressentiment which grows stronger as the bureaucratic forces become more anonymous and impregnable, as they are increasingly removed from the realm of personal give and take.

In his discussions with the workers in Northern England, Richard Hoggart encountered both the feeling that no authority is justified, and the tendency to rely on it. This tendency is particularly obvious in the use of phrases like, " 'They ought to do something about it,' 'They ought to get us out of it,' 'They ought to do this about the Health Service and that about the schools.' " However, the dislike of authority implied no desire for independence. What is frequently manifested is a "sullen shaking-away of the idea of authority, coexisting with an assumption that nevertheless something or somebody outside should provide. The joint effect of these two attitudes will be to increase the . . . unresponsiveness of many people towards calls upon them from outside their personal and domestic lives." Hoggart adds that people are turning into "what Alex Comfort has called 'irresponsible obedients'; it would be better if more were 'responsible disobedients.' "[17]

The continuous transfer and accumulation of responsibility from independent social groupings to administrative offices and central organizations develops in close connection with the expansion of rational forms of thought. There is a relationship between rational ideas and the "will to do everything." Responsibility is delegated to the best informed author-

[17] Richard Hoggart, *The Uses of Literacy: Changing Patterns in English Mass Culture* (Fair Lawn, New Jersey, 1957), p. 162.

ity. Traditional, independent social groupings were never able to withstand efficient administrative technology. But efficient administrative technology is quite capable of coming into conflict with actual social attitudes, which are of course determined by values and goals.

Seen from rational-technical angles, it may ultimately appear irrational that differences of opinion and hence dissension are tolerated in society. Eduard Heimann has observed that from such a point of view it seems necessary to run society like "a system of logic," in which "the minor propositions are derived from and subordinated to the higher ones, so [that] society is organized in a strict rationality of functions from the top down. Dictatorship is the logical form of social rationalism. And being the incorporation of collective reason itself, the dictatorship necessarily claims to be infallible."[18]

Wherever bureaucratic control becomes all-encompassing it also creates an obsession with power which overshadows rational tendencies—as has been shown by the Russian example. But what developed to its fullest extent under special historical conditions is everywhere inherent in the bureaucratic mind. From the very beginning the "will to do everything" includes a striving to increase power.[19] That is how the concept developed that the assumption of power was the decisive reason for the adoption of a rational form of life in all societies and that "administrative apparatuses" could readily be set up for completely new goals because no serious restrictions existed to prevent manipulation."[20] This is evident in the practice of large corporations which abandon their production goals as they expand. Their further expansion is frequently designed to promote the power of the managing bureaucracy. But the search for power does not only cause conflict with rational aims in the relations between the bureaucracy and the surrounding world. There is also conflict between administrative departments in their attempts to gain authority. Consequently, the *Economist,* in April 1965, pointed out to the British Foreign Minister that other "overlords" before him had already discovered the center of governmental power to reside less in a minister than in his ministry.

---

[18] Eduard Heimann, "Rationalism, Christianity and Democracy," in *Synopsis: Festgabe für Alfred Weber* (Heidelberg, 1948), p. 168.

[19] But the striving to increase power need not be the predominating motive. Montesquieu had already realized that the more zealously a servant of the state works for public welfare, the more he is tempted to gain power since he knows what is good for the people.

[20] Wiegand Siebel, "Rationalität und Normenorientierung in der Organisation," *Zeitschrift für die Gesamte Staatswirtschaft,* CXX, 4 (October, 1964).

All studies of bureaucratic institutions refer to "departmental imperialism." The struggle to expand departmental authority, which is based on departmental loyalty, leads to a preoccupation with interdepartmental problems of coordination, and to the contrast between departmental interests and functions. American sociologists use the term "dysfunction" when referring to an operation which does not correspond to rational aims and their optimal technical fulfillment, and whose emphasis has been shifted from goals to procedures which develop from the nature of bureaucracy itself.[21] In his well-known satire, C. Northcote Parkinson states that civil service personnel increases faster than the volume of work. He refers to it as a "law of growth."[22] In this sense as well as in the popular concept, bureaucracy is seen as an "organizational sickness."[23]

While administrative agencies seek to acquire and to extend their authority, it appears to those who consult them that the individual official tries to suggest that he is unable to deal with specific problems. Although the "will to do everything" is inherent in the bureaucratic mind, people feel that bureaucrats are unwilling to do anything. The official needs to be able to refer to official channels and to regulations, for this corresponds to the separation of the individual from his office. But for those who have to deal with officialdom it provides an example of bureaucratic inhumanity. What struck Max Weber first and foremost about bureaucracy was its precision, promptness and "efficiency"; the general public, however, has quite the opposite view of it. This attitude did not develop suddenly, but has accompanied the bureaucratic process from its beginnings. Von Justi, who took the Chinese system of government as an example in his work in 1762—because China possessed not merely a few powerful ministers but an entire administrative apparatus—cited as its "only flaw" the fact that "there is a not infrequent tendency toward procrastination."[24]

In the nineteenth century, Balzac made a somewhat similar criticism of bureaucracy in a novel devoted almost entirely to the subject:

Bureaucracy, that gigantic power started up by midgets . . . created a principle of inertia called The Report. . . . The best decisions ever made in France were

[21] Robert K. Merton, *Social Theory and Social Structure* (New York, 1959), esp. pp. 51 and 53.

[22] C. Northcote Parkinson, *Parkinson's Law and Other Studies in Administration* (Boston, 1957), pp. 3 and 4.

[23] Fritz Morstein-Marx, *Einführung in die Bürokratie* (Neuwied, 1959). English edition, *The Administrative State: An Introduction to Bureaucracy* (Chicago, 1957).

[24] Johann Heinrich Gottlob von Justi, *Vergleichungen der Europäischen mit den Asiatischen und anderen vermeintlich Barbarischen Regierungen* (Berlin, Stettin, Leipzig, 1762).

taken before Reports existed and decisions were spontaneous. . . . [But later] . . . a superior man found it very difficult to make his way through the mud of these sinks of iniquity where unusual accomplishments frightened everyone. . . . The only ones who came or remained were the lazy, the incompetent and the stupid. Thus the mediocrity of the French Administration was slowly established. Entirely made up of small minds, the bureaucracy placed obstacles in the way of prosperity, buried in its files for seven years a canal project that would have stimulated the productivity of an entire province.[25]

However, the contemporary French sociologist Michel Crozier, who made a study of the "bureaucratic phenomenon," countered the popular concept of the "bureaucracy as a sickness." He pointed out that those "bureaucratic" characteristics which engender public indignation had actually had far greater opportunity of developing in traditional organizations than in modern ones. The older types of administrations were ruled by those ritualistic officials who pedantically observed the regulations for fear of punishment. They used ritualistic interpretation against their own office as often as against a client.

In modern organizations, in which the official is no longer at the mercy of a superior, and in which his status and future are assured, the procedures used are more rational.[26] Official agencies certainly no longer conduct their business as they did at the time of Balzac, or in the manner of Charles Dickens' "Circumlocution Office" through which "all the business of the country went . . . except the business that never came out of it; and *its* name was Legion."[27] The "Circumlocution Office" was in fact situated on a boundary. Dickens' satire was part of the attack waged by England's bourgeoisie against the degenerate aristocratic administration, whose main aim was to provide for its office holders. "Parkinson's Law" certainly contradicts Crozier's optimism, and new fears have replaced the old ones in departments plagued by "status" problems. Nevertheless administrative efficiency has increased. There is no doubt but that the bureaucratic mind no longer needs to function purely by means of red tape. It has in many cases adapted itself to the laws of motion of an automated society.

The social effect of bureaucracy does not derive as much from the

[25] Honoré de Balzac, *Les Employés,* eds. M. Bouteron and H. Longnon (Paris, 1910), pp. 16–19. English edition, *Bureaucracy; or a Civil Service Reformer,* tr. Katherine Prescott Wormeley (Boston, 1889).

[26] Michel Crozier, *Le Phénomène bureaucratique* (Paris, 1964), pp. 244–245. English edition, *The Bureaucratic Phenomenon,* tr. author (London, 1964).

[27] Charles Dickens, *Little Dorrit* (London, 1868), p. 96.

efficiency of administrative institutions—its most striking quality—as from the way in which the bureaucratic mind affects interpersonal relationships. The negative effect of the bureaucratic mind on the minds of those it controls becomes more evident as bureaucratic influence expands and encompasses greater domains. Because industrial nations have developed into "organizational societies," citizens have increasingly come to feel powerless and removed from participation in decision-making.[28] The feeling of powerlessness contradicts the human striving for security. The sense of self-esteem without which man feels insecure develops through his participation in social intercourse. Neurotic tensions result from the individual's attempt to compensate for the feeling of powerlessness and the inability to participate. Alice Rühle-Gerstel maintains that "Neurosis is not a sickness but a way of life. In neurosis the separation of the individual from his sense of association (*Gemeinschaft*) with other individuals becomes a distinguishing category of the mind."[29]

Neurotic tensions are calmed with substitutes. One such substitute is prestige, the appearance of power, which is supposed to outweigh the feeling of powerlessness. This has given rise to the mania for status and its symbols, which has been much discussed, and which has been excellently described as "the paradox of the intensified irrationality of human existence in a thoroughly rationalized world."[30]

Governmental Bureaucracy—Authority or Tool?

The political role of governmental administration, as well as the conduct and working procedures of its officials, depends on the political and economic structure of the state and the national character of the population. This study does not intend to detail the changes which took place from one era to another, or the differences existing between nations. But a permanent officialdom and a "continuous, regulation-bound fulfillment of administrative functions," as Max Weber defines it, have been established in all industrial nations.

The permanence of this officialdom governed by strict administrative regulations, and its independence from day-to-day politics and changes

[28] Robert Presthus, *The Organizational Society: An Analysis and a Theory* (New York, 1965), pp. 9 and 35.
[29] Alice Rühle-Gerstel, *Der Weg zum Wir* (Dresden, 1927), p. 79.
[30] Ernst von Schenck, "Überwindung der bloss formalen Demokratie," in *Zweites Europäisches Gespräch: Arbeiter, Manager und Kultur* (Köln, 1951).

159

in the political hierarchy, have made it a necessary factor in the maintenance of the efficient, continuous administration on which industrial nations are built. "Well-planned, methodical procedure, expertise and mastery of administrative technology—these," writes Fritz Fleiner, "are the virtues of officialdom."[31]

However, in those instances where the administrative machinery had not been established and bequeathed by the absolute monarchy—as was the case in the United States—the principles of a permanent administrative machine conflicted with democratic principles. When Andrew Jackson was made President in 1828 with the help of a radical-democratic movement, the people turned against administrative officials whom they saw as having been corrupted by their self-aggrandizement. Jackson explained to Congress that "Office is considered as a species of property, and government rather as a means of promoting individual interests than as an instrument created solely for the service of the people." He believed that "official duties could be made so plain and simple that men of intelligence may readily qualify themselves for their performance."[32]

Arthur Schlesinger sees the "doctrine of rotation-in-office" as having been conceived as a genuine, democratic measure of reform. However, in actual fact it brought about the spoils system, by which the office was made a reward for political service. Those who received such rewards exploited them as much as possible before the next election took place. Schlesinger demonstrated that "its historical function was to narrow the gap between the people and the government—to expand popular participation in the workings of democracy. For Jackson it was an essential step in the gradual formulation of a program for democratic America." Jackson realized that a body of permanent officials represented a threat to democracy.[33]

Almost all investigations of the bureaucratic system deal with the problem of whether bureaucracy represents "an authority or a tool." Karl Jaspers used the following definition: "Bureaucracy is a means. But it tends to make itself into its own end."[34]

At first Max Weber described bureaucracy as a rational and effective

---

[31] Fritz Fleiner, "Beamtenstaat und Volkstaat," in *Festgabe für Otto Meyer* (Tübingen, 1916).

[32] Cited by Arthur M. Schlesinger, Jr., *The Age of Jackson* (Boston, 1953), p. 46. Lenin expressed an almost identical sentiment.

[33] Between one fifth and one tenth of all federal office holders were dismissed by President Jackson. Schlesinger, *op. cit.*, p. 47.

[34] Karl Jaspers, *Vom Ursprung und Ziel der Geschichte* (Frankfurt-Main and Hamburg, 1955). English edition, *The Origin and Goal of History*, tr. Michael Bullock (London, 1953).

institution for the fulfillment of definite goals, functioning to serve those who have established those goals. Nevertheless, he always pointed out that bureaucracy acquires increasing authority over expanding areas of social life, no matter who is in control. He came to the conclusion that whoever controls bureaucratic organizations has what is technically the most highly developed instrument of power. However, this does not determine to what extent bureaucracy can impose its own opinions on a particular social structure, whence the term "the ruling servants."[35]

Attention is always drawn to the fact that a "servant" bureaucracy survives its masters when there is a change in the political regime.[36] Max Weber noted that because of its "impersonal" character, the bureaucratic machine is easily available to whomever has gained control over it. But the virtue of neutrality also has its drawbacks:

Hence it is possible that the civil service, because of its self-imposed commitment to the interests of the general public, begins to see rational behavior as contradictory to party politics, and finally takes up an exaggeratedly neutral stance. This is revealed by its indifference to constitutional principles, disregard for party feuds, insensitivity toward any change in political leadership, and the arrogance with which it relies on its own judgment. Indeed, when the ship founders on the sands, the bureaucracy might even convince itself of the necessity of placing itself at the political wheel as a "nonpartisan" solution.[37] The principle of neutrality among competing interest groups can be exaggerated to the point of self-cancellation, so that seemingly the official is not committed to anything except the ingenious defense of his public status.[38]

The ministerial bureaucracy of the Weimar Republic was of particular significance in this connection. It was apparently neither antidemocratic nor prodemocratic, and was quite indifferent to the form of the government and state. The higher official regarded the state more or less as a business enterprise which had to be successfully organized. He had

[35] See Eric Strauss, The Ruling Servants: Bureaucracy in Russia, France—And Britain? (New York, 1961).

[36] For example: "The observation originally made of France that governments rise and fall but the bureaucracy remains appears particularly applicable to Germany. Although this century has seen Germany ruled by four regimes whose ideological perspectives and power bases were fundamentally different, the civil service remained stable." Herbert Jacob, German Administration Since Bismarck: Central Authority Versus Local Autonomy (New Haven and London, 1963), p. 200.

[37] Karl Dietrich Bracher noted the establishment of "specialists" in the Weimar Republic which came about when the parties were unable to agree. This tended to limit further the power of the Reichstag. More and more power was taken away from the legislature, because of the collaboration of bureaucrats with private interest groups, and put into the hands of state and private bureaucracies. Karl Dietrich Bracher, Die Auflösung der Weimarer Republik: eine Studie zum Problem des Machtverfalls in der Demokratie (Villingen, 1964).

[38] Fritz Morstein-Marx, Einführung . . ., op. cit.

the same cynicism as the successful businessman. Political problems were reduced to technical administrative exercises. Essentially this was of course an antidemocratic and authoritarian attitude. Success was rated higher than law or social justice. Power was esteemed as the guarantor of success.[39]

The essential result of the development of such rational neutrality is the restriction of the political sphere by the administrative machine. The latter becomes so all-enveloping and complex that legislation cannot keep up with its demands and the need for administrative regulation becomes more pressing. The laws themselves become mere authorizations for the administration which determines their interpretation. The parliamentary regime is dependent on the legislative control exercised by its executive bodies, but this control is no longer able to supervise all the technical details and ramifications of public administration. For in order to be effective, parliamentary control needs information, for which it depends in large measure on the administrative apparatus. The member of parliament is bewildered by the skilled way in which the administration advances its explanations; and parliament is also dependent on the administration for the legislation to be enacted, since the latter works it out.

Although the direction of the administration is controlled by parliamentary ministers, their functions are largely dependent on the ministerial bureaucracy. Each new minister confronts a smoothly running machine through which his political directives must pass. These are screened by the department of justice, the department of foreign affairs, and various other sections. Any plans for the future which the politician might have hoped to see realized are strangled and pushed aside by a wealth of official administrative business.

Bureaucracy, whose essential responsibility covers day-to-day administrative operations, can sabotage directives issued by an impractical man in charge, if that becomes necessary. According to Arnold Brecht, officials would not just say "no" to new proposals, but they would "adjust the political plans to expeditiousness, and would take the fundamentals off the radical proposals and reduce them to cautious experiments . . . The most serious case of bureaucratic sabotage arises when large portions of the civil service act in concert to cross the legitimate policy of the government."[40]

It is doubtful whether the virtue of "neutrality" does in fact exist;

[39] Franz Neumann, *Behemoth: The Structure and Practice of National Socialism* (Toronto, New York, London, 1942), p. 370.

[40] Arnold Brecht, "Bureaucratic Sabotage," *The Annals of the American Academy of Political and Social Science,* CLXXXIX (January, 1937), pp. 51 and 53.

mostly it exists only within certain limits. The continuity of the bureaucratic machine favors a predominantly conservative attitude, and in addition the upper echelons of the administrative structure are recruited mainly from among those who are interested in maintaining the existing system.

In his study of the socialist government of the Canadian province of Saskatchewan, Seymour Lipset noted that the program of the Cooperative Commonwealth Federation, which came into power in 1944, was considerably modified by the existing bureaucratic administration. The ministers had assumed that they would set the policy to be carried out by their official deputies. Some of these deputies were able to convince their ministers that certain proposed changes were administratively impractical or that they would result in too much opposition. They also exchanged information among themselves as to how to control their ministers. In fact, some "key officials boasted of 'running my department completely,' and of 'stopping harebrained radical schemes.' " One minister discovered that "members of his staff continued to grant leases and farming privileges to well-to-do persons who had secured them under previous governments, though it was now government policy to give them to poorer farmers and landless veterans." Another cabinet minister decided that some types of government work, previously contracted out to private concerns, should now be given to government employees. His deputy, however, continued to send the work out to private companies.[41]

Bureaucratic sabotage is obviously an instrument of power. When the German Social Democratic theoretician Rudolf Hilferding—who had the reputation of being a radical Marxist—was appointed Minister of Finance in 1923, all ministerial documents were handled in such a way that he found himself sitting at an empty desk. This caused him to suffer a nervous breakdown; it was not until he had assured the ministerial bureaucracy that he would refrain from making any radical changes that conditions became normal.

The policy of governmental bureaucracy under the Weimar Republic demonstrates the doubtfulness of bureaucratic neutrality and the importance of a conservative civil service ideology. The German Prussian civil service considered itself as a governing institution. After initially admitting members of the bourgeoisie to the bureaucratic administration, the nobility secured the key positions for itself, and used its hereditary title system to introduce a caste structure which segregated the upper from

---

[41] Seymour Martin Lipset, *Agrarian Socialism: The Cooperative Commonwealth Federation in Saskatchewan. A Study in Political Sociology* (New York, 1968), pp. 316, 318 and 320.

the lower echelons of the bureaucracy.[42] The latter were relegated to the petty bourgeoisie, which thus became tied to the prevailing ruling system.[43]

As the civil service so constituted represented the interests of the aristocratic upper class, and later on of the upper middle class affiliated with it, it was not contested or limited in its administrative efforts. An administrative class was thus created. Such a class always bases its motivation on the assumption

that a certain category of persons voluntarily dedicates itself to the state, offers its professional services to the state, and that the right to conduct the state's business is limited to this class. It alone has the judicial and moral responsibility, for better or worse, for the welfare of the state. As a German saying has it "The State is its civil servants."[44]

When the fundamentally democratic orientation of the government under the Weimar Republic threatened the existence of the civil service, and when individuals from previously unprivileged categories were placed in it, the administrative bureaucracy opposed the new system and had some share in its downfall. As Karl Dietrich Bracher has shown, this downfall was predetermined; the democratic principle could not be enforced at the beginning because the need for administrative continuity strangled at birth all attempts at radical reform.

National socialism carried to its extreme the process of bureaucratization which is structurally characteristic of modern society. Democracy had left certain opportunities for choice between competing organizations. However, the totalitarian transformation of the structure into a one-party system—with its ideological substructure of an exaggerated leader cult and the nebulous theory of a community of the people—made the bureaucracy of authoritarian entities omnipotent, especially in the party and the government.[45]

In the new industrial nations possessing a parliamentary system, the overt difference between political and administrative systems is lessened

[42] Fritz Morstein-Marx, *op. cit.*

[43] Writing in the nineteenth century, Engels found similar conditions in governmental bureaucracy: "The present organization of the German government is nothing more than a compromise between the nobility and the petty bourgeoisie which amounts to putting the administration into the hands of a third class: the bureaucracy. The two high contracting parties participate in the composition of this class according to their different stations: the nobility, which represents the more important sectors of production, keeps the higher positions; the petty bourgeoisie contents itself with the lower positions, and only manages to place its candidates in the higher administration as a rare exception." Friedrich Engels, "Der Status Quo in Deutschland," in Karl Marx-Friedrich Engels, *Werke*, IV (Berlin, 1964), p. 44.

[44] Fritz Fleiner, "Beamtenstaat und Volkstaat," *op. cit.*

[45] Bracher, *Die Auflösung* . . .

by the fact that members of parliament themselves largely come from the bureaucratic machines of interest groups and of political parties. There is consequently a close connection between public bureaucracies and those of such groups.

A Comment Regarding England

The evolution of a permanent state bureaucracy into a powerful instrument of government on the European continent was part of a long development which had begun with absolute monarchy. In England, however, the process was different, since its geographical position did not force the country to become militarized and centralized.

By the sixteenth century royal authority had grown relatively strong. The feudal magnates were overpowered by the Tudors. An extended executive system was established with an administrative body increasingly drawn from the middle class. Although they did not possess a professional army, the Tudors were able to put the Reason of State above the letter of traditional law, and augment the Crown's police power. Taxation increased since the wars waged by Edward VI and Elizabeth required large sums. But the government still depended on cooperation at the local level. The crown was not represented by appointed officials. The Justice of the Peace (usually a member of the country gentry and a man of property), performed most administrative functions in addition to his judicial duties. Although a royal administrator, he was not a professional official and was not paid. Local autonomy remained the basis of political life and found its expression in the House of Commons. The struggle for power between the Crown and the House of Commons finally culminated in the Puritan Revolution, and the subsequent subordination of dynastic bureaucracy. "The destruction of the royal bureaucracy in 1640–41 can be regarded as the most decisive event in the whole of British history."[46]

The arrested growth of administrative centralization permitted the aristocratic rule of the eighteenth century and the autonomy of local institutions with amateur and unpaid officers who often failed to perform their duties. Otto Hintze describes conditions of that period as follows:

The entire system of government was characterized by a more companionate, corporative tendency. . . . The administration was conducted in a dignified, patriarchal manner, with that easy going nonchalance which is usually typical

[46] Christopher Hill, *Reformation to Industrial Revolution: A Social and Economic History of Britain 1530–1780* (London, 1968), p. 76.

of uncontrolled, aristocratic self-government, and which forms a marked contrast to the stringency and industry with which continental administrative agencies are run.[47]

Mercantilist interference was thus contained, a fact which was to influence the Industrial Revolution. Merchants and manufacturers could pursue their business without fear of governmental intervention, even when it came to tax assessment. Yet, ironically, the needs of industrialized England induced the gradual formation of a bureaucratic state, beginning with the Poor Law Amendment Act of 1834.

A more modern type of administrative bureaucracy did not begin to develop until the second half of the nineteenth century. By instituting competitive civil service examinations, the bourgeoisie put an end to the old system which guaranteed positions for the aristocracy, and opened the administration to their own sons graduated from Oxford or Cambridge. They modelled the civil service on the rational pattern they had already used in the administration of the East India Company, which had, no doubt, learnt many things from the Chinese. The reformers wanted to coordinate administrative reform with the changes inspired by the Industrial Revolution. Many hoped that Parliamentary Reform would result in a decrease in taxation and state intervention. They found, however, that the opposite took place; under Liberalism there was an even greater measure of governmental activity.[48]

A study conducted in 1961 shows that government expenditure remained fairly constant from the beginning to the middle of the nineteenth century. However, expenditures rose by one-third between 1850 and 1860, and then continued to rise slowly. Expenditures in 1880 were about 25 percent higher than those of 1860, and continued to rise gradually. These figures refer to total expenditures at current prices, but they are justified since "the absolute level of government expenditure at current prices was uppermost in the minds of the Chancellors of the Exchequer."[49]

A Comment Regarding the Third World

The Third World adopts bureaucracy in whatever form suits its requirements. Since the countries belonging to the Third World have no

[47] Otto Hintze, "Machtpolitik und Regierungsverfassung," in *Staat und Verfassung: Gesammelte Abhandlungen zur Verfassungsgeschichte*, ed. Gerhard Östreich (Göttingen, 1962).

[48] G. M. Trevelyan, *History of England* (London, 1964), pp. 647–648 and 614.

[49] Alan T. Peacock and Jack Wiseman, *The Growth of Public Expenditure in the United Kingdom* (Princeton, 1961), p. 36.

traditional bourgeoisie or entrepreneur class, it is up to the bureaucracy to satisfy the wish to imitate industrial nations. But state bureaucracy—with Asian exceptions—is not traditional either. Frequently it develops as an aid to colonial bureaucracy. In exercising its functions, usually established by itself, the bureaucracy frequently comes into conflict with the traditional ways of life of tribal organizations or village communities, and with their chiefs and dignitaries. The new bureaucracy is full of ressentiment against the traditional authorities from whom it derives and on whom it looks down, as well as against the "developed" world to which it looks up. It grows increasingly arrogant because it considers itself far above its primitive surroundings and needs a mask to hide its insecurity from the developed world. This governmental bureaucracy is torn between feelings of inferiority and the need for acceptance, because it is confronted with tasks which are beyond its competence and with goals which are often too high. Those on the outside dream of becoming part of the administration. Anyone who has invested in education and knowledge expects a bureaucratic position. Seen subjectively, corruption often appears justified because it rewards special efforts; but this leads to conflict with that rectitude necessary for the established goals of primitive accumulation.

The bureaucracy tends to be concentrated in the capital cities, most of which were established by the colonial powers, and it represents decided centralist tendencies. The development of new economic systems and techniques is often promoted contrary to local interests. The bureaucratic interest in centralized governmental institutions is strengthened by the knowledge that it is a progressive force of higher value than the regional communities with their backward tendencies. It is quite obvious that systems of direct bureaucratic control are attractive to the political imagination of such administrations, particularly since they almost automatically acquire direct control.

However, since social advancement is essentially linked to being admitted into the state bureaucracy, and the number of aspirants is likely to grow faster than the amount available in the state treasury, people become interested in the forcible removal of those holding office. Hence it is understandable that the Maoist Communist movement, recognizing that most countries of the Third World lack an industrial base and consequently a proletariat, tries to gain support from a "class struggle" within the bureaucracy. This idea was discussed in an article "The Class Struggle in Africa," in the pro-Chinese journal *Revolution*, I, No. 9: "The fact

167

is that the social class begotten by colonialism which had the mission of liquidating its domination was not the proletariat, but the class of minor functionaries. . . . The political consciousness of the workers was not—and could not be—more advanced than that of the minor officials."[50] The dysfunction of bureaucratic administration, which is in part due to the influx of aspirants not always suitable for official positions, presents a much more momentous problem for a poor, nonindustrialized country in the process of primitive accumulation than for a modern industrialized nation. It is far more difficult in such situations to stem the increase of all those phenomena produced by the "bureaucratic sickness," as there is no other control but that of the bureaucracy itself. Thus a general trend is strengthened by which bureaucracy creates more bureaucracy. An illustration of this point can be found in a report from Cuba in *The Times* (London, December 12, 1966), referring to a speech by Fidel Castro, in which he complained about the failure of the fight against bureaucracy: "We must debureaucratize the commissions of the struggle against bureaucracy." *The Times* went on to say that "Some offices had a staff of 100 when twenty would be enough. Their administrators had become enemies of the revolution, generous with the people's money, wasting the people's time and wasting the people's intelligence."

---

[50] Cited by Leopold Labedz, *"The End of an Epoch,"* Survey, LIV (January, 1965), p. 18.

10

ANTIBUREAUCRATIC ATTITUDES

Democratic Ideals

In his attempt to describe the special characteristics of the West, Karl Jaspers states that its intellectual heritage contains the concept of political freedom developed in Greece. "Its radiance has permeated and found response in our Western history."[1] European constitutional philosophy could not fail to be influenced by this radiance, although it derived from the distant past and had been buried for a long time. Although many of its original ideas will have to remain in obscurity, the principle of Attic democracy has always reappeared as an ideal, in defiance of existing reality. The oration given at the funeral of Athenians fallen in the Peloponnesian War, which was ascribed to Pericles by Thucydides, contained phrases dealing with Attic political democracy which have resounded throughout European intellectual history. This oration, as Ernst Cassirer indicates, although not pronounced as we have it but composed by Thucydides, represented the ideal rather than the empirical reality of that time.[2]

In repeatedly returning to the ideas of that era, European thought had to determine their ideal truth apart from the historical circumstances in which they were realized. It had to consider that Attic freedom applied to those who were free. Athenian society was based on a slave economy, and there was far less freedom for the individual than exists in Europe in modern times. Jacob Burckhardt said of that period:

The Periclean Age in Athens was in every sense of the word an age in which any peaceful and prudent citizen of our time would refuse to live, in which he could not but be mortally unhappy, even if he was neither a member of the slave-majority nor a citizen of a city under the Attic hegemony, but a free

---

[1] Karl Jaspers, *Vom Ursprung und Ziel der Geschichte* (Frankfurt-am-Main and Hamburg, 1955). English edition, *The Origin and Goal of History,* tr. Michael Bullock (London, 1953).
[2] Ernst Cassirer, *An Essay on Man* (New York, 1954), p. 205.

169

man and a full citizen of Athens itself. Huge contributions levied by the State, and perpetual inquisitions into the fulfillment of duties towards the State by demagogues and sycophants, were the order of the day. Yet the Athenians of that age must have felt a plenitude of life which far outweighed any security in the world.[3]

The phrase from the funeral speech, "It is as free men that we conduct our public life" expressed a feeling which has persistently appealed to men through the ages.[4] It conjured up the vision of a social alternative, of a different way of life, in which "the system was not divided up into a series of rationalized functions; and in which the professionalization of public life was unknown."[5]

Although European usage asked that "each man sweep in front of his own door," and held that "the first duty of each citizen is to keep the peace," the Attic example continued to find response in intellectual life. As Pericles said: "The same persons attend at once to the concerns of their households and of the city, and men of diverse employments have a very fair idea of politics. If a man takes no interest in public affairs, we alone do not commend him as quiet, but condemn him as useless; and if a few of us are originators, we are all sound judges of a policy."[6] Of course by today's standards such ideas coming from a much smaller world are seen merely as myth, but even so, the ideal provides a yardstick for measuring reality. As long as this myth "radiates luster and suscitates a response in us," the present cannot be accepted as the best of all possible worlds.

No doubt it was the smallness of the city state, its surveyability, which made this type of self-governing urban community possible. The Greeks themselves realized that the *polis* had to remain small and wanted it that way, so that every resident could be assigned a suitable role. But the fact that they stressed that aspect—which has to be remembered when considering the polis as a prototype—has encouraged our mistrust of the centralist tendencies of a larger world. It has also kept alive in political thought the possibility of dividing social operations. It is not merely a matter of imitating former institutions, although their spirit has shown considerable tenacity. Political concepts which favor the participation and joint responsibility of the greatest number of people have

---

[3] Jacob Burckhardt, *Force and Freedom: Reflections on History,* ed. and tr. James Hastings Nichols (New York, 1954), p. 357.

[4] Thucydides, *The Peloponnesian Wars,* tr. Benjamin Jowett (New York, 1962), p. 67.

[5] Alfred Weber, "Bürokratie und Freiheit," *Die Wandlung* (December 20, 1946).

[6] Thucydides, *op. cit.,* p. 68.

looked to that spirit time and again for sanction. The essence of Pericles' political philosophy, according to Lord Acton, was the idea that "power ought to be so equitably diffused as to afford equal security to all."[7]

Criticism of the bureaucratic system was inherent in Attic democracy, with its rotating official positions assigned by election or lot, and an administration responsible in everything to the assembly of the people. The model of Attic democracy as an ideal social structure consistently lent support to those concepts of political philosophy which found bureaucracy repugnant. An ideal survived which ran counter to the decisive trend towards bureaucracy, and not merely in the remoter spheres of political philosophy. This was the concept of direct democracy, which allied itself to socialist theory when the latter took hold among the masses in the nineteenth century.

Two differing currents met in socialist ideology. One was derived from rationalist concepts developed when the modern state was formed under the absolute monarchy. These concepts were a model for utopian societies in which rational administration was to bring about universal happiness.[8] The other trend, however, contained notions of direct democracy. It originated in the precapitalist era and brought with it fundamental valuations which became characteristic of the socialist movement. A high regard for labor and the endeavor to constitute cooperative forms of life date back to the democratic life of medieval cities.[9] As Alfred Weber expressed it, a decisive role was played by "the little man who came to the city to be an artisan, with his knapsack on his back, who possessed nothing, but who was prepared for communal relationships and was attuned to the idea of collective subsistence."[10] Cooperative organization

[7] John Emerich Edward Dahlberg, Lord Acton, *Essays on Freedom and Power* (Cleveland and New York, 1964), p. 61.

[8] Paul Valéry was one of the few who recognized the connection between socialist utopias and absolute monarchies: "The system established by Richelieu and Louis XIV sanctioned and favored theorizing à la Blanqui." Paul Valéry, *Regards sur le monde actuel* (Paris, 1945), p. 70. English edition, *Reflections on the World Today*, tr. Francis Scarfe (London, 1951).

[9] The importance of the autonomy of European cities in the relationship between democracy and bureaucracy can hardly be overemphasized. Where it did not exist, bureaucracy developed as the sole type of administration. As mentioned in Chapter VIII, this autonomy was destroyed early on in Russia. In China, as Max Weber has said, "The City like the mandarin's estate, possessed no self-government." Although the saying had it that in Europe "city air makes one free," Chinese cities were far from being bastions of freedom. They were centers of governmental administration, controlled by officials who represented the imperial government. In exact contrast to what happened in Europe, all those who rebelled against the oppressive might of the official hierarchy fled to the villages to escape from the bureaucracy. *See* Etienne Balazs, *Chinese Civilization and Bureaucracy: Variations on a Theme*, tr. H. M. Wright, ed. Arthur F. Wright (New Haven and London, 1966), p. 70.

[10] Alfred Weber, *Kulturgeschichte als Kultursoziologie* (Leiden, 1935).

in medieval townships laid the cornerstone in Europe for socialist ideology. This developed essentially as a protest against that disintegration of protective systems which was characteristic of the early stages of capitalism. It was not mere chance that the impetus toward modern socialism was created by those perceptive artisans who first came into conflict with the capitalist industrial economy. They carried the tradition of the democratic way of life into the first cities; cooperatives in particular were an outcome of this tradition.[11]

Marx recognized this historic connection and made it his point of departure in the *Critique of Hegel's 'Philosophy of Right.'* He found that popular life and political life in the Middle Ages were still identical. "Man was the actual principle of the state, but he was unfree man." Or, "The Middle Ages was the democracy of nonfreedom." In using this designation, Marx emphasized that the bureaucratic partition between individuals and public life must be broken up. As he saw it, "true democracy" only exists where there is no separation of private affairs of the individual from those of the universal system. "In democracy the *constitution* . . . is *itself* only *a* self-determination of the people, and a determinate content of the people."[12]

The first German editors of Marx' early writings were struck by the similarity between the concept of "true democracy" and the idea of the ancient polis:

[11] For instance, Wilhelm Weitling (1808–1871), the first apostle of German socialism and communism, was a tailor. The first Communist organization, the "Bund der Gerechten," consisted almost exclusively of artisans, as Friedrich Engels testified. He remarked rightly that the latter still clung to a great number of inherited guild ideas, but he underestimated the importance of the connection. *See Introduction* to Karl Marx, *Enthüllungen über den Kommunistenprocess in Köln* (Zürich, 1885). The fact that the early socialist movement consisted almost exclusively of artisans has been documented in detail by Wolfgang Schieder, *Anfänge der deutschen Arbeiterbewegung* (Stuttgart, 1963). But even August Bebel, leader of the German Social Democratic party prior to World War I, was an independent masterturner.

Thomas Hardy, founder and Secretary of the London Corresponding Society—the English equivalent of the "Bund der Gerechten"—was a shoemaker. *See* E. P. Thompson, *The Making of the English Working Class* (New York, 1964).

Early socialist concepts regarding government were enthusiastically naive. Weitling, for example, wrote, "Communism is the administration of everyone's consumption and production by means of their collective knowledge . . . No one may be elected to the government who expects a good salary and who does not give up all his worldly goods to society." Wilhelm Weitling, *Das Evangelium des armen Sünders* (Birsfeld, 1846). A pamphlet issued in 1834 by the "Bund der Geächteten" (Association of Pariahs), entitled *Glaubensbekenntnis eines Geächteten* (Confessions of a Pariah), stated that the entire population should assemble in precincts and vote on the legislation suggested by its representatives. Executive authority was to be exercised by officials elected either directly or indirectly.

[12] Karl Marx, *Critique of Hegel's 'Philosophy of Right',* ed. Joseph O'Malley, tr. Annette Jolin and Joseph O'Malley (Cambridge, England, 1970), pp. 31 and 32. Later on Marx still felt that "it is entirely too convenient to be 'liberal' at the expense of the Middle Ages." *Das Kapital,* I, Chap. 24.

This theory of "true democracy" contains an old relic of the European past, the old ideal of community which Rousseau had in mind in his *Social Contract* and which was included in the whole idea of Natural Law. His covert model is the concept of the ancient polis with its identity of private and public life, in which there was no differentiation between being a man or a citizen, for they were one and the same. The polis is also the original source for the idea of the "classless society," as Marx later called "true democracy."[13]

Marx did not consider the mere possibility of people's social advancement as an important factor in determining democracy. For him the realization of democracy did not lie in the fact that anyone could become a civil servant:

That each has the possibility of gaining the privilege of another sphere proves only that *his own* sphere is not the actuality of this privilege.

In a true state it is not a question of the possibility of every citizen to dedicate himself to the universal in the form of a particular class, but of the capability of the universal class to be really universal, i.e., to be the class of every citizen.

In a rational state, taking an examination belongs more properly to becoming a shoemaker than an executive civil servant, because shoemaking is a skill without which one can be a good citizen of the state, a social man; but the necessary state knowledge is a condition without which a person in the state lives outside the state, is cut off from himself, deprived of air.[14]

The theory of "true democracy" was not taken up again by Marx as a special subject, but the idea remained the basis for his concept of social transformation. It is found in a sentence of the *Communist Manifesto:* "Instead of the old type of bourgeois society, with its class system and class contrasts, there is an association in which the free development of each individual is the condition for the free development of one and all." Marx' critique of the state in *The Eighteenth Brumaire* expressed the same idea, and he finally stressed it again in his great celebration of the Paris Commune.[15] Marx saw socialist society as the totality of the associations which control national productivity according to a joint plan.

This Marxian ideal of society had little influence on the practical policy of the parties which referred to his theories. It was only in opposition to party leadership that the Marxist credo met with any response. Thus Rosa Luxemburg saw the essence of democracy as, "necessary to the working class because it creates the political forms (autonomous adminis-

---

[13] Karl Marx, *Der Historische Materialismus: Die Frühschriften,* eds. S. Landshut and I. P. Mayer (Leipzig, 1932).

[14] Marx, *Critique* . . ., pp. 50 and 51.

[15] *See* Chapter VII, above, section 2, n. 14.

tration, electoral rights, etc.) which will serve the proletariat as fulcrums in its task of transforming bourgeois society." She also concluded that "The production relations of capitalist society approach more and more the production relations of socialist society. But on the other hand, its political and juridical relations establish between capitalist society and socialist society a steadily rising wall."[16]

Even if the ideal and the real do manage to grow so far apart, ideals must continue to influence reality. The effect of ideals as counterparts to reality is noticeable precisely when the distance is greatest between them. That is why the Marxist credo became the basis and starting point for East-European philosophers and writers in their opposition to despotic bureaucratic regimes.

Ressentiments

Centralization of social functions and governmental intervention in heretofore uncontrolled domains, together with all other curtailments of privileges entailed in the expansion of bureaucracy, are always seen as the loss of prestige or actual power by both small and large groups of individuals. Such losses of prestige and power are invariably accompanied by ressentiments, directed against bureaucracy as the obvious usurper of the lost sphere of power. Those forced to relinquish their position by the course of history, have always warned the victors that they are headed for destruction. They generally look on their lost privileges as losses to humanity. But because their vision is intensified by their ressentiment, they are able to recognize the victors' weaknesses, and to see through the justifications and ideological embellishments of the new type of government.

Reactionary critics of absolutism, the defenders of feudal liberties, were able in many respects to criticize absolutist bureaucracy much more pertinently than their progressive and revolutionary opponents managed to do later.[17] Nevertheless, Heinrich von Treitksche who was a definite defender of the bureaucratized Prussian state, was right in his own way when he wrote:

It is undeniable that absolutism was responsible for spreading freedom precisely at the time of the Great Elector. All the interpreters of freedom—Leibnitz, Pufendorf, Thomasius—to whom we owe Germany's reawakening, were strict

[16] Rosa Luxemburg, *Reform or Revolution*, tr. Integer (New York, 1937), pp. 24 and 45.
[17] *See* Chapter IV above, Sections 1-3.

absolutists. Who were the reactionaries of that time? They were the representatives of so-called freedom, men like Konrad von Burgsdorf and General Kalkstein, leaders of the Diet Party, who wanted to make the common man a slave to the interests of the upper classes.[18]

Those who harbored ressentiments against the bureaucracy for taking away their privileges, and those whose social progress was hampered by bureaucracy, intermittently voiced the same criticism. Karl Ernst Jarcke interpreted von Haller's theories as requiring, "in opposition to everything, even the most beneficent absolutism . . . a degree of freedom for the individual" which his times were not able to countenance.[19] But Adam Smith also supported a greater amount of individual freedom than that granted by absolutist-mercantilist policy; except that in his case a quite different sort of freedom was involved, intended for a completely different set of people.

The rising bourgeoisie and its intellectual supporters demanded a free hand in their use of capital, turning against the bureaucracy whenever it no longer served their specific needs: "And most of what the merchant and the manufacturer felt to be irksome or silly interference associated itself in the collective mind of the capitalist class with this bureaucracy or civil service. Such an association is an extremely durable thing . . ."[20]

Small businessmen become filled with ressentiments as the economy becomes increasingly organized, as industrial and governmental administrations tend to interlock, and as the market loses its significance in contrast to organized distribution, administered prices and regimentation of working conditions. Their independence shrinks quickly, and their reactions may be compared to those of the feudal classes against absolutist bureaucracy. Complaints about governmental arbitrariness, about interference with acquired privileges, about curtailment of the freedom to use one's own property, and about the growth of a revenue-consuming bureaucracy, are not new.[21] Edgar Salin points out: "Things are no different today than they have been during the entire course of capitalist history: in addition to intellectuals, politicians and theoreticians, it is

[18] Heinrich Gotthard von Treitschke, *Politik*, 2 vols. (Leipzig, 1899–1900), I, p. 160. English edition, *Politics, by Heinrich von Treitschke,* tr. Blanche Dugdale and Torben be Bille (New York, 1916).

[19] Karl Ernst Jarcke, *Vermischte Schriften,* 3 vols (München, 1839).

[20] Joseph A. Schumpeter, *Capitalism, Socialism and Democracy* (New York, 1950), p. 206.

[21] In the United States, where the principles of a market economy have become a national faith, large sections of the public are disillusioned with the omnipotent Washington bureaucracy. This sentiment played an important part in Senator Goldwater's election campaign (1964), when he promised to do away with the "welfare state" and income tax.

precisely those economic groups threatened by new developments who constitute themselves the heralds of freedom. Up to that point they represented a very different system . . ."[22]

The erosion of this "very different system" upsets the traditional justification of policy and conduct. Speaking about competition in the United States, John Kenneth Galbraith says, "Like marital fidelity, decent plumbing, or clean underclothing, competition is a prerequisite of respectability in our society."[23] If such a belief loses its basis, and it becomes obvious that it is impossible to reconstitute it, a ressentiment has to develop which seeks a culprit and finds it in governmental bureaucracy. Those who feel this way find their complaints justified by certain national economists who believe in the ideal type of traditional system, which they plainly consider the best assurance of a well-organized world. They support free enterprise and a free market system as an ideal contrast to state intervention, in the same way that local dignitaries once supported freedom of the estates in the face of absolutist pressures.

Antibureaucratic ressentiment finds its justification in the idealization of a market economy and the "natural" condition of free competition, as opposed to the despotism and bureaucratic regimentation so artificially remote from life.[24] Even Karl Ludwig von Haller entitled his critique of absolutist bureaucracy *Theorie des natürlich-gesellschaftlichen Zustandes* (*Theory of the Natural-Social Condition*). Yet contemporary theoreticians discussing the "natural-social" condition have shown neither the pragmatic realism possessed by Justus Möser, the defender of "local rationalism," nor the ability to construct a grandiose utopia of the past in the manner of von Haller. Thus F. A. von Hayek expressed antibureaucratic, liberal ressentiment in the title of his book, *Der Weg zur Knechtschaft* (*The Road to Serfdom*). He claimed there were only two alternatives: "either there could be the impersonal discipline of a market without duties and price agreements, or a system controlled by the will of a few individuals." Yet he did not perceive just how "impersonal" the effect of a large bureaucracy could be. He did not conceive of governmental bureaucracy as intimately connected with the decisive economic forces of the industrial state, but rather as a sort of independent power, placed above society. Hayek's idealization of the liberal forces inherent in a freely competitive

[22] Edgar Salin, "Kartellverbot und Konzentration," *Kyklos,* 2 (1963).

[23] John Kenneth Galbraith, "The Defense of Business: a Strategic Appraisal," *Harvard Business Review,* 2 (March–April, 1954), p. 41.

[24] Max Scheler points out that "all praise of the 'past' has the implied purpose of downgrading present-day reality." Max Scheler, *Ressentiment,* tr. William W. Holdheim (New York, 1961), p. 68.

market system was an ideological contribution welcomed by managers of large industrial organizations as material for official speeches. In comparison with those who actually transmitted antibureaucratic ressentiments, however, his prescriptions for the revival of a laissez-faire economy had little actual influence.[25]

In 1929, Ludwig von Mises published his critique of interventionism, in which he argued, among other things, that the establishment of unemployment benefits would prevent the wage rate from being depressed in a natural market which could supply work to all those seeking it.[26] Fifteen years later, it was his main concern to "demonstrate that no profit-seeking enterprise, no matter how large, is liable to become bureaucratic provided the hands of its management are not tied by government interference."[27]

But even the criticism deriving from ressentiment can be revealing, and there may be some actual connections between the criticism of the bureaucracy by those favoring a free market and those defending vested interests. There is, however, a touch of the ridiculous about the criticism of bureaucracy born of the ideal of a market economy—as there is, incidentally, about all protest by theoreticians representing a section of society which has been relegated to the background. For such protest defends a structure whose façade is cracking and even demands the restoration and embellishment of the broken-down building. The rapid advance lately made by bureaucracy has created still another ressentiment, which has manifested itself in a tragic way. This occurs when value systems lose their basis in reality, when their perspectives become obscure, when theories of social development lose touch with reality and when philosophy is overwhelmed by a feeling of impotence. The ressentiment formed by such unhappy conditions has given rise to fundamental attacks on the administered world. Since the points of departure of those making the attacks are very different, it becomes obvious that the issue is not merely any *one* specific theory or ideology.

The "clercs" of whom Julien Benda writes, or Lewis Coser's "custodians of abstract ideas," who hold up an impractical ideal in reproach to society—those who constitute what Karl Mannheim calls a "free intelligentsia," who transform conflicts of interests into conflicts of ideas—are distressed by a feeling of being superfluous and helpless in the administered

[25] Friedrich August von Hayek, *Der Weg zur Knechtschaft* (Zürich, 1944). English edition, *The Road to Serfdom* (Chicago, 1945).

[26] Ludwig von Mises, *Kritik des Interventionismus: Untersuchungen zur Wirtschaftspolitik und Wirtschaftsideologie der Gegenwart* (Jena, 1929).

[27] Ludwig von Mises, *Bureaucracy* (New Haven, 1944), p. 12.

177

world. They are torn between being part of and opposing the system.[28] They are no longer allowed to speculate freely but are forced into becoming specialists. They are expected to deal with the practical technology of society instead of developing theories of social criticism; they learn that they are to offer "social-technological recommendations and social-organizational suggestions."[29] That certain independence they enjoyed in the interstices of society decreases as the latter are closed. They react with uncertainty towards the securities offered them. They are alienated from society because they are confused between wanting to reveal that society to itself and wanting to serve it. The concept of alienation has turned into a constantly repeated formula of ressentiment, far beyond its meaning and usage in the thought of Hegel and Marx.

Spinoza and Hegel both clearly indicated that "correct conduct develops out of the true representation of reality, out of an understanding of that which exists."[30] But the diagnostician of the present is overcome by frustration because he cannot find a point from which to proceed. Vainly he asks, like Archimedes, to be given a point of leverage outside of the world so that he can lift it out of its hinges. So it happens that conservative and radical social criticism arrive at almost identical conclusions, acquire the same sense of alienation and the same resignation as to how they should proceed.

The disappearance of originality and the repression of spontaneity and freedom in the bureaucratized world caused similar reactions among those whose value judgments were formed by the tradition of European philosophy and social criticism. This was the case despite their quite diverse attitudes and social theories. Paul Valéry expressed these feelings when he wrote that the surface of freedom had begun to shrink as of the beginning of the century, that it was becoming *une peau de chagrin.* But he also emphasized that it was incorrect and superficial only to consider legal constraints: "Modern man is the slave of modernity. There is no longer any form of progress which does not end by completely enslaving man."[31]

---

[28] Although an exact definition is not necessary, it seemed appropriate simply to avoid the word "intellectual." For the above-mentioned concepts, *see* Julien Benda, *La Trahison des clercs* (Paris, 1927); Lewis A. Coser, *Men of Ideas* (New York, 1965), and Karl Mannheim, *Ideology and Utopia: An Introduction to the Sociology of Knowledge* (New York and London, 1952).

[29] Jürgen Habermas, *Theorie und Praxis: sozialphilosophische Studien* (Neuwied, 1963).

[30] Max Horkheimer, "Ideologie und Wertgebung," in *Soziologische Forschungen in unserer Zeit,* ed. K. G. Specht (Köln, 1951).

[31] *Une peau de chagrin* (a wild donkey's skin) refers to Balzac's novel *La Peau de chagrin,* published in 1830. Its principal symbol is a magic skin which shrinks as the hero expends his life energy (translator's note). *See* Valéry, *op. cit.,* pp. 72–73.

The convergence of opposing intellectual theories in the same diagnosis was clearly the result of opposition to real situations, rather than of legal conflicts. This has been demonstrated in distinguished works by Hans Freyer, the conservative German philosopher, and Herbert Marcuse.[32] Neither man is concerned with "legal constraints" but with the tendency inherent in the real world to "completely enslave man." As Marcuse sees it:

By virtue of the way it has organized its technological base, contemporary industrial society tends to be totalitarian. For "totalitarian" is not only a terroristic political coordination of society, but also a nonterroristic economic-technical coordination . . .

At its most advanced stage, domination functions as administration, and in the overdeveloped areas of mass consumption, the administered life becomes the good life of the whole, in the defense of which the opposites are united. . . .

The totalitarian universe of technological rationality is the latest transmutation of the idea of Reason.[33]

In discussing the problem of alienation Hans Freyer writes:

Today man is overwhelmed by the machine. . . . An entire preconceived . . . system of alienation is connected with it. . . . But functional man is affected by an additional driving force, similar to that of remote control, which derives from the administration. . . .

Manipulated man is the carefully worked-out product of an equally carefully developed administration of objects. . . .

Hence the ideological formula is only too correct: men are not controlled, but objects are administered. Only the formula forgot to add: objects including mankind, and man necessarily along with objects.[34]

Conservative as well as radical social theorists see alienation as the basic contemporary condition. Marcuse expresses it this way: "The organizers and administrators themselves become increasingly dependent on the machinery which they organize and administer." Thus "a vicious circle" is formed, which "encloses both the Master and the Servant."[35] Freyer notes that the alienation which Marx ascribed to the proletariat, that is, being considered part of a system of objects, is now universally applicable.

[32] *See* Hans Freyer, *Theorie des gegenwärtigen Zeitalters* (Stuttgart, 1958), and Herbert Marcuse, *One Dimensional Man: Studies in the Ideology of Advanced Industrial Society* (Boston, 1964).

[33] Marcuse, *op. cit.,* pp. 3, 123, and 255.

[34] Freyer, *op. cit.*

[35] Marcuse, *op. cit.,* p. 33.

Both authors, as "custodians of abstract ideas," conclude that ideas no longer contain guidelines for action; the world of which they are custodians is an alien one. There is no alternative for existing conditions in the one-dimensional world. The alienated proletariat, from whom Marx' critical theory expected a break-through to an alternative, has now, according to Marcuse, become "a prop of the established way of life." He goes on, "Dialectical theory is not refuted, but it cannot offer the remedy." Its greatest weakness lies in "its inability to demonstrate the liberating tendencies *within* the established society." And "confronted with the total character of the achievement of advanced industrial society, critical theory is left without the rationale for transcending this society."[36]

Freyer views the adaptation which is required and promoted in the present age as "a renunciation of freedom, of wealth and autonomy;" that is, a denial of the confidence which should have been maintained through a growing historical heritage. But since "historical social strata cannot be drilled like oil wells," the problem arises, "to what depth and undisturbed extent the historical heritage still exists." The alienated system of the present is one of those historical creations which cannot be "predetermined," that is, "they determine their own conditions and elements and hence need no foundation to be penetrated. That is how the heritage is disowned."[37]

Both Freyer and Marcuse lament the loss of a tendency toward transcendency inherent in the social system; that is, the loss of a tendency to orient oneself to those truths contained in ideas. The more they evaluate the present in terms of that loss, the gloomier it appears. Hence they tend logically to look to the past, which seemed to possess more viable alternatives. In any case, Freyer holds the view that "the alienated system must be countered with a humanity which does not derive from it and which cannot be developed from it, but which must rather be drawn from our historicity." Freyer is aware of the greatness of the loss when the present is compared with the past, "what a great deal Western man has given up in terms of naïveté, of original attitudes, of the ability to improvise, and of the sureness of his instincts."[38]

Marcuse also looks at the culture which has been invalidated by technical society. "In the verse and prose of this pretechnological culture is the rhythm of those who wander or ride in carriages, who have the time and the pleasure to think, contemplate, feel and narrate." To be

[36] *Ibid.*, pp. 252, 253, 254, and xiv.
[37] Freyer, *op. cit.*
[38] *Ibid.*

sure, "this romantic pretechnical world was permeated with misery, toil and filth, and these in turn were the background of all pleasure and joy. Still there was a 'landscape,' a medium of libidinal experience which no longer exists."[39]

The sense of having lost something which cannot be recalled and which lies in the past, is part of the alienation complex. It is a feeling originally expressed by the Romantics, who were the first to recognize the artificiality of the state as that which drives away the vitality and originality in life. As Novalis expressed it: "Those were wonderful, brilliant times, when Europe was a Christian country." But then "religion was sacrilegiously enclosed within state frontiers, thus establishing the basis for the gradual corruption of religious cosmopolitan interest."[40]

The essential reason for Marcuse's appealing pathos is that he is also affected by the loss of *that* "good old era" when socialists still lived in their intellectual paradise; when they could, in all innocence, consider themselves to be the instrument of universal consciousness preparing for the transition from the realm of necessity to that of freedom.[41] Marcuse may well say, "the truth of a historical project is not validated *ex post* through success," but hard reality shows otherwise. And the truth of an idea which cannot be verified creates the hopelessness of ressentiment.

Thus Marcuse is left with only the "absolute refusal," since every opposition to the administered totality is absorbed by it for lack of an alternative theory. He does not enter the lists against the bureaucratized world; he acts as the herald of destiny. As such, he foresees no "happy ending."

Antigovernmental Tendencies in the Course of History

In the course of recent history governmental power structures have repeatedly been faced with sudden hostile assaults which, in addition to being strictly time-bound, seem to have been rooted in antiadministrative tendencies deeply embedded in the popular masses.

[39] Marcuse, *op. cit.*, pp. 59 and 73.

[40] Novalis, *Die Christenheit oder Europa* (Stuttgart, 1947). English edition, *Christianity in Europe*, tr. J. Dalton (London, 1844).

[41] Marcuse could have chosen as his motto what Karl Gustav Jochmann said about Robespierre: it is "with nostalgia that we look back on a time in which each of its hopes was a *lie*, in which each of our sentiments was part of the *truth*." Karl Gustav Jochmann, "Robespierre," in *Die Rückschritte der Poesie und andere Schriften* (Frankfurt, 1967), p. 116.

These tendencies surfaced here and there, like an underground stream, when the existing power structures were disturbed. They were expressed by attempts to substitute more popular and direct forms of social organization for the bureaucratic organisms of the state. During all revolutionary periods a radical wing developed in the revolutionary movement which embodied such antigovernmental sentiments. Such opposition developed against even the earliest attempts at centralization. Hans Nabholz, the Swiss historian, discusses the importance of antigovernmental tendencies during the German Peasants' War as follows:

In the course of the fifteenth century, the government began to standardize the administration of individual domains. This action resulted from those general changes occurring in the regional administration at that time; it involved the final elimination of feudal administrative institutions in favor of a system whose legal jurisdiction was based on a central executive. This led to the revolt among the peasants, who wanted to assert their special local privileges and their considerable independence vis-à-vis the centralizing tendencies of the regional government which wanted to enlarge its jurisdiction on its own authority. . . . The peasants' complaints reveal a thoroughly conservative trend, a rigid, inflexible way of holding on to traditional customs and rights. This was the only way they felt they could stand up to the increased demands of those in authority and preserve the remnants of their self-determination.[42]

It was this conservative clinging to traditional conditions, this resistance to the development of governmental influence, which induced Ferdinand Lassalle not to classify the Peasant Wars as a revolutionary movement in history.[43]

The repeated rebellions of the Russian peasants and cossacks took place essentially in opposition to the creation of an administrative authority which tended toward Asiatic despotism. Nicolas Berdyaev notes:

On the one hand the Russian people meekly abetted the organization of a despotic and autocratic State, but on the other hand they also fled from it; they revolted against it and took refuge in the assertion of their liberty. Stenka Razin, who is a characteristically Russian type, was a representative of the "barbarian Cossacks." Colonization was the work of the free Cossacks . . . [who] represented the anarchic element in Russian history as a counterweight to the absolutism and despotism of the State. They demonstrated that it is possible

---

[42] Hans Nabholz, "Zur Frage nach den Ursachen des Bauernkrieges 1525," in *Gedächtnisschrift für Georg von Below* (Stuttgart, 1928).

[43] *See* Ferdinand Johann Gottlieb Lassalle, *Franz von Sickingen: eine deutsche Tragödie* (Berlin, 1926); also "Arbeiter-Programm," in *Ferdinand Lassalle's Reden und Schriften*, 2 vols. (Berlin, 1892–1893). English edition of the latter work, *The Working Man's Programme*, tr. E. Peters (London, 1884).

to find a way of escape from the State when it has become intolerable, into the free and open Steppes.[44]

The English Revolution, which substituted the Parliamentary Grandees for the king and his favorites, and which replaced the "king's prerogative" with "parliamentary privileges," encouraged that powerful trend of self-determination and radical democracy in the Revolutionary Army which found expression in the militant Council of the Army:[45]

Once it had abolished royal absolutism, Parliament began to abolish the royal provincial representatives who had suppressed local government. But then, in its own absolutist fashion, it promptly established Deputy-Lieutenants and County Committees which differed in no way from their royal predecessors.

The Levellers remained the sole opponents of Parliament which refused to agree to its own dissolution. To them the counties were close-knit communities, whose overriding reality lay in the fact that they were composed of enfranchised individuals, living under similar conditions.

The Levellers and their leader, John Lilburne, wanted to prevent any corruption in office:

Each county is to have its different districts from which a representative will be elected, so that several representatives of each parish . . . may participate in electing all those magistrates who are to be appointed in a specific county. . . . If we are to remain permanently content we must remove any opportunity for corruption, and this can only come about by means of frequent elections.

The movement which began in the Revolutionary Army in April 1647 with the election of two delegates or "Agitators" from each regiment, seemed at first to be limited to the soldiers' immediate organizational interests. However, from its very beginnings it was linked to the Levellers' radical democratic concepts. Already in May of that year, when the "Advertisements for the Managing of the Counsels of the Army" was issued, demands were made public which went beyond the economic grievances of the soldiers. An extension of democratic rights was called for, and the question raised as to whether the aims for which the war had been fought had been accomplished. The Council movement compelled the army leadership to allow the formation of a central democratic institution. The General Council was thus created, consisting of repre-

---

[44] Nicolas Berdyaev, *The Russian Idea,* tr. R. M. French (London, 1947), p. 11.

[45] Wilhelm Kottler, "Der Rätegedanke als Staatsgedanke: Demokratie und Rätegedanke in der grossen englischen Revolution," *Leipziger rechtswissenschaftliche Studien,* XV (1925). The ensuing discussion of the Leveller movement and the Army Council is based on this article.

sentatives and officers of the regiments whose task it was to provide the army with a democratic constitution. However, the endeavors of the appointed executive committee were frustrated because it was impossible to prevent the generals from influencing the General Council. The Agitators began to be persecuted and executed, and the General Council was turned into an officers' Council of War. "The English revolution continued, although the concept of the Councils, which had dominated the political situation for some years, was unable to influence the form the English constitution was to take."

The history of the conflict between the forces of direct democracy and federated self-government on the one hand, and those of a centralized bureaucratic executive power on the other, constitutes an important phenomenon of the French Revolution, which has been carefully studied by Peter Kropotkin and Daniel Guérin. Those institutions of direct democracy which developed spontaneously were partially responsible for giving new content to previously existing ones. In this way the first Paris Commune was created in the tradition of the old freedom of the city. But contemporary conditions were the determining factor. The division of Paris into electoral districts led to the formation of the Parisian "Sections" which on the eve of August 10, 1792, took away the Legislative Assembly's right to be in "permanent" session—that is, the right to convene at any time. From that time on they regarded themselves, in Jaurès' words, as the sovereign's genuine representatives. The uprising of August 10 was their uprising, but the concept of direct democracy affected the entire country. Communes patterned on the Paris model came into being everywhere, and the idea of a federation of the communes was necessarily part of the agenda.

But already in 1793 the two contrasting tendencies of the social system were locked in their final struggle. The Convention took away the right of the Paris Sections to meet permanently. The government's commissaires fought with the local administrations in the provinces. Commissaire Ysabeau wrote to Bouchotte, the Minister of War, on November 10, 1793: "What is this new force which has arisen against legitimate authority? Or is there a dual government in France?" Once the Revolutionary regime was established in December 1793, the Paris Sections lost their right to elect arbitrators, to establish relief committees and engage in their own welfare work. The country's revolutionary committees were integrated into the governmental machinery, their members became paid officials and local administrations were no longer elected. Thus the Paris

Sections and the provincial revolutionary institutions died out for lack of independence. The hiring of officials turned out to be extraordinarily expensive—for instance almost the entire Jacobin Club was taken over by the administration—and contributed to the worsening of the financial situation. The Paris Commune was forbidden to have direct communication with the city's revolutionary committees. The other Communes in the country were not allowed to have contact with each other, and any assembly of representatives of several localities or departments was also forbidden.[46]

At the end of the French Revolution, Babeuf and his *Société des Egaux* tried to draw some precepts which they could continue and revitalize on a new basis. Babeuf's *Tribune du Peuple* was the forum of "true democracy." His society wanted to see sovereignty confined exclusively to local assemblies, while a central assembly was supposed merely to coordinate their deliberations. They believed that the system of equality they were striving for should avoid having a class of people solely concerned with administration, because they would soon learn to acquire privileges.[47] These ideas disappeared underground in the postrevolutionary period, only to reemerge with elemental force in the Paris Commune of 1871.[48]

The discord between democratic theories of self-government and the bureaucratic mind was far less radical and apocalyptic in tone when the concept of Workers' Councils appeared in the political arena with the collapse in 1918 of the German empire and its war machinery. Wilhelm Kottler called the formation of Councils "the concrete expression of political longing." He saw the idea behind them as

a reminder of democracy's basic idea, the liberation of the individual from the enveloping mechanism of the state, the rescue of his personality, as well as recognition of a necessary commitment by the individual to the community, especially in the confines of his life and work. The concept of councils in its various forms is concerned with valorizing the individual neither as a free individual, nor as a member of the community as a whole, but as a *member of his own community*. There is only one idea at the back of all these phenomena, past and present. Although expressed in diverse forms and transmitted through differing intellectual traditions, it always appears when certain conditions obtain. The latter involve the ideal of self-government as expressed, for example, in

[46] *See* Daniel Guérin, *La Lutte des classes sous la première republique: bourgeois et "bras nus" 1793-1797*, 2 vols. (Paris, 1946); and Peter Kropotkin, *The Great French Revolution, 1789-1793*, tr. N. F. Dryhurst (London and New York, 1909).

[47] Guerin, *op. cit.*, pp. 347 and 348.

[48] *See* Chapter VIII, Section 2.

185

the old German cooperatives or the shop committees which are their modern counterparts. The basic idea is the right of self-determination, but not by way of parliamentary democracy which, although it allows the individual . . . to participate in government, considerably waters down that participation. The concept of councils goes beyond the problematical relationship of the individual to the state, jolting the traditional system and revealing the fact that the problem is the structure of the state itself.[49]

The importance of this concept in German history and in the history of world bureaucratization lay not so much in the revolutionary movement of a utopian-chiliastic minority affected by the tailwinds of the Russian revolution, as in the more limited efforts by the majority of the German working class to institute a method of control in the social system which would not be part of the government. These efforts, and the events surrounding them, have been elucidated in a detailed study by Eberhard Kolb, who has also shown why the Council movement failed in practice. The atmosphere was such that the more liberal administration of the Social Democratic party allied itself with the antidemocratic Prussian bureaucracy against what both considered the antibureaucratic interference of a democratic movement.[50]

Workers' Councils (*Arbeiterräte*) first developed in Germany during the great strikes of 1917–1918. At first they were no more than strike committees, but already they contained something new in their make-up. These Councils, which were established everywhere by the local Social Democratic party leadership in November, 1918, were improvised and hardly clear as to their precise role.

Their "consciousness" first developed in practice. As Kolb says, "It was indicative of the development of the Workers' Councils in the German revolutionary movement of 1918–1919 that this consciousness only led to tangible results when the basis of any political effectiveness had been taken away from them." When the state's power structure collapsed in November 1918, the administrative bureaucracy submitted to the Workers' and Soldiers' Councils (*Soldatenräte*) which took power. But underneath the new surface, "the old administrative apparatus, with its old system of authority, continued undisturbed." From the beginning

[49] Kottler, *op. cit.*

[50] Kolb rightly concludes: "Previous research into the history of revolutionary and council movements has completely overlooked the attempts of the *Arbeiterräte* (German Workers' Councils) to democratize the administration." Eberhard Kolb, *Die Arbeiterräte in der deutschen Innenpolitik 1918 bis 1919* (Düsseldorf, 1962). In fact, history and political analyses have dealt mainly with discussing such alternatives as Bolshevism or parliamentary democracy. The following discussion of the Workers' Councils refers to the volume by Kolb, unless otherwise stated.

there was "collaboration between the new government and previous state institutions against the Workers' Councils."

In Prussia, particularly, there was a prompt and rapid growth of Workers' Councils paralleling the many-layered governmental administration. Thus the presidents of the Local Councils (*Ortsräte*) formed a County Workers' Council (*Kreisarbeiterrat*), and elected an Executive Committee which was empowered to control the County Government Office (*Landratsamt*). The County Councils then formed a District Workers' Council (*Bezirksarbeiterrat*), to supervise the District Government (*Regierungspräsidium*). A Provincial Council (*Provinzialrat*) was elected to establish a central supervisory office in the chief administration of the Province of Prussia (the *Oberpräsidium*). By mid-December the organizational system was completed.

According to Kolb, "When the Councils held their first Congress in Berlin on December 16, 1918, it was not an assembly of representatives of incidental, arbitrarily constituted organizations. At this point the improvisational stage had been passed; an official structure of Workers' Councils had been developed, which corresponded to the governmental administrative system in its comparatively clearly defined powers, responsibilities and areas of jurisdiction."

But now the struggle for power set in. Contrary to the wishes of the Social Democratic Party (*SPD*)—to which the majority of the participants belonged—the Congress did pass resolutions concerning the military command which, if they had been put into effect, would have altered the power balance.[51] But because the Congress did not establish an authority to enforce the resolutions, it sealed the fate of the Councils.

Already at the beginning of December, Ebert had challenged the right of the Executive of the Councils to send delegates to the central government's ministries for orientation. At the same time, the Social Democratic leadership was not aware, "that although the top executives had been replaced when the imperial government was overthrown, the massive substructure of the administration and the military machine had not been affected. Thus the new government would remain in jeopardy, until far-reaching changes were undertaken in those institutions."

But it was not merely a question of what Kolb described as "lack of awareness." With their bureaucratic interpretation of the situation,

---

[51] The resolutions stated, among other things, that "The high command of the army, navy and colonial troops will be exercised by the people's representatives under the control of the Executive Council . . . The soldiers are to elect their leaders themselves."

the Social Democratic leadership allied itself from the very beginning with those key men of the bureaucratic administration who were kindred spirits, despite their opposing political ideology. The Social Democratic leaders regarded nongovernmental democratic organizations as the monstrous product of a temporarily chaotic period. However, the Congress of the Workers' Councils was unaware of the inevitable conflict between bureaucratic centralization and democratic institutions of self-government. When Lüdemann, a leading Social Democrat, put forward a motion unobtrusively demanding that the entire political power be given to an Assembly of the people's representatives, that is, to the central government, the Congress voted unanimously in its favor.[52] It did so because the motion provided for the appointment of a Central Committee of the Councils, which was to supervise the German and Prussian cabinets. But the government, having obtained complete political power, soon ignored that Central Committee. A motion put forward in February 1919, to give the Central Committee the right of veto in the National Assembly, was received by that body with "amusement" and rejected.

Kolb points out that no one today denies that "one of the main causes of the Weimar Republic's internal weakness was the central government's (*Reichsregierung*) inability immediately to undertake prompt and far-reaching reforms in the personnel structure of the administrative bureaucracy." The examples which he cites clearly show how bureaucratic opposition stifled political reform, and how ministers who had come from the party bureaucracy were drawn into the bureaucratic routine, or at least gave in to it. Republicans were unable to obtain executive administrative positions, even when trained for such posts, because the bureaucracy would maintain that it was another's turn, according to the seniority rule. When a County Director (*Landrat*), who had previously been censured for insufficient respect for the Hohenzollerns, was to be appointed President of the Province (*Oberpräsident*), the other County Directors threatened to strike. The ministers always gave in. Any decrees the bureaucracy did not want to see implemented were accidentally left in the record-office.

In his detailed attempt to deal with the phenomenology of the German Workers' Councils, Kolb discovered that the Councils could be divided into two groups, despite their diversity. One group wanted solely to act as a regulatory agency for a given time and to help reconstruct the ad-

---

[52] On November 23, the Executive Council of the Workers' and Soldiers' Councils issued a statement in Berlin on the constitutional status of the Councils and people's representatives, which declared that the Councils had political authority.

ministration. The other aimed at expanding the power of the Councils, which they desired to be given a permanent place in the new government. However, both of them realized from their practical experience in November and December of 1918 that "a determined take-over of the administrative apparatus was necessary if the power won through the overthrow of the government was not soon to be lost." Thus practical experience brought the Councils to the same insight Max Weber had formed in 1917 after careful analysis of the bureaucratic structure of the modern state: "In a modern state real authority—which expresses itself neither in parliamentary speeches nor in promulgations by monarchs, but in the administration of daily life—is vested inevitably and necessarily in the bureaucracy."[53] Since the Workers' Councils were concerned with "real authority" and "its implementation in daily life," they had to demand the democratization of the administration—over and above equal voting rights and elections of parliamentary bodies. In their opposition to a "party leadership which did not undertake any firm measures to reform the administrative machine, they found themselves in conflict with their own principles of party loyalty."

The Social Democratic ministers for their part firmly maintained "that the controlling function of the Workers' Councils was irreconcilable with 'democratic principles,' and systematically abolished them without simultaneously reforming the administrative machine." This struggle exhausted the energy of the democratic Workers' Councils before they had had a chance to dedicate their political energies to establishing a sound *democratic* foundation for the young republic.

Discussing the activity of the Workers' Councils Kolb concludes:

They concentrated on solving social and social-political problems: on guaranteeing food supplies, on combating the black market, eliminating the housing shortage and providing employment. They tried to gain influence and power in government institutions, in order to destroy the supremacy of the conservatives and to assure a permanent democratic structure. All their efforts were aimed at creating a new type of administration whose institutions would be closer to the people. They had the experience necessary to accomplish this, because they mostly acted out of a sense of justice and sound common sense, because they enjoyed the participation and were conscious of their responsibilities. The "unpretentious, objective conduct" which had impressed Max Weber during his membership in the Heidelberg Workers' and Soldiers' Council, can be considered as being characteristic of all the democratic Workers' Councils.

[53] Max Weber, *Gesammelte Politische Schriften* (München, 1921), p. 139.

The origin of the council concept has been traced by Kurt Wolzendorff in a work dealing with the principles of constitutional philosophy:

It was said of that bleak, harsh and soulless state—which had just been demanding "unlimited human sacrifice,"—"L'État est mort, vive l'État!" That is when hope turned away from the state and sought to create a new "system," not through governmental machinery but fashioned out of man's daily experience, with his own hands, a system in which he would be his own master and not be employed for alien ends: the Councils.[54] The concept of councils is the expression of a universal attitude toward the problem of social life. It has a role—and a very different role—in political and social party doctrines. . . . But the essence of this concept cannot be realized from studying the roles played by it in our public intellectual life. Its essence is much more universal and has developed out of the intellectual needs of our social life rather than having been implanted from the outside. It is the intellectual rejection of the mechanics of the state, which continued to function in its soulless, unperturbed way during the most dreadful catastrophe to have befallen mankind. Even in those instances where those mechanics broke down, they automatically rebuilt themselves and made those who directed them act in as mechanical a fashion as their predecessors. That is the *entirely universal* mood which was expressed in the "demand for the councils." The fact that it was first expressed by the proletariat and first seized on by socialism resulted in concomitant, visible social developments. But the mood is in itself neither proletarian nor socialist, and that is its universal significance for political thought and life, however frequently that mood failed to find effective expression.

The idea which emerged from this mood is that man is entitled to fashion a system for himself, basing it directly on his own social, economic and intellectual experience.[55]

---

[54] Here Wolzendorff cites H. Sinzheimer, *Das Rätesystem*, 1919.

[55] Kurt Wolzendorff, "Der reine Staat: Skizze zum Problem einer neuen Staatsepoche," *Zeitschrift für die gesamte Staatswissenschaft*, LVII, 1 and 2 (August, 1920), pp. 203-204.

11

NEW TASKS
FOR GOVERNMENT

Towards the end of World War II, Joseph Schumpeter attempted to forecast the future of the capitalist world, and saw in the development of governmental machinery one of its major trends: "The bureaucracies of Europe . . . are the product of a long development . . . that went on through the centuries until the powerful machine emerged which we behold today . . . it grows everywhere, whatever the political method a nation may adopt. Its expansion is the one certain thing about our future."[1]

This forecast is "certain" to be reliable, especially since the state has grown increasingly involved with satisfying the demands of organized pressure groups for a bigger share of the national income. It has become responsible for helping those who need economic support and for giving aid in economic emergencies. The subsidies and investments which this intervention requires enlarge the role of the state in industry, both directly and indirectly. For while there is an increase in the credit requirements of the government and its influence on the capital market, the growing commitments of a self-expanding social security system also require further investment.

But new and greater tasks will result from the enormous technological changes due to the process of automation. The reorganization of manpower and of the regional distribution of industry will call for new forms of state intervention. Since the world undergoes fundamental change within the space of a single generation and previous education is rendered obsolete, it is necessary to retrain and integrate the upcoming generation. The employment rate becomes a problem once the work force required for the production of goods decreases drastically. In almost all predictable changes of this nature the individual has to rely on the state.

The introduction of atomic technology will alter the living conditions of entire regions in the foreseeable future, and will require massive tech-

---

[1] Joseph A. Schumpeter, *Capitalism, Socialism and Democracy* (New York, 1950), p. 294.

nical administrative procedures. It has been pointed out, for instance, that whole districts could be transformed if one reactor were capable of producing both electric current and fresh water from the ocean. Agreements would have to be reached between sovereign states and their subdivisions regarding the control of such large investments and their revenue.[2]

One can reasonably anticipate that *control* will be the key concept in future sociological thought. Not only that which pertains to the economy, but also the "numbers and location of the population, its genetic quality, the manner of social domestication of children, the choice of lifework" may become increasingly subject to "scientific investigation and control."[3]

Interlocking international companies will continue for their part to strengthen the role of the state in industry. The export of capital will continue to be an important business of the state in the form of credits and transfers to the nonindustrialized world. An increasing number of international economic agreements will entail corresponding regulations of national economies.

This further growth in state functions leads to the numerical increase in state employees. Administrative expansion requires measures of coordination as well as supervision and control. Thus the administration of administration also becomes more extensive.

An ever closer connection between management and administrative bureaucracy must develop owing to the exploitation and deepening of the government's intervention in industry. A conference of Swiss sales and marketing organizations, meeting in November, 1966, came to the following conclusions:

It can be anticipated that the private sector in the economy will cease to function. It will be replaced by continuous and concentrated reciprocal action between industry and the government. National economy will cease being an ideological problem. Instead numerous groups, whose interests are time- and situation-bound, will become the focal point of endless minor conflicts and of a bargaining for influence. The structure of the state will be determined by the way in which these associations and trade unions coordinate their interests.

The convergence of government and industry is already revealed by the fact that the state must now be concerned not only with managing

---

[2] List Gesellschaft, *Planung ohne Planwirtschaft* (Basel, 1964).
[3] Robert L. Heilbroner, *The Limits of American Capitalism* (New York, 1966), p. 129–130.

192

economic cycles, but with fostering economic expansion, since it must increase the total demand to correspond to the long-term planning of large corporations.

When England's Conservative government suggested the formation of a National Economic Development Council in 1961, Selwyn Lloyd defined its functions as follows:

The NEDC has to exercise constant supervision over the economic efficiency of the country, in the course of which the future development of the public and private sectors of the economy must be carefully planned. The NEDC is supposed to track down the obstacles which prevent the economy from achieving faster growth, and submit suggestions for their elimination as well as for increasing economic productivity. In addition, the problem of whether the country's economic resources are being used to their optimal advantage must also be investigated. Thus the Council must develop methods for strengthening British competitive ability.[4]

The desire for state involvement is assuming greater urgency as industrial consolidation in Western nations is pushed to extremes. A 1967 forecast mentioned that apart from the public sector, it is probable that even before the end of this century about 75 percent of the industrial capital will be controlled by as few as 300 large corporations. The composition of this group of three hundred naturally depends largely on the outcome of the power maneuvers during the next decade. It may be anticipated that about 175 American and 125 European and Japanese firms will be included in that final group.[5]

The origins of the process of consolidation are to be sought not only in industrial-technological and market policies, but also in attempts to achieve power and prestige which are so characteristic of the bureaucratic mind. This is especially the case where conglomerate consolidation is concerned. In the United States there has been a particular increase in the mergers of companies which function in completely different areas and which have no buyer-seller relationships.[6]

Administrative functions show greater than proportional increase in conglomerate consolidation and hence there is also an increase in administrative expenditures, as Eugen Schmalenbach already pointed out:

[4] Excerpted from *Neue Zürcher Zeitung*, July 9, 1965.

[5] The forecast originally appeared in the *Sunday Times* (London) and was cited in *Der Volkswirt*, February 24, 1967.

[6] For instance, the fact that the textile company Textron has undertaken the manufacture of helicopters, chicken feed, bathroom accessories, men's shoes, rocket parts, spectacle frames and hearing aids, is perhaps an extreme but significant example of conglomerate consolidation.

193

"Administrative expenditures have a tendency to increase overproportionally in ratio to industrial plant expansion, once the optimum has been exceeded. As the company continues to grow, the lack of adequate supervision by management necessitates more comprehensive control in the form of auditing and similar departments. Eyes and ears have to be replaced by paper and ink." As to real savings in the economy, that is, the decrease of production costs, the point is soon reached in the process of consolidation "where the increase in administrative costs per unit is greater than the reduction in the net production costs per unit."[7] Statistical surveys show the steady increase of fixed administrative costs in ratio to production costs.[8]

Although Schmalenbach's "paper and ink" are being superseded, it is uncertain whether the introduction of data-processing machines has effected savings. As pointed out by E. Böhler, the use of these machines developed from a fascination with the prospect of obtaining additional information; and the immediate outcome has been the hiring of further highly-specialized personnel:

It has been estimated that the management of all paperwork connected with business enterprises in the United States amounts to more than 100 billion dollars per year; about 50 million steel filing cabinets house about 250 billion business papers.

Experience in the United States shows that in the end management personnel drown in reports whose purpose they fail to see; this *wealth of information* decreases their decision-making capacity because the diversity of the points of view to be considered tends to confuse them. In addition, there is also the psychological fact that personal opinion and experience is lost in processing statistical material, whereas decisions taken are unconsciously and predominantly based on instinct.[9]

In spite of the complexity and increased costs of administration which accompany bureaucratic expansion in growing enterprises, the latter continue operating on a profitable basis owing to their strong position in

[7] Hans Otto Henel, *Ursachen der Konzentration* (Tübingen, 1962); *see also,* Eugene Schmalenbach, *Der freien Wirtschaft zum Gedächtnis* (Köln, 1949).

[8] Seymour Melman, *Decision-Making and Productivity* (New York, 1958), pp. 119–128. Other authors, such as Reinhard Bendix and Peter M. Blau, have argued on the basis of their studies that large corporations do not have disproportionately high administrative costs. There is no reason to doubt their findings which, however, do not exclude a later excessive growth of the administrative apparatus as the tendency towards a "displacement of goal by means" (as Robert Merton puts it) becomes stronger. It has also been pointed out that the efficiency of the productive worker is often increased by extension of the administration. This, again, is probably as true as its reverse. Neither observation, however, "measures" the existential problem of bureaucracy.

[9] E. Böhler, "Die Inflation der Dienstleistungen," *Neue Zürcher Zeitung,* May 22, 1966.

the market and their other business advantages.[10] But the fact that American top executive pay is now related to the sales volume rather than company profit also ties in with the bureaucratic concept of expansion.[11]

The administration of the greater part of the invested capital of Western industrial nations by comparatively few large corporations also indicates that they are becoming ever more internationally interlocked. Hence sales planning and management will increase and acquire a greater importance. The consumer will be most carefully "conditioned" to purchase goods exactly as they are produced. This means that the aims and opinions of branch offices and production divisions located in different areas must be reconciled with those of the head office. The pluralistic objectives must become clarified by means of reciprocal action by the individual concerns. Thus the top management must first of all indicate specific basic goals to local managements, as a sort of guideline. Subsequently, the national or regional companies can set their own achievable goals, in accordance with the particular conditions of their market, but in line with the overall plans. The head office responsible for the general planning of the enterprise is faced with vast problems. Not only does it have to check to see whether the various individual goals and plans are realistic: it has to determine whether the goals established by the lower levels of an international business hierarchy are not set too low to be compatible with a seemingly above average level within the company generally.[12]

Concentration of power increases among international corporations as a result of this global planning by head offices. They influence civilization and culture in their planning of the consumption of goods. They do so not only because they determine the type and quality of goods produced, but because they condition the consumers. This means that the bureaucratic apparatus of large corporations is confronted with problems very similar to those experienced by the government bureaucracy. The fact that—in the interests of advancement—output goals are falsified by those operating at lower levels, is only one such problem.

The main office and regional divisions of large corporations often expe-

[10] Henel, *op. cit.*

[11] *See* Arch Patton, "Top Executive Pay: New Facts and Figures," *Harvard Business Review*, XLIV, 5 (September–October, 1966), p. 96. The article complains that this trend means that profit is no longer the real "basic goal of industry" and the "top management rewards are . . . being based on the less demanding objective of sales volume."

[12] Jan. S. Kŕuli-Randa, "Die Praxis der multinationalen Marketing-Politik und Planung," *Neue Zürcher Zeitung*, December 28, 1967.

rience difficulty in communication and understanding. Plans and guide-lines are frequently misinterpreted or deliberately sabotaged; the main office tries to protect the general interests of the entire enterprise, while the regional offices often believe that their own problems are not under-stood by those at the head office who specialize in management and are supposed to provide assistance. Regional personnel often do not know what kind of assistance they can expect from the main office: *what they are aware of is the growing number of forms to be filled out. Large concerns suffer from the chronic problems of bureaucracy.* Multinational enterprises are no exception. Hence they are subject to the danger of inflexibility, which naturally hampers decision-making. One of the most frequent complaints by affiliated managements is that the main office is unable to make decisions in time for local requirements. At times the regional staff is altogether unable to determine *who* in the main office is supposed to pass on specific decision.[13]

Governmental bureaucracy for its part is also influenced by the power-ful industrial bureaucracy. The two bureaucracies are interrelated but they also conflict, for in their interaction the government represents the interests of society as a whole. Sales-oriented business policy is not inter-ested in the real usefulness of its products as long as an illusory usefulness is in demand. The automobile industry has always found that "safety does not sell," but variety in models does. However, controlling the quali-ty of products is only one of many tasks the state will have to assume. Above all, it will become involved in controlling the increased pollution of air and water, and the destruction of the ecological balance of nature. The administrative structure is bound to be enlarged, because people are less and less able to cope with their own problems, and wait for and expect assistance from specialized agencies. As Galbraith maintains, "Only the state can defend the landscape" against encroachment by industry, and regulate "patterns of consumer consumption . . . [which] are inconsistent with aesthetic goals."[14]

---

[13] Hovard V. Perlmutter, "Menschliche Aspekte der internationalen Unternehmung," *Neue Zürcher Zeitung,* December 28, 1967.

[14] John Kenneth Galbraith, *The New Industrial State* (Boston, 1967), p. 350.

12

THE CONFLICT OF VALUES AND REALITY

Bureaucracy and its Growth

Bureaucracy is not an unambiguous term. Although it generally refers to a group of people concerned with organization and management, its usage is often limited to government officials. The term has also acquired a derogatory meaning which points to such shortcomings in the performance of administration as slowness and cumbersomeness.

There are many variants among bureaucracies, especially state bureaucracies. They can conduct themselves rationally or arbitrarily. Their performance can be efficient and precise, or protracted and inefficient. A bureaucracy may be characterized by honesty or corruption. Its political orientation and social origin, as well as its status in society can vary greatly. It may function collectively, even if its hierarchical structure permits only a very uneven distribution of authority, to the point where it may be nonexistent among the lower echelons. Bureaucracy can serve as the mere tool of authority and still be significant enough to influence those in control.[1]

Differences exist not only between the upper and lower levels within bureaucracies, but also between specialists and administrators.

The bureaucratic *concept*, however, refers to a system of social interaction which forms in all varieties of bureaucracies and bureaucratic organizations. Franz Neumann has provided a detailed analysis: "Bureaucratization, correctly understood, is a process operating in both public and private spheres, in the state as well as in society. It means that human relations lose their directness and become mediated relations in which

---

[1] The extent to which bureaucracy holds power varies greatly and is sometimes manifested in paradoxical fashion. Thus history records bureaucracies which have been constituted by slaves. The Ottoman Empire at the height of its glory had such slave bureaucracies, while the free nobility were excluded from government functions. Similarly, the Mamelukes were a slave bureaucracy in Egypt until they acquired full governmental power. *See* Arnold Toynbee, *Study of History,* I–VI (New York and London, 1947), I, pp. 174–176.

197

third parties, public or private functionaries seated more or less securely in power, authoritatively prescribe the behavior of man." This has become a comprehensive process in modern society. Neumann points out that a gigantic organizational network surrounds almost every aspect of human life, even including culture. Sports and the arts are also administered by professional bureaus, and special departments in the mass-media system figure out how much light and how much classical music, how many lectures and how much news are to be presented to the public.[2]

(The *real problem* posed by the bureaucratic process is its relationship to democratic values. However, the public pays much more attention to the way in which the bureaucracy functions than to its actual influence. Perhaps it is precisely this fact which shows to what extent the process has succeeded. The negative factors in the bureaucratic system are seen in the way it conducts its business, which has been described as "the disease of bureaucracy." The fundamental difficulty does not stem from its "superfluous," but from its "indispensable" aspects. Bureaucracy holds disintegrated society together. The nature and history of the bureaucratic system have to be studied so we can understand the interpersonal relationships which it forms. After all, the administrative bureaucracy itself complains about its "superfluous" aspects and the "disease of bureaucracy" and wants to rationalize its organization.)

Whether the "disease" is curable, whether it is part of the system, whether indispensable bureaucracy must always include superfluous administration, are by no means unimportant questions to which varied answers can be given. "Parkinson's Law" shows how the bureaucratic balloon is permanently inflated, how it wastes funds and promotes the selection of mediocrities. There is no lack of examples. However, there is also evidence that modern offices function more efficiently than they did in the past; electronic machinery has replaced red tape, and the efficiency of many skilled administrative officials is noticeable. It has been shown that bureaucratic business management is not a uniform phenomenon, but is subject to many influences. Government and industrial bureaucracies, and those of the unions and political parties, react differently and reveal variants in their conduct which have provided the topics of innumerable individual investigations. What is apparently evident in intrabureaucratic relationships, and in relationships between administrators and those they administer, is considerable "dysfunction."

[2] Franz Neumann, *Behemoth: The Structure and Practice of National Socialism* (New York and London, 1942), p. 368.

"Dysfunction" is inherent in bureaucracy, but it is only one of the many difficulties connected with it, and not even the essential one.

The problem presented by bureaucratization in social interaction is only seen clearly when the former is considered in the light of its irrevocability:

Bureaucratic organization is a first-class sociological work of art which has been fashioned over many centuries. It is an illusion to maintain that it could be suppressed and replaced by "self-government." The contrary is proved by "communal bureaucracy" . . . [and] the bureaucracy of political parties in all countries possessing a parliamentary and democratic system. It is the indispensable machinery of an official administration which orients itself toward formal law. Its systematic structure, the way in which it turns all that is personal into something functional, is a necessary attendant symptom of the inevitable process by which it becomes a large-scale enterprise.[3]

From an historical as well as objective point of view, the expansion of government activity and the centralization of its social responsibilities and actions must be considered particularly problematical since they concern society as a whole. These special problems were already touched upon by Wilhelm von Humboldt in 1792:

It has been from time to time disputed by publicists whether the State should provide only for the security, or for the whole physical and moral well-being of the nation. Concern for the freedom of private life has in general led to the former proposition; while the idea that the State can give something more than mere security, and that the injurious limitation of liberty, although a possible, is not an essential, consequence of such a policy, has influenced the latter theory. And this belief has undoubtedly prevailed, not only in political theory, but in actual practice. This is shown in most of the systems of political jurisprudence, in the more recent philosophical codes, and in the history of constitutions generally. Agriculture, handicrafts, industry of all kinds, business, the arts and learning itself, all receive life and direction from the State.[4]

The conclusion reached in the last sentence is particularly surprising when one considers to what extent the state has increased its functions since then. However, in view of the new areas which fall to the responsibility of government, the problem as described by von Humboldt must

---

[3] Otto Hintze, "Nationale und europäische Orientierung in der heutigen politischen Welt," in *Soziologie und Geschichte: Gesammelte Abhandlungen zur Soziologie, Politik und Theorie der Geschichte*, ed. Gerhard Östreich (Göttingen, 1964).

[4] Wilhelm von Humboldt, *The Limits of State Action*, ed. and tr. J. W. Burrow (Cambridge, England, 1969), p. 14. *See also* Chapter VII, Section 1.

be dealt with on quite a different level. The basis for extensive changes in the social structure is being established in the area of industry in particular, where the "new industrial state" must constantly submit to new regulations. Schumpeter has already pointed out that capitalist economics invariably tend toward a socialist model. But he could not conceive of a socialist organization except as an all-embracing bureaucratic apparatus. Schumpeter was not unaware of the problems presented by a comprehensive bureaucracy, nor of the "diseases" which accompany administrative activity. Yet he maintained of the latter: "The elimination of the profit and loss motive that is often exclusively stressed is not the essential point. Moreover, responsibility in the sense of having to pay for one's mistakes with one's own money is passing anyhow . . . and the kind of responsibility that exists in the large-scale corporation could no doubt be reproduced in a socialist society." Schumpeter also recommended the expansion of bureaucratic activity:

It is not enough that the bureaucracy should be efficient in current administration and competent to give advice. It must also be strong enough to guide and, if need be, to instruct the politicians who head the ministries. In order to be able to do this it must be in a position to evolve principles of its own and sufficiently independent to assert them. It must be a power in its own right. This amounts to saying that in fact though not in form appointment, tenure and promotion must depend largely—within civil service rules that politicians hesitate to violate—on its own corporate opinion in spite of all the clamor that is sure to arise whenever politicians or the public find themselves crossed by it as they frequently must.[5]

The danger envisaged by Schumpeter is not the limitation of political activities by bureaucracy but the way in which politicians might jeopardize a true understanding of administrative relationships. Inefficient political interference could endanger the results of long-term administrative labor. The official who identifies with his particular task might be forced into defending himself against political showmanship. The administration is often better able to recognize and to represent society's needs in the face of the egoistic interests of pressure groups and the indifference of all those who do not consider themselves concerned.

It is not possible to deal with the heart of the problem until this reality has been acknowledged. As Schumpeter phrases it, "recognition of the

---

[5] Joseph A. Schumpeter, *Capitalism, Socialism and Democracy* (New York, 1950), pp. 206 and 293.

inevitability of comprehensive bureaucratization does not solve the problems that arise out of it."[6] The accumulation of power is promoted by the fact that a growing number of functions have become centralized. There is no guarantee that this power is administered in the interests of one and all. But this is only part of the difficulty. The conflict between reality and democratic values cannot be seen in its entirety until one takes into account the reaction of those who are administered to the continuous accumulation of central power and responsibility—an accumulation which renders them impotent and undermines their responsibility.

Concerning Democratic Values and the Ideology of Non-ideology

But what are these democratic values? Schumpeter believed that democracy could and should be limited to a restricted sphere of activity: "Democracy means only that the people have the opportunity of accepting or refusing the men who are to rule them. But since they might decide this also in entirely undemocratic ways, we have had to narrow our definition by adding a further criterion identifying the democratic method, viz., free competition among would-be leaders for the vote of the electorate."[7] To be sure, the presence or absence of these two criteria determine the nature of a political system. But in the actual operation of parliamentary systems, election and competition are largely restricted by the preliminary decisions of bureaucratic party authorities.

The democratic principle cannot, however, be reduced to such a limited formula. Democracy is not only a principle of social organization, it is also a system of values.[8] It is a system of values which evolved from and was molded by what Alfred Weber has described as the "European consciousness of freedom."[9] Otto Stammer says of these democratic values: "The classic theory of democracy was also based on certain values: for instance, those related to the principles of freedom of the individual, of equality of political rights and opportunities, of the legality of government and administration, of the ability to understand and control the

[6] *Ibid.*, p. 206.
[7] *Ibid.*, p. 284–285.
[8] Neumann, *op. cit.*, p. 78.
[9] Alfred Weber, *Kulturgeschichte als Kultursoziologie* (Leiden, 1935).

political process, and of the division of governmental authority."[10] It goes without saying that Schumpeter's definition of democracy as a principle of social organization requires freedom of expression. But over and above that, the democratic system of values contains the concept of direct participation in the organization of society. Problems have arisen precisely because with the waning of this participation, the effectiveness of the democratic organizational principle itself has become uncertain.

It might be well to recall de Tocqueville's conclusion: That those who do not participate in at least the most minor of administrative duties would forget how to make proper use of their franchise and, finally growing tired of all representatives, would submit to the rule of a dictator—a combination soldier and bookkeeper. This sociological analysis was fulfilled in the twentieth century, when the bookkeeping records of a certain totalitarian state duly noted the number of gold teeth extracted from those it had murdered.

But it would be imprudent to believe that this prophecy has now been fully realized, since its preconditions still exist. Of course, whether or not these preconditions lead indeed to substantive changes in the existing principle of social organization depends on the interplay of several factors of varying origins; but this is where the special nature of bureaucracy comes into play. Although there is a significant difference between bureaucracies which exercise direct control and those which do not, bureaucratic domination inevitably encourages the growth of antidemocratic tendencies inherent in it.

The "nature" of bureaucracy, its conduct, and the way in which it functions, largely depend on the social climate as it affects the bureaucratic mind, and as it affects the internal structure of the machinery—in particular the apparatus of government. A bureaucratic system uses an authoritarian attitude for external as well as internal purposes. As a result, such safeguards as ritualism, procrastination and sabotage, are more frequently resorted to in a bureaucracy than elsewhere. The only control which exists is the hierarchic autocontrol practiced by the bureaucracy. The contrast between different organizations—the state, the political party or industry—is one of internal structure, and is not a conflict between independent organizations and interests. The state more or less comprises the whole of society and encloses all its groups; "conflict,"

[10] Otto Stammer, "Politische Soziologie und Demokratieforschung," *Kölner Zeitschrift für Soziologie und Sozialpsychologie*, VIII (1956).

which is an important source of social progress, is buried by governmental bureaucracy as a matter of principle.[11] Business management is also impaired by the authoritarian comprehensiveness of government. "Large-scale organization," Galbraith maintains, "also requires autonomy. The intrusion of an external and uninformed will is damaging."[12] In such cases, the productivity of large-scale industrial corporations suffers, hence it has been suggested *they* be given autonomy—which is what modern Communist theoreticians refer to as "reform."

Intrabureaucratic relationships in a dominant administration provide the best example of the effects of influences stemming from a generally repressive atmosphere in state and society. Such "bureaucratic bureaucracies" reveal dominant authoritarian trends. But where external conditions are different, where bureaucracies are still open to democratic influence, administration functions differently. Michel Crozier had rightly emphasized that the best results are produced by a permissive department head. The most productive organization is not the rational type described by Max Weber, but the one that is most alive; that is to say, the one in which the subordinates are encouraged to participate in the formation of decisions which they have to implement.[13]

The existence and extension of this type of organizational management obviously require a social climate which respects democratic values. But the difficulty inherent in creating and maintaining such a climate is precisely part of the problem prevailing in the administered world. The open society, which accompanied the creation of national states and which shaped their social climate tends to fall apart:

The openness of modern society . . . developed as the growth of modern social structure compelled the individual to emerge from the purely communal social interaction of small groups. It came about because the individual considered himself part of numerous social categories and special interest groups, entailing participation in the abstract conflicts of interest and action of a multilayered social organization. However, precisely these multiple social identifications . . . have come increasingly to be considered . . . an oppressive overburdening of man in modern society . . . and are constantly being reduced . . . The "will

---

[11] Pierre Naville, "Critique de la bureaucratie," in *Cahiers internationaux de sociologie* (Paris, 1953). On the function of conflict in the development of society, *see* Lewis A. Coser, *The Functions of Social Conflict* (Glencoe, 1956).

[12] John Kenneth Galbraith, *The New Industrial State* (Boston, 1967), p. 390.

[13] Michel Crozier, *Le Phénomène bureaucratique* (Paris, 1964). English edition, *The Bureaucratic Phenomenon*, tr. author (London, 1964).

203

of the people" is turning more and more into one of those abstract concepts manipulated by bureaucracy for polemic purposes, as a vehicle for its demands, and as a symbol of its own policies. Although it serves the function of expressing conflicts between organizations, it can hardly generate any conflict within the individual, since he is engaged in trying to escape to the conflict-free and peaceful area of his private life.[14]

The main phenomenon of an open society is the formation of public opinion. This can be achieved by active participation and interest in public affairs, and by the interplay and clash of ideas. But public opinion can also be a smoke screen over society as a whole produced by public relations firms.

Since its creation, the concept of "public opinion" has always implied a free-floating institution of criticism and control of those in authority. It has always been a court of appeal, part of a productive process in which ordinary individuals, as well as personalities, have exerted influence. Many also participate "silently," so to speak, solely by their outward behavior. In his investigation of the structural changes of public opinion, Jürgen Habermas has demonstrated its transformation from a critical, productive institution into one that is manipulated for consumption. Modern communications media, with their set programs and constant stream of advertising and "public relations" material, constitute a pseudo-public opinion, which might produce echoes but no answers. At best, says Habermas, public opinion becomes

a possible means of frictional resistance to government and administration, but one which can be appropriately manipulated according to circumstances and the findings of public opinion surveys. According to H. Schelsky, "this enables the government and its institutions to face the reality of a situation created by the responses of those especially affected by government policies. The public opinion poll performs this task in the sense of providing a feedback of reliable sample opinions of the situation to those authorities and institutions whose task it is . . . to see that the public is in accord with political objectives." Public opinion analysis is a type of market research, to find out how the consumer has digested that which public relation firms have prepared for him.[15]

Essentially, social climates depend on how societal forces resolve their conflicts, and on the political demands with which they confront one

[14] Helmut Schelsky, *Wandlungen der deutschen Familie in der Gegenwart: Darstellung und Deutung einer empirisch-soziologischen Tatbestandaufnahme*, 2 vols. (Stuttgart, 1955). English edition of Vol. I, *Changing Family Structures under Conditions of Social and Economic Development* (The Hague, 1958).

[15] Jürgen Habermas, "Strukturwandel der Öffentlichkeit," *Politica*, IV (Neuwied, 1965).

another. And because the decisive forces are represented by established bureaucratic organizations, the conflict does not remain on the level of competition among opposing structural ideas and the corresponding attitudes of those who hold them. Parties and unions lump together fluctuating ideas which they feel bound to represent, and promise certain results as determined by given situations and periods of time. Political parties which represent diverse groups—control of which bureaucracy considers its main task—do not stand for a politically structured ideological system, nor are their efforts directed toward social change. They are concerned with their clients' demands. Thus electoral propaganda becomes unpolitical and is turned over to public relations specialists. The ability to select political leadership—which de Tocqueville feared would be lost—is no longer called for. Since political propaganda has assumed the characteristics of advertising, it has also lost its credibility. Unions have maintained their credibility to a greater extent. The malaise that arises from the conditions of factory existence and from the workers' general "discontent with society" bears most directly on them.[16] However, these dissatisfactions are mainly projected as mere demands, without being directed towards any real change in the worker's way of life, and hence they lose their effective influence on society.

Democratic values no longer have a real conceptual domain. This is what is meant by the frequently cited "end of the age of ideologies." It is "*a development from politics to administration,* from principles to technique."[17]

The term "ideology" is used in many different contexts and thus gives rise to confusion. When the "end of ideologies" is referred to, ideology is equated with political ideas, the postulation of what ought to be. This is the area where give and take have in fact decreased. Political parties avoid political theories because they might limit their influence. The demand for them is lacking, because a skeptical and cynical point of view has formed toward politics. This is not only due to the use of the total lie by the total state, but also to the loss of credibility produced by the advertising techniques of political parties. Although advertising influences the public, it does so without engaging the latter's belief. The fact that people without political commitments also seek refuge in party

[16] Heinrich Popitz et al., *Das Gesellschaftsbild des Arbeiters* (Tübingen, 1957). For a discussion of this problem as it affects American workers see *Dissent* (Winter, 1972), a special issue devoted to *The World of the Blue Collar Worker.*

[17] Herbert Tingsten, *The Problem of Democracy* (Totowa, New Jersey, 1965), p. 196.

systems or dogmatic sectarianism is a confirmation of the point, not a contradiction.

But "ideology" ought properly to be used in another or real sense, namely, as a justification internal to any social system, and the representation of the system as the best of all possible worlds:

For ideologies are not simply lies; they are truthful statements about what a man thinks he sees. Just as the medieval knight saw himself as he wished to see himself and just as the modern bureaucrat does the same and just as both failed and fail to see whatever may be adduced against their seeing themselves as the defenders of the weak and innocent and the sponsors of the Common Good, so every other social group develops a protective ideology which is nothing if not sincere.[18]

If we were to take ideology in both senses simultaneously, we could speak of the ideology of non-ideology which is the justification of the administered world. This ideology interprets the lack of a concept of what ought to be, and the decline of public opinion, as the positive result of the progress and prosperity which have now been achieved. It regards adaptation as a virtue, and thus not only justifies the existing system, but also that manipulation which concerns itself with producing the required conformity.

However, the individual who has adapted himself is not the guardian of democratic values. Marx' observation has proved correct: "The individual is the social being. . . . He exists in reality as the representation and the real mind of social existence, and as the sum of human manifestations of life."[19] Individuals recognize the existence of the administered world, where responsibility is held by competent authorities, simply by declaring themselves incompetent, and thus abdicating responsibility. There is nothing which the individual considers as a social responsibility—he is taxed in order that such matters be dealt with on his behalf. The individual is the consumer of the social product, and he tends less and less to identify himself as a participating member of any social unit. Children grow up in a social vacuum.[20] Sharing responsibility is not part of experience.

[18] Joseph A. Schumpeter, "Science and Ideology," *The American Economic Review,* XXXIX, 2 (March, 1949), p. 349.

[19] Karl Marx, *Early Writings,* tr. T. B. Bottomore (New York, 1964), p. 158; cited in Karl Marx, *Critique of Hegel's 'Philosophy of Right,'* ed. Joseph O'Malley, tr. Annette Jolin and Joseph O'Malley (Cambridge, England, 1970), p. xliv.

[20] *See* Paul Goodman, *Growing Up Absurd: Problems of Youth in the Organized System* (New York, 1960).

Robert Presthus has dealt with the connection between organizational society and the "indifferent" types it produces.[21] Indifference is the way in which the individual accommodates himself to a world organized by others. In instances where the tradition of civic responsibility is still maintained, it is actually done so only as an empty gesture:

The Swiss city of Fribourg had 9,231 enfranchised voters at its last election. All civic business is conducted by a General Council numbering eighty members. However, Fribourg law states that taxes must be determined by an *assembly of all taxpayers,* of which there are 14,300. These were therefore called on, at the end of December, to fix the tax rate for 1968. *Twenty-five* people attended the meeting. For years this assembly of tax payers has been a farce, as is shown by the fact that in 1966 only thirteen people attended this assembly. Several years ago no one attended at all, so that the President of the Council had to summon two policemen from the street. This enabled him to observe the protocol of the law, which requires two signatures.[22]

Indifference promotes alienation between the lower level of the organization and the decision-makers at the top. The gap between the two increases as those at the top shoulder all the responsibility, and the employees find themselves less able to understand administrative activity and its political significance. Thus the latter's resignation with regard to events which cannot be influenced becomes ever greater. Since education is oriented toward professional specialization rather than decision-making, it reinforces the concept that no one is able to have any say in that which is the concern of another.

However, accommodation which is based on resignation and indifference does not have a firm foundation. It has been learnt at too great a cost that man, who has largely been turned into an object and whose accommodation appears to be such a rational act, is quite willing to act irrationally under given circumstances. He will follow a pied piper into an abyss if he is offered something to compensate him for his ressentiment born of impotence.

A critic of Weber's overestimation of the rationality of the administered world has pointed out that mechanization of work, depersonalization of functions and oppressive routine can produce a dual effect: the loss of liberty incurred might be partially expressed and partially repressed to form an all-the-more virulent reservoir of aggressions. Thus the prevailing,

[21] Robert Presthus, *The Organizational Society: An Analysis and A Theory* (New York, 1965), esp. pp. 205–256.
[22] Cited in *Neue Zürcher Zeitung,* January 7, 1968.

businesslike rationality ends by arming its opponents: the forces of irrationality. A large powerful vacuum then develops in the bureaucratized world in which everyday routine craves and reaches for that which is extraordinary, unusual—and which redeems.[23]

The apparent rationalization of the administered world and its "nonideology" reveals itself as the mere reification of human interaction. Accommodation remains questionable; it is accomplished by means of repressions which create havoc in the unconscious, and in this nonpolitical realm the fantasies of those who are irresponsible bear their fruit. The routine of our world gives rise to dissatisfaction with civilization. Youth is angry and turns into beatniks, bohemians or hippies. It becomes criminal out of boredom; it craves and grows enthusiastic over noble acts of violence carried out by bearded guerillas in distant lands. Even its political attitude consists of nonpolitical protest. Opposition to the bureaucratic mind is also of a negative kind. The principle of authority is met with defiance which is the neurotic, manly form of protest, and a means of overcoming systems of authority in an unproductive fashion. Those who are concerned about the failure of accommodation tell themselves that the young must be given a sense of belonging—but they are unable to provide it, because that sense of belonging has no place in contemporary reality. The behavior of individuals as a collective body "superimposes over them," as Marx says, "an *alien* authority." The alienation which endangers democratic principles, the disintegration of general belief in these principles, the social reality in which these principles are progressively devalorized—these are the problems which the growth of bureaucracy sets before us.

---

[23] Eduard Baumgarten, *Max Weber: Werk und Person* (Tübingen, 1964).

THE POSSIBILITIES
OF DEMOCRACY

(Since democratic principles are threatened by the existence of an administered world, how will they survive?|We can only determine this by considering the socio-economic bases of society and the trends they suggest.

Technological innovations of enormous proportions are in the process of reshaping the economic foundation of the "new industrial state." Industrial conglomerates are being established with ever greater amounts of capital. Wage expenditures which decrease in relation to capital expenditures are coming to be considered fixed costs. The results produced by technological changes permit great alterations in the conditions of life, but in their unplanned and uncontrolled use they also present a danger to human existence. Large-scale corporations are already demanding state control of overall economic conditions, so as to maintain their financial position. This entails regulations which include long-term planning. But at the same time, society needs to do more than simply share in technological improvements.(It demands protection from the pollution of water, air, and earth as well as from damage to human health which it suffers as the by-product of an economic system solely interested in profit.

(Demands for planning and control are opposed by the myth of free competition and free markets. This myth has little significance in terms of future development, as long as it only expresses the ressentiment and ideology of one section of society oriented toward the past.) But it also serves other purposes. Because of the complexity of administering large corporations and the need to make decisions in changing circumstances, management presses toward autonomy. Of course management bases its decisions on what it considers to be the general interests of the whole undertaking. Not only do its material interests come into play, but also the simple fact that it identifies with the organization. However, the profit calculations of private enterprise and the cost accounting of the public economy by no means coincide. This results in conflicts of interest between industrial and state bureaucracies, between the general welfare and the special interests of large industrial concerns. Regulatory measures taken in the interests of the national income could restrict the powers of self-determination in such concerns.(Yet the myth of free enterprise and the task of its market policies can be used in defense of autonomous administration. It can prevent the general public from seeing economic conditions as they really are, and can help justify the establishment of certain companies in positions of great power—or rather, to deflect the public's attention from the power achieved in the market.)Democratic endeavors, however, are concerned with influencing economic objectives and opposing the special interests of the self-perpetuating oligarchies and affiliated groups.

Such objectives, concerned with increasing the national income and its distribution, are of a much more genuine and rational nature. Of course, the proper way in which to use the fruits of man's labor, and the ability to place the interest of the general public over those of special groups, was the concern of all utopias. The contemporary skeptical and cynical view of the world is not interested in the promises they contained.[1] With the aid of computers and input-output calculation, contemporary methods of administration have improved to such an extent that economic policy designed to establish universal prosperity is no longer utopian. A good while before the present level of productivity was achieved and before modern economic theory was developed, H. G. Wells remarked that the concept of utopia does not stand or fall with its ability to solve problems of socialism—which, as a matter of fact, can be solved with modern technology—but with its ability to resolve problems of democracy.[2]

Karl Loewenstein sees the present-day aspect of this question as lying essentially in "the shadow of the Leviathan." He does not consider the dismantling of the "corporate *mystique*" such a difficult task. But this does not resolve the "problems of the interest groups in the power process and their relations to the official power holders"; nor does it resolve the additional difficulties presented by political parties and socio-economic

---

[1] It is noteworthy that never before has the future been so much written and spoken about as in the middle of the twentieth century. But there is hardly any mention of new forms of interpersonal relationships in these reflections on the future.

[2] H. G. Wells, *A Modern Utopia* (London, 1905).

interest groups. There is the constant danger that the entire "complex, plural mechanism will break down," and that "individual liberty and self-determination will become further eroded and destroyed and, with it, constitutional democracy." It may be, then, that human ingenuity will devise a new approach to politics. Loewenstein believes that the crucial issue facing society today "is that of overcoming the untrammeled laissez-faire pluralism of our age" and of bringing the plural groups, parties and interest groups, as well as the "oligopolies" under social control by means of "effective and socially enforcible legal arrangements." He admits that he cannot understand, or even imagine, how this is to be accomplished. But he is certain that the "supreme arbiter" must be "the state itself." He maintains:

The only alternative to more private government is more public government. Only the political government, installed in power by democratic processes uncontrolled by the interest groups, is able to function as the custodian of the individual against his collectivization by the plural forces. To save the ultimate values of political democracy, plural democracy will have to be regulated. But this development carries with it the incalculable risk that the individual, rescued from the tyranny of the free-wheeling plural forces, will have to submit to the authoritarian direction of the state.[3]

(Thus the social scientist is caught in a contemporary vicious circle: in his analysis he progresses from the point at which the democratic process is obviously made ineffective by the pressure of socioeconomic interest groups, to the other extreme, where governmental bureaucracy is invested with an uncontrollable concentration of power. However, the crucial issue can be stated in one question: *how can concentrated power* be controlled, *regardless* of whether it is private or state power?)

The extreme modernity of the problem becomes clear when one compares it with the naive and sanguine viewpoint of Marx. He accepted Saint-Simon's theory that government of people would be replaced by the administration of objects. Today it seems surprising that *the* sociologist who revealed the human relations behind the material relations of economics could be content with such a theory. Hans Freyer observed that: "Man is subsumed under things and under the laws governing their progress; hence it is necessary to submit him to administration insofar as he is connected with the manipulation of things. It must be assumed that these interventions will have to increase and become more drastic

[3] Karl Loewenstein, *Political Power and the Governmental Process* (Chicago, 1957), pp. 384–385.

211

as the system becomes more complex."[4] But what are the alternatives for democracy from the viewpoint of the skeptical and disillusioned present, and in the face of bureaucratic progress?

The practical issue raised is obviously merely that of coming to terms with bureaucratic circumstances. The Italian political scientist Gaetano Mosca, who gave up his earlier authoritarian viewpoint in favor of democratic principles, came to see the essential issue as being whether a nation was prepared to acknowledge the productive collaboration of democracy and bureaucracy.[5] He felt that

the great superiority and the main strength of modern political systems lie in the ingenious balancing that they admit of between the liberal principle and the autocratic principle, the former represented by parliaments and local councils, the latter by permanent bureaucracies. We have also seen that this joint participation is essential if all political forces and capacities are to make themselves felt in public life, and if all sovereign powers are to exercise the reciprocal control and limitation that is the indispensable condition of political liberty. On any other basis liberty becomes a mere word devoid of any practical significance. Liberty of the press and, in general, all personal liberties—in other words, all the safeguards that the citizen has against arbitrary conduct on the part of the public official—would be insufficiently guaranteed once elective elements came to have little or no weight on the scales of public power.[6]

However, contemporary sociology is aware that what is involved is not only collaboration between two different principles, but also between two differing types of organization, and that the expansion of bureaucracy implies a continuous threat to democracy. Peter Blau defines bureaucracy as "an organization established for the explicit purpose of achieving spe-

[4] Hans Freyer, *Theorie des gegenwärtigen Zeitalters* (Stuttgart, 1958). In the light of accumulated experience, such criticism of Marx' theories has been put forward by very differing authors in the second half of the twentieth century. A dissertation, written at the University of Basel in 1952, states: "the concept by which the government of people in a classless society could be replaced by the mere administration of things and the management of production procedures, is no less utopian than the ideal societies of the utopian socialists. For each administration of things also signifies an administration of people; and the management of production procedures is at the same time the management of individuals . . . ." (Laurent Tschudi, *Kritische Grundlegung der Idee der direkten Rätedemokratie im Marxismus* [Basel, 1952]). A similar viewpoint was expressed by a member of the Central Committee of the Communist Party of Poland. Adam Schaff, *Marxismus und das menschliche Individuum* (Zürich, 1966).

[5] The attitude expressed in those of Mosca's books which appeared in the last two decades of the nineteenth century was later transformed by his impression of the fascist dictatorship as seen in the last edition of the volume, *Elementi de Scienza politica* (Turin, 1923). My discussion is based upon this final version of his thought.

[6] Mosca used the term "liberal" instead of "democratic," and considered the democratic tendency as "the tendency which aims to replenish the ruling class with elements deriving from the lower classes . . ." The English edition used for the passages cited is Gaetano Mosca, *The Ruling Class*, tr. Hannah D. Kahn (New York and London, 1939), pp. 487-488 and 395.

cific objectives" and maintains that "the organizing principle is administrative efficiency." However, "democracy is an organization established to ascertain the common objectives among men on the basis of the will of the majority . . . and the organizing principle is the freedom of dissent necessary for majority opinions to form." He concedes that "The bureaucratic manager may have democratic convictions" but he is expected to base his decisions on "the criterion of efficiency." Blau does not consider bureaucracy "suited for deciding between alternative ends"; however, he does admit it is more capable of "implementing these decisions." Thus the two systems are complementary. But bureaucracies "threaten to destroy democratic institutions," because power is concentrated among a few small groups in business and government. "If this is a paradox, it is also a challenge."[7]

In terms of present-day international politics, the "threat to democracy" does not only lie in the conflict between democratic and bureaucratic principles. The political turmoil which exists in the world contributes considerably to the deterioration of democracy. Throughout history the military mentality has given impetus to the bureaucratic mentality. Sismondi wrote to a friend in 1835 that "As war becomes more sophisticated, it continuously increases governmental authority and decreases the power of the people." Today's gigantic war machine not only possesses its own powerful bureaucracy, but since it is preparing for all-out war it has extended its activities far beyond the military sphere. The general inscrutability of bureaucratic functions is here thickened by the veil of military secrecy. The danger of war as a permanent condition moreover justifies the development of vast secret agencies, which affect the whole of society and which infiltrate many areas of activity lending them a dubious character. These are no longer the espionage and informer services of the past; they are, rather, independent bureaucracies with ever-expanding documentation, with the ambition of acquiring information about everyone, and with the technical means to penetrate into every area. They are thus always able to interfere in social conflicts, either secretly or publicly. Like all bureaucratic machines with an independent existence—and perhaps even more than others—they aim to move beyond the role of mere instrument. Their main interest is to increase their autonomy and to evade democratic control; consequently they easily become a means of undermining the democratic process.

---

[7] Peter M. Blau, *The Dynamics of Bureaucracy: A Study of Interpersonal Relations in Two Government Agencies* (Chicago and London, Revised Edition, 1966), pp. 264 and 265.

213

The upheavals which the international situation can bring about at any time, and the fears which it generates, can provide demagogic forces with an opportunity to utilize ressentiments and aggressive instincts by manipulating public opinion. Highly rationalized methods are available for such manipulation. The "antibureaucratic" sentiments of those who believe their demands have not been given adequate consideration provide a basis for demagogic exploitation. The prevailing apathy and "non-ideology" offer no protection against irrational, antidemocratic outbursts; on the contrary, they represent a hidden potential that can be activated under the right circumstances.

Social upheavals setting off such processes could also result from the regrouping and structural social changes connected with automation, unless these are properly channelled and directed:

Automation could involve a division of society. All those who are gainfully employed—the minority of people concerned with the essential aspects of production and administration, including the "professionals" from the liberal and other highly specialized professions who belong to this category by virtue of their social status—might be separated from that nondescript majority of those who have no special qualifications, who are incapable of understanding the ways of society and the economy, and whose work is, moreover, largely "unproductive" in terms of classic economics. In a fully developed, automated system of production, the minority of "productive" engineers, administrators, qualified workers, and remaining semi-skilled workers could produce everything needed—both by them and the vast majority of those individuals uninvolved in production—for the maintenance, and if possible the enhancement of the standard of living. . . . Obviously that type of social structure would present a very unsound foundation for a liberal society. The concentration of power in the minority, as well as the human impoverishment of the majority, could reach a point prior to the completion of the suggested development at which the transition to an authoritarian social system would be unavoidable.[8]

The human impoverishment to which Pollock refers would contribute further to the nonresponsibility of those lacking authority and to the apathy of the "indifferents," who have now to be reckoned with in the evolution of society.

In his book *The Organizational Society* Presthus describes two other personality types, besides the "indifferents." The second category, the "upward mobiles," presents a contrast to that of the "indifferents." The "upward mobile" is an authoritarian, extroverted, pragmatic type of person,

[8] Friedrich Pollock, *Automation* (Frankfurt-am-Main, 1964). English edition: *Automation: A Study of its Economic and Social Consequences,* tr. W. O. Henderson and W. H. Chalonet (New York, 1957).

who is willing to accommodate himself to hierarchical structures.[9] Otto Rühle has a similar type in mind, whom he calls "the status-conscious man." As he puts it: "This is not only the type of person who has status, but the one who needs it, who cannot live without it. This status is not part of an illusory world; it is part of direct reality. It represents standing, importance, prestige, power, superiority."[10] This is the kind of individual an organization needs. He may be able to organize, but he will also play the status game, and he will compete for power and prestige. He will thus contribute to the factors which encourage undemocratic actions and the growth of an authoritarian society.

The third personality type mentioned by Presthus is the "ambivalent." This is an introverted type with strong intellectual interests, a sensitive individual, who is isolated, out of step with organizational society. He is a nonconformist and belongs to that category which falls between the authoritarian, status-conscious people tied to the organization and the apparatus, and those who are comparatively indifferent. This type can provide democratic alternatives. The nucleus of democratic opposition takes shape—even under authoritarian forms of government—in the ranks of the middle category constituted by such persons. This group consists of those who become shop stewards in business enterprises, who represent the working force in negotiations with management, who generally represent the collective will against the organizational apparatus, or who, as simple individuals, provide impetus for social action.[11] Welfare or protective measures which often appear to be government policy, on closer examination turn out to result from social pressure by such types. Enlightened proponents of the welfare state, political scientists and economists—men as varied as the Prussian Professor von Justi, and his American colleague Galbraith who reiterated his ideas two hundred years later—have, for example, set governmental bureaucracy the task, among other things, of protecting society from business egoism and of controlling the quality of goods produced. Of course a government organization is necessary to impose regulations on an automobile industry which maintains that safety is not saleable. But it required the participation of an individual who had been involved in a David-like struggle with the Goliath of corporative bureaucracy before American governmental machinery could be set in motion.

[9] Robert Presthus, *The Organizational Society: An Analysis and a Theory* (New York, 1965). The "indifferents" are dealt with on pp. 205–256. The "upward mobiles" are discussed on pp. 164–204.
[10] Otto Rühle, *Der Mensch auf der Flucht* (Berlin, 1932).
[11] *See above*, Chapter VII, Section 3, Labor Unions.

The "ambivalent" type of person can penetrate the bureaucratic process and can provide a democratic influence. The posing of alternative decisions and the carrying-out of such decisions, do not always occur on different organizational levels. Consequently democratic and bureaucratic principles need not be isolated from each other. Bureaucratic organizations, unions or political parties can be headed by "ambivalent" types who resist the bureaucratic mind, and whose main difficulty consists in having to overcome the indifference of their own constituency. But yet in bureaucracies such types can become "permissive leaders" guided by exceptions to rules and committed to finding compromise solutions.[12]

The outline of this "ambivalent" personality type is not intended to support an "elite theory." It is rather a means of demonstrating concisely the existence of a behavior pattern which is partially manifested, but which also remains partially below the surface as a mere potential—until such time as it can become active, or until it atrophies from frustration. The predisposition toward this behavior pattern—which is generally related to a certain intellectual curiosity—can be found on all levels of society. But unless it can express itself intellectually it has difficulty in manifesting itself at all. Potentially, it represents a possible activation of democratic forces. Where there is a sudden collapse of central government or of organizational and administrative apparatus, there is often a surprising demonstration of spontaneous action by local democratic leaders.

Richard Hoggart encountered individuals of this sort in his investigation of mass media influence on the working class in the north of England. In the thirties these people had a sense of purpose, which led them to become members of the most varied organizations. The urge to join was still present in the later fifties, even if it had lost force. They " 'want to do something about things' but feel frustrated," Hoggart writes, because although they are supposed to know and have opinions on many things "like good democratic citizens," there is no way in which they can effectively participate in solving any problems. They frequently hide "an undefiant moral courage" under a cover of shyness. They also disguise their "sense of being lost, without purpose" beneath a kind of cynicism. But they are interested, they care, they want to do something. At a time when society is in danger of "reducing the larger part of the population to a condition of obediently receptive passivity . . . these few, because they are asking important questions, have a special value." The questions

---

[12] For a discussion of the "ambivalent" personality type, *see* Presthus, *op. cit.*, pp. 257–286.

that concern them have to do with those ideas by which men try to give meaning to their lives. "People such as this are therefore among the more sensitive, though now bruised, tentacles of society." They are mostly ignored. Yet, Hoggart observes, the conclusion Bishop Wilson came to a hundred years ago could be applied to them: "The number of those who need to be awakened is far greater than that of those who need comfort."[13]

The task of combining "the awareness of limitation with a vital utopian vision" as Karl Mannheim formulates it, falls to this third or "ambivalent" type.[14] The survival of democracy depends on reconciling the necessary centralized, planned economy with the expansion of responsible activity and participation in the shaping of society. A method is needed which would combine central decision-making with decentralized enactment. Richard N. Goodwin, who was an advisor to the late President Kennedy, concludes from his experience that the realization of certain essential objectives depends on finding new and appropriate techniques. For instance, poverty in its present form "cannot be abolished by friendly edicts from remote officials, and even if it could, the result would be sterile, vacuous, and purely material." Methods must be devised to meet specific ills which "in themselves enlarge the sense and reality of individual relevance and participation." This can be accomplished, at least on the political front, by way of decentralization. Private groups and small communities must be urged to reassume greater responsibility. "In other words, both burden and enterprise must be shifted into units of action small enough to allow for more intimate personal contact and numerous enough to widen the outlets for direct participation and control."[15]

The endeavor to expand participation in the social process and achieve the decentralization of responsibility must not be confused with attempts to defend local self-interests. Particularly in the United States, the defense of states' rights against the central government is maintained by an opposition whose ressentiment has carried over from the past, and which by no means reflects democratic interests. On the contrary, it only represents limited and antisocial private interests. Decentralization is not merely a matter of spatial displacement; the problem is one of social organization and not geography:

[13] Richard Hoggart, *The Uses of Literacy: Changing Patterns in English Mass Culture* (Fair Lawn, N.J., 1957), pp. 256–259.
[14] Karl Mannheim, *Ideology and Utopia: An Introduction to the Sociology of Knowledge* (New York and London, 1952).
[15] Richard N. Goodwin, "The Shape of American Politics," *Commentary*, XLIII, 6 (June, 1967), p. 36.

Federalism, as it is called, creates more rather than less bureaucracy. The murky offices, where important decisions are reached without public participation, tend to multiply. . . . For the requisite central decisions have to be passed on and prepared according to office procedures. Thus instead of a *single* bureaucracy, one has several of them superimposed on each other—those of the subordinate branches and that of the central federal organization—and thus one lives with a complexity both superfluous and paralyzing. . . . Intellectually and politically speaking, however, the malfunction is just as great if the federative concept is exaggerated. This overdevelopment facilitates control, but also favors the mushrooming of small bureaucratic cliques of all sorts, which would otherwise be easily lost in the noncompartmentalized spaces of larger social structures.[16]

Ultimately, however, social structure and the behavior of individuals will continue to depend largely on forms of production. The expectation that the mechanizing and depleting effects of production might be compensated for by an increase in speed and leisure time has not been realized. The process of production has a far-reaching influence on social interaction. The hierarchical organization of large corporations, the mechanical utilization of the labor force, and the fact that the worker is accustomed to acting as a not-yet automated link in the manufacturing process, have all contributed greatly to the predomination of a certain type of individual. This is the type who is socially indifferent, who seeks stimulating entertainment, and who is easily manipulated by those catering to his leisure time. Can automation produce any alternatives? Friedrich Pollock refers to investigations which show that it would be possible to decentralize large-scale enterprises by dividing them up into units with a limited labor force. Such automated enterprises with only a few hundred people could encourage a new type of interaction in the work process. It is assumed that if such factories were integrated into small communities, the workers would also be willing to take on responsibilities in public affairs. Members of a smaller working staff would be curious and intellectually more stimulated, and would want to be better informed. Paradoxically, a decrease in the manpower necessary to production would mean that workers would have to be treated more like individuals, and that more understanding would have to be shown for constructive nonconformism.[17]

It appears possible that in those enterprises where wages are part of the fixed costs and employment contracts are permanent contracts, identification with the organization and an esprit de corps could develop.

---

[16] Alfred Weber, "Bürokratie und Freiheit," *Die Wandlung* (December 20, 1946).
[17] Pollock, *Automation.*

It is precisely when relationships of this sort become clear that new possibilities of worker participation can develop which would go beyond the issues of the working milieu itself and even touch on managerial prerogatives. A union policy which effectively satisfies the need for security, justice, freedom and dignity by a sensible wage policy, could also lead to a needed stimulation of independence in the membership. Members would have a better understanding of demands concerned with *their* work pace, *their* working conditions, and the guarantee of *their* job. There would be a shift of power in the unions from the managing committee and district managements to factory wage commissions. Thousands would have to become members of these commissions.[18]

But even before automation becomes the overall method of production, it might be asked whether the system—under which the worker is given a bare minimum of responsibility and appears to be a mere supplementary part of the mechanism—is a technical necessity? Seymour Melman's studies led him to the conclusion that it is possible to organize large corporations by other means than unilateral management decisions. He points out that the "growth in the cost of managing can be reversed . . . highly mechanized plants can be operated at a high level of productivity with [alternative] management methods that are at once simple, inexpensive and effective."[19]

Examples proving this theory do exist. Non-Linear Systems, Inc., a San Diego, California, electronics company "threw out time cards and put all production workers on a salary—sixty cents an hour higher than the prevailing wage in San Diego. Then . . . the assembly line which carried electronic equipment through wiring, soldering, testing, inspections, and packaging [was torn down], and replaced with sixteen independent production units of six or seven workers each." These "teams" were headed by an electronic technician, and were free to organize their work as they saw fit: "They can decide to break the work down and specialize in different assembly operations, or they can decide that each man should take an entire product unit through every phase of the operation, including test and final checkout, himself." Although at first production was disrupted, within three months production again reached "the old assembly line level," and finally it topped that level by 30 percent.

There have been other tangible benefits. As skills increased, rejects dropped almost to nil. NLS [Non-Linear Systems] eliminated the job of inspector. . . .

[18] Hans Matthöfer, "Die Bedeutung der Mitbestimmung am Arbeitsplatz und im Betrieb für die politische Bildungsarbeit der Gewerkschaften," *Die Neue Gesellschaft,* I, 15 (1968).
[19] Seymour Melman, *Decision-Making and Productivity* (New York, 1958), p. 9.

With sixteen assembly teams instead of one production line, NLS gained flexibility. Where it used to take eight to ten weeks to crank up for a new model, now it takes two or three.

Given their head, some employees bore out the theorists—they expanded their work roles, showed unsuspected talents. Former hourly wage earners are now writing their own assembly instructions.[20]

Might it not be possible to improve certain procedures currently accepted as "given"? Paul Goodman has shown the possibilities of decentralization, which would be feasible without going back to obsolete types of governmental organization, and which would result in greater efficiency at less cost to society. Goodman indicates that decentralization creates more decision-making centers and increases the number of those involved in determining policy. He recognizes that many functions must be centralized, "epidemic-control, setting of standards, certain kinds of production and distribution, unification and scheduling of transportation." Enterprises requiring vast amounts of capital "like the moon shot," ought even to be internationally controlled.

Decentralization need not merely result from spontaneous action. "To decentralize, to delegate autonomy to many centers, can also be a political decision of a central power, usually compelled by the fact that the centralization is not working." A great deal more decentralization could be undertaken if the necessary research or experiments were undertaken. However, there is a superstition "that no other method of organization could be more efficient or is even possible" than the present system. "Breakdowns in the centralizing system are handled not by examining the system but by patchwork or imposing new levels of control." There are hidden costs in the process of centralization.

The danger of modern urbanization is "*anomie,* the rootlessness and helplessness of individuals. . . . When it tries at all to cope with this, centralized administration tries to encourage 'participation,' but participation is empty unless it involves the possibility of initiating and deciding." What matters is not that people belong to an association, but that they actually participate in some undertaking.

Goodman notes that "this vast machinery of social power is almost powerless in most simple practical matters. Everyone in society . . . shares the sneaking suspicion that 'Nothing Can Be Done.' "

A mixed system of centralized and decentralized organization is needed in such areas as schools, universities and mass communications. Their

[20] Cited in *Business Week,* March 20, 1965, p. 94.

present-day bureaucratic structure involves an enormous expenditure, far greater than that of institutions run by private or amateur groups.[21]

There can be no doubt that there are practical solutions for making inroads in the bureaucrattic network, for loosening it and for developing alternatives to centralized decision-making power. Faced with the difficulty of finding a way to express initiative outside of the existing bureaucratic system, social criticism always ends by calling on the machinery of government. Thus Galbraith, in attempting to solve the problem of the increasing destruction of nature and culture by industry, suggests that "where there is a conflict between industrial and aesthetic priorities, it is the state which must assert aesthetic priority against the industrial need."[22] But Galbraith himself also notes the fusion of state and industrial bureaucracies, and ultimately one must consider what sort of aesthetic priorities the state could establish. Decisions would then have to be enforced by governmental institutions, but in that case what of initiative and the establishment of goals?

Another American economist, Calvin B. Hoover, envisages similar responsibilities for government in the new industrial state, but he also warns "that while new patterns of enlarged economic functions of the state are emerging and indeed must emerge, the state power cannot automatically be assumed to be wielded in the public interest and that the limitation of state power to a practicable minimum still remains requisite for the maintenance of personal liberty."[23]

All of these concepts contain an apparent paradox to which those who express a conservative ressentiment can refer. But this is not so much a paradox as a dilemma which confronts the industrialized world when it tries to determine how welfare and freedom can be achieved at the same time. The dialectical irony of world history is that the bureaucratic limitation of freedom has been brought about largely by the freeing of individuals and the loosening of all social ties associated with that process; and that the preservation and expansion of individual freedom depend in many respects on a new socialization of individuals. De Tocqueville's warning that democratic liberties could not survive unless new *pouvoirs sécondaires* were established in society is still valid.

The main issue, writes Kurt Wolzendorff "is no longer the border-line between state power and the sphere of individual freedom, but the demar-

---

[21] Paul Goodman, "Notes on Decentralization," *Dissent*, XI, 4 (Autumn, 1964), pp. 389, 390, 391, 393, and 403.

[22] John Kenneth Galbraith, *The New Industrial State* (Boston, 1967), p. 350.

[23] Calvin B. Hoover, "What kind of new partnership?" *Business Week*, July 17, 1965, p. 92.

221

cation between the *social responsibilities of the state, and those of nongovernmental organizations.*"[24]

The inscrutability of social interrelations, the remoteness of administrative power, the apathy of the majority of people, and the authoritarian attitude of the status-seeker—all these conditions oppose the establishment of organs of social initiative and control. The concept of such organs, however, is closely related to the defense of democratic principles. However much politics are influenced by power structures and by the conflicts between them, political models and norms have their place in the shaping of society. (That is why the future of democracy is so dependent on the restoration of a politically aware public.) The ideology of a non-ideology" would suggest that political models have lost their meaning. What has proved meaningless is only the faith in a compact system of regulations for organization and political activity which—according to its proponents—would bring about a better world if properly carried out. As such faith disappears, so does the belief in the possibility of founding *the* party capable of faultlessly instituting such a system. In any case, once it is recognized that popular parties necessarily develop bureaucratic machines, the hope disappears that political models based on democratic principles would be furthered by the reorganization of parties. Yet there are types of organizations which can activate machinery for developing political purpose. Ostrogorski's idea of reducing parties to temporary associations had no basis in reality. But alliances—of a more or less temporary nature—which would hold governmental and party bureaucracy accountable in specific areas, which would exercise control, which would offer alternative solutions to particular problems, and which would take the initiative in areas of vital interest, could generate a politically conscious public and become a complex of those "free associations" which de Tocqueville hoped might preserve freedom and democracy.[25] He noted in his memoirs that there are far more ways of structuring society than man, living in a specific society, is able to envisage.

[24] Kurt Wolzendorff, "Der reine Staat: Skizze zum Problem einer neuen Staatsepoche," *Zeitschrift für die gesamte Staatswissenschaft*, LVII, 1 and 2 (August, 1920).

[25] In this connection it might be worthwhile to consider the civic associations which exist in the United States and which, better than political parties, are able to protect themselves against those seeking power and promote reform measures. *See* Richard S. Childs, "Citizen Organization for Control of Government," *The Annals of the American Academy of Political and Social Science*, CCXCII (March, 1954), pp. 129–135.

BIBLIOGRAPHY

Abramov, Fyodor. *The Dodgers*. Tr. David Floyd. London, 1963.

Acton, John Emerich Edward Dahlberg, Lord. *Essays on Freedom and Power*. Cleveland and New York, 1964.

d'Allais, Denis Vairasse. *Histoire des Sevarambes*. Paris, 1677.

Allen, V. L. *Power in Trade Unions: A Study of their Organization in Great Britain*. London, New York and Toronto, 1954.

Amburger, Erik. *Geschichte der Behördenorganisation Russlands von Peter dem Grossen bis 1917*. Leiden, 1966.

Andrieux, André and Jean Lignon. "Gewandelte Vorstellung vom Wesen der Demokratie," *Gewerkschaftliche Monatshefte* (February, 1966).

Armstrong, John A. *The Soviet Bureaucratic Elite: A Case Study of the Ukrainian Apparatus*. New York, 1959.

Aron, Raymond. "Social Structure and the Ruling Class," in *Political Sociology*, ed. Lewis A. Coser. New York, 1967.

d'Avenel, Georges. *Richelieu et la monarchie absolue*. Paris, 1884.

Bahrdt, Hans Paul. "Fiktiver Zentralismus in den Grossunternehmungen," *Kyklos*, 4 (1954).

Bain, Joe S. *Barriers to New Competition: Their Character and Consequences in Manufacturing Industries*. Cambridge, Mass., 1962.

Balazs, Etienne. *Chinese Civilization and Bureaucracy: Variations on a Theme*. Tr. H. Wright; ed. Arthur F. Wright. London and New Haven, 1966.

Balzac, Honoré de. *Les Employés*. Eds. M. Bouteron and H. Longnon. Paris, 1910. In English: *Bureaucracy; or A Civil Service Reformer*. Tr. Katherine Prescott Wormeley. Boston, 1889.

Barton, John. *An Inquiry into the Causes of the Progressive Depreciation of Agricultural Labour in Modern Times, with Suggestions for its Remedy*. London, 1820.

――――. *Observations on the Circumstances which Influence the Condition of the Labouring Classes of Society*. London, 1817.

Baudeau, Nicolas. *Première Introduction à la philosophie économique ou analyse des états policés, par un disciple de l'ami des hommes*. Paris, 1776.

Baudin, Louis. *Der Sozialistische Staat der Inka*. Hamburg, 1956. In English: *A Socialist Empire: The Incas of Peru*. Tr. Catherine Woods. Princeton, 1961.

Baumgarten, Eduard. *Max Weber: Werk und Person*. Tübingen, 1964.

223

Benda, Julien. *La Trahison des clercs.* Paris, 1927.

Berdyaev, Nicolas. *The Russian Idea.* Tr. R. M. French. London, 1947.

Berle, Jr., Adolf A. *The Twentieth Century Capitalist Revolution.* New York, 1954.

——. and Gardiner C. Means. *The Modern Corporation and Private Property.* New York, 1932.

Blau, Peter M. *The Dynamics of Bureaucracy; A Study of Interpersonal Relations in Two Government Agencies.* Revised ed. Chicago and London, 1966.

Bloch, Marc Léopold Benjamin. *La Société féodale.* Paris, 1939. In English: *Feudal Society.* Tr. L. A. Manyon. Chicago, 1961.

Bode, Barbara. "Sowjetliteratur 1964," *Ost-Europa,* XVI, 1 (January, 1966), 30–52.

Böhler, E. "Die Inflation der Dienstleistungen," *Neue Zürcher Zeitung,* May 22, 1966.

Bonald, Louis Gabriel Ambroise de. "Theorie du pouvoir politique et religieux," in *Oeuvres.* 2 vols. Paris, 1854.

Borkenau, Franz. *Der Übergang vom feudalen zum bürgerlichen Weltbild: Studien zur Geschichte der Philosophie der Manufakturperiode.* Paris, 1934.

Borrelli de Serres, Léon Louis. *Recherches sur divers services publics du XIIIᵉ au XVIIᵉ siècles.* Vols. I–III. Paris, 1895.

Boulainvilliers, Henri de. *Histoire de l'ancien gouvernement de la France.* 3 vols. The Hague and Amsterdam, 1727. In English: *An Historical Account of the Ancient Parliaments of France, or States-General of the Kingdom.* Tr. Charles Forman. 2 vols. London, 1739.

Boulding, Kenneth E. *The Organizational Revolution.* New York, 1953.

Bracher, Karl Dietrich. *Die Auflösung der Weimarer Republik: eine Studie zum Problem des Machtverfalls in der Demokratie.* Villingen, 1964.

Brecht, Arnold. "Bureaucratic Sabotage," *The Annals of the American Academy of Political and Social Science,* CLXXXIX (January, 1937), 48–57.

Bukharin, Nikolai. *Ökonomie der Transformationsperiode.* Tr. Frieda Rubiner. Hamburg, 1922.

Burckhardt, Jacob. *Force and Freedom: Reflections on History.* Ed. and tr. James Hastings Nichols. New York, 1943.

——. *Die Kultur der Renaissance in Italien.* Bern, 1943. In English: *The Civilization of the Renaissance in Italy.* Tr. S. G. C. Middlemore. New York, 1944.

Calverton, V. F. *The Making of Society.* New York, 1937.

Campanella, Tommaso. *Civitas solis poetica idea reipublicae philosophicae.* Utrecht, 1643. In English: *Campanella's City of the Sun.* Tr. Thomas W. Halliday. London, 1885.

Capitant, René. "Hobbes et l'état totalitaire," *Archives de philosophie de droit et de sociologie juridique,* VI (1936).

Cassirer, Ernst. *An Essay on Man.* New York, 1954.

Cheruel, Adolphe. *Histoire de l'administration monarchique en France depuis l'avènement de Philippe-Auguste jusqu'à la mort de Louis XIV.* 2 vols. Paris, 1855.

Childs, Richard S. "Citizen Organizations for Control of Government," *The Annals of the American Academy of Political and Social Science,* CCXCII (March, 1954), 129–135.

Churchward, L. G. "Soviet Local Government Today," *Soviet Studies*, XVII, 4 (April, 1966), 431–452.

Clarendon, Edward Hyde, Earl of. *A brief view and survey of the dangerous and pernicious errors to Church and State in Mr. Hobbes Book entitled Leviathan.* Oxford, 1676.

Colbert, Jean-Baptiste. *Lettres, instructions et mémoires.* Ed. Pierre Clément. 9 vols. Paris, 1861.

Coser, Lewis A. *The Functions of Social Conflict.* Glencoe, Ill., 1956.

——. *Men of Ideas.* New York, 1965.

Crozier, Michel. *Le Phénomène bureaucratique.* Paris, 1964. In English: *The Bureaucratic Phenomenon.* Tr. by author. London, 1964.

Custine, Adolphe Louis Léonard, Marquis de. *La Russie en 1839, par le marquis de Custine.* Paris, 1843. In English: *Russia, Translated from the French of the Marquis de Custine.* New York, 1854.

Descoeudres, Eric. "Les coopératives et la protection des consommateurs," *Coopération* (Geneva), 46, November 13, 1965.

Dickens, Charles. *Little Dorrit.* London, 1868.

Dorn, Walter L. "The Prussian Bureaucracy in the Eighteenth Century," *Political Science Quarterly*, XLVI, 3 (September, 1931), 403–432; XLVII, 1 (March, 1932), 75–94; and XLVII, 2 (June, 1932), 259–273.

Drucker, Peter F. "The Employee Society," *The American Journal of Sociology*, LVIII, 4 (January, 1953), 358–363.

Dupont-Ferrier, Emile Marie Joseph Gustave. *La Formation de l'état français et l'unité française, des origines au milieu du XVI siècle.* Paris, 1934.

——. *Les Origines et le premier siècle de la cour du trésor.* Paris, 1936.

Dupont-White, Charles Brook. *L'Individu et l'état.* Paris, 1857.

Eckermann, Johann Peter. *Gespräche mit Goethe in den letzen Jahren seines Lebens.* Wiesbaden, 1959. In English: *Conversations with Goethe in the last Years of his Life.* Tr. S. M. Fuller. Boston, 1852.

Eichendorff, Joseph Freiherr von. "Der Adel und die Revolution," in *Aus dem Literarischen Nachlass.* Paderborn, 1866.

Eisenstadt, Shmuel Noah. "Bureaucracy and Bureaucratisation: A Trend Report and Bibliography," *Current Sociology*, VII, 2 (1958), 99–124.

——. *The Political Systems of Empires.* London and New York, 1963.

Engels, Friedrich. "Der Status Quo in Deutschland," in Karl Marx-Friedrich Engels, *Werke.* IV. Berlin, 1964.

Ensslin, Wilhelm. "The Emperor and the Imperial Administration," in *Byzantium: An Introduction to East Roman Civilization.* Eds. Norman H. Baynes and H. St. L. B. Moss. Oxford, 1948.

Fabroni, Giovanni Valentino Mattia. *Dei provvedimenti annonarj.* Firenze, 1817.

Fainsod, Merle. *How Russia is Ruled.* Cambridge, Mass., 1962.

——. *Smolensk under Soviet Rule.* Cambridge, Mass., 1958.

Feuerbach, Paul Johann Anselm von. *Anti-Hobbes, oder aber die Grenzen der höchsten Gewalt und das Zwangsrecht der Bürger gegen den Oberherrn.* Erfurt, 1798.

Fleiner, Fritz. "Beamtenstaat und Volkstaat," in *Festgabe für Otto Meyer.* Tübingen, 1916.

Ford, Henry. *My Life and Work.* London, 1924.

Franck, Sebastian. "De Tocqueville, Prophet of the Total State," *Politics,* III, 4 (April, 1946), 127–128.

———. *Zur Kritik der politischen Moral: Kritik des politischen Verhaltens.* Offenbach, 1947.

Freyer, Hans. *Theorie des gegenwärtigen Zeitalters.* Stuttgart, 1958.

Fried, Ferdinand. *Das Ende des Kapitalismus.* Jena, 1931.

Friedrich, Carl J. "Constitutionalism versus Absolutism," in *Synopsis: Festgabe für Alfred Weber.* Heidelberg, 1948.

——— and Zbigniew K. Brzezinski. *Totalitarian Dictatorship and Autocracy.* Cambridge, Mass., 1956.

Frölich, Paul. *1789, die grosse Zeitwende: von der Bürokratie des Absolutismus zum Parlament der Revolution.* Frankfurt-am-Main, 1957.

Gablentz, Otto Heinrich von der. "Industriebureaukratie," *Schmollers Jahrbuch,* II (1926).

Galbraith, John Kenneth. "The Defense of Business: a Strategic Appraisal," *Harvard Business Review,* XXXII, 2 (March–April, 1954), 37–43.

———. *The New Industrial State.* Boston, 1967.

Gitermann, Valentin. *Geschichte Russlands.* 3 vols. Hamburg, 1949.

Göhre, Paul. *Drei Monate Fabrikarbeiter und Handwerksbursche: eine praktische Studie.* Leipzig, 1891.

Goethe, Johann Wolfgang von. *Faust, Part Two.* Tr. and intro. Philip Wayne. London, 1962.

Goodman, Paul. *Growing Up Absurd: Problems of Youth in the Organized System.* New York, 1960.

———. "Notes on Decentralization," *Dissent,* XI, 4 (Autumn, 1964), 389–403.

Goodwin, Richard N. "The Shape of American Politics," *Commentary,* XLIII, 6 (June, 1967), 25–40.

Gordon, R. A. *Business Leadership in the Large Corporations.* Washington, 1945.

Guérin, Daniel. *La Lutte des classes sous la première republique: bourgeois et "bras nus" 1793–1797.* 2 vols. Paris, 1946.

Guizot, François. *Histoire des origines du gouvernement représentatif.* Bruxelles, 1851. In English: *History of the Origin of Representative Government in Europe.* Tr. Andrew R. Scoble. London, 1861.

Habermas, Jürgen. "Strukturwandel der Öffentlichkeit," *Politica,* IV (1965).

———. *Theorie und Praxis: sozialphilosophische Studien.* Neuwied, 1963.

Haller, Karl Ludwig von. *Restauration der Staatswissenschaft oder Theorie des natürlich-gesellschaftlichen Zustandes der Chimäre des künstlich-bürgerlichen entgegengesetzt.* Winterthur, 1816.

Hallowell, John H. *The Decline of Liberalism as an Ideology.* London, 1946.

Hanotaux, Albert Auguste Gabriel. *Origines de l'institution des intendants de province d'après des documents inédits.* Paris, 1884.

Hayek, Friedrich August von. *Der Weg zur Knechtschaft.* Zürich, 1944. In English: *The Road to Serfdom.* Chicago, 1945.

Hegel, G. W. F. *Naturrecht und Staatswissenschaft, oder Grundlinien der Philosophie des Rechts.* Jubliäumsausgabe, Vol. VII. Stuttgart, 1928. In English: *Hegel's Philosophy of Right.* Tr. T. M. Knox. Oxford, 1945.

――――. *Die Verfassung Deutschlands.* Ed. Hermann Heller. Leipzig, 1922. In English: *Hegel's Political Writings.* Tr. T. M. Knox. Oxford, 1964.

――――. *Vorlesungen über die Philosophie der Geschichte.* 2 vols. Berlin, 1952. In English: *Lectures on the Philosophy of History.* Tr. J. Sibree. New York, 1956.

Heichelheim, Fritz. *Wirtschaftsgeschichte des Altertums.* Leiden, 1939. In English: *An Ancient Economic History: from the Paleolithic Age to the Migration of the Germanic Slavic and Arabic Nations.* Tr. Joyce Stevens. Leiden, 1958.

Heilbroner, Robert L. *The Limits of American Capitalism.* New York, 1966.

Heimann, Eduard. "Rationalism, Christianity and Democracy," in *Synopsis: Festgabe für Alfred Weber.* Heidelberg, 1948.

Henel, Hans Otto. *Ursachen der Konzentration.* Tübingen, 1962.

Herder, J. G. von. *Ideen zur Philosophie der Geschichte der Menschheit.* 2 vols. Berlin, 1952. In English: *Outlines of a Philosophy of the History of Man.* Tr. John Godfrey. London, 1800.

Herzen, Alexander Ivanovich. *The Memoirs of Alexander Herzen.* Tr. J. D. Duff. Parts I and II. New York, 1967.

Hilferding, Rudolf. *Das Finanzkapital.* Vienna, 1927.

Hill, Christopher. *Reformation to Industrial Revolution: A Social and Economic History of Britain 1550–1780.* London, 1968.

Hintze, Otto. "Der Beamtenstand," in *Soziologie und Geschichte: Gesammelte Abhandlungen zur Soziologie, Politik und Theorie der Geschichte.* Ed. Gerhard Östreich. Göttingen, 1964.

――――. "Der Commissarius und seine Bedeutung in der allgemeinen Verwaltungsgeschichte: eine vergleichende Studie," in *Staat und Verfassung: Gesammelte Abhandlungen zur allgemeinen Verfassungsgeschichte.* Ed. Gerhard Östreich. Göttingen, 1962.

――――. "Machtpolitik und Regierungsverfassung," in *Staat und Verfassung: Gesammelte Abhandlungen zur allgemeinen Verfassungsgeschichte.* Ed. Gerhard Östreich. Göttingen, 1962.

――――. "Nationale und europäische Orientierung in der heutigen politischen Welt," in *Soziologie und Geschichte: Gesammelte Abhandlungen zur Soziologie, Politik und Theorie der Geschichte.* Ed. Gerhard Östreich. Göttingen, 1964.

Hobbes, Thomas. *Behemoth.* London, 1680. New York, 1962.

――――. *De Cive, or the Citizen.* Ed. Sterling P. Lamprecht. New York, 1949.

――――. *Elemens philosophiques du citoyen: traicté politique où les fondemens de la société civile sont découverts. Traduicts en françois par un de ses amis.* Amsterdam, 1649.

――――. *Leviathan or the Matter, Forme and Power of a Commonwealth Ecclesiasticall and Civill.* Ed. W. G. P. Smith. Oxford, 1965.

Hoenigswald, Richard. *Hobbes und die Staatsphilosophie.* München, 1924.

Hoggart, Richard. *The Uses of Literacy: Changing Patterns in English Mass Culture.* Fair Lawn, N.J., 1957.

Hoover, Calvin B. "What kind of new partnership?" *Business Week,* July 17, 1965, 92.

Horkheimer, Max. "Ideologie und Wertgebung," in *Soziologische Forschungen in unserer Zeit.* Ed. K. G. Specht. Köln, 1951.

Humboldt, Karl Wilhelm von. *Ideen zu einem Versuch die Grenzen der Wirksamkeit des Staates zu bestimmen.* Ed. Alexander von Gleichen-Russwurm. Berlin, n. d. In English: *The Limits of State Action.* Ed. and tr. J. W. Burrow. Cambridge, England, 1969.

Jacob, Herbert. *German Administration Since Bismarck: Central Authority Versus Local Autonomy.* London and New York, 1963.

Jacoby, Henry. "Hobbes und de Tocqueville," *Zeitschrift für die gesamte Staatswissenschaft,* CIX, 4 (1953).

——— and Lewis A. Coser, "Rückblick auf Utopia," *Aufklärung,* II, 4–6 (1953).

Jaeggi, Urs and Herbert Wiedemann. *Der Angestellte in der Industriegesellschaft.* Stuttgart, 1966.

Jarcke, Karl Ernst. *Vermischte Schriften.* 3 vols. München, 1839.

Jaspers, Karl. *Vom Ursprung und Ziel der Geschichte.* Frankfurt-am-Main and Hamburg, 1955. In English: *The Origin and Goal of History.* Tr. Michael Bullock. London, 1953.

Jochmann, Karl Gustav. "Robespierre," in *Die Rückschritte der Poesie und andere Schriften.* Frankfurt-am-Main, 1967.

Justi, Johann Heinrich Gottlob von. *Die Grundfeste zu der Macht und Glückseligkeit der Staaten: oder ausführliche Vorstellung der gesamten Polizeiwissenschaft.* 2 vols. Königsberg and Leipzig, 1760.

———. *Vergleichungen der Europäischen mit den Asiatischen und anderen vermeintlich Barbarischen Regierungen.* Berlin, Leipzig and Stettin, 1762.

Kafka, Franz. *The Castle.* Tr. Willa and Edwin Muir. New York, 1962.

Kantorowicz, Ernst H. *Kaiser Friedrich der Zweite.* Berlin, 1927. In English: *Frederick the Second.* Tr. E. O. Lorimer. London, 1931.

———. *The King's Two Bodies: A Study in Medieval Political Theology.* Princeton, 1957.

Keynes, John Maynard. *The End of Laissez-Faire.* London, 1926.

———. *The General Theory of Employment, Interest and Money.* New York, 1936.

Kolb, Eberhard. *Die Arbeiterräte in der deutschen Innenpolitik 1918 bis 1919.* Düsseldorf, 1962.

Kool, Frits and Erwin Oberländer, eds. *Arbeiterdemokratie und Parteidiktatur.* Olten, 1967.

Korb, Johann Georg. *Diarium Itineris Moscoviam.* Vienna, 1700. In German: *Tagebuch der Reise nach Russland.* Graz, 1968.

Kottler, Wilhelm. "Der Rätegedanke als Staatsgedanke: Demokratie und Rätegedanke in der grossen englischen Revolution," *Leipziger rechtswissenschaftliche Studien,* XV (1925).

Kovalevsky, Maxim. *Instutitions politiques de la Russie: naissance et développement de ses institutions des commencements de l'histoire de Russie jusqu'à nos jours.* Paris, 1905. In English: *Russian Political Institutions: The Growth and Development of these Institutions from the Beginnings of Russian History to the Present Time.* Chicago, 1902.

Kritzmann, Lev. *Die heroische Periode der Grossen russischen Revolution: ein Versuch der Analyse des sogenannten "Kriegskommunismus."* Berlin and Wien, 1929.

Kropotkin, Peter. *The Great French Revolution, 1789–1793.* Tr. N. F. Dryhurst. London and New York, 1909.

Kruli-Randa, Jan S. "Die Praxis der multinationalen Marketing-Politik und -Planung," *Neue Zürcher Zeitung,* December 28, 1967.

Labedz, Leopold. "The End of an Epoch," *Survey,* LIV (January, 1965), 3–28.

Laffemas, Barthélemy. *Règlement général pour dresser les manufactures en ce royaume.* Paris and Rouen, 1597.

Laski, H. J. "Alexis de Tocqueville: A Biographical Essay," in *The Social and Political Ideas of Some Representative Thinkers of the Victorian Age.* Ed. F. J. C. Hearnshaw. London, 1953.

Lassalle, Ferdinand Johann Gottlieb. "Arbeiter-Programm," in *Ferdinand Lassalle's Reden und Schriften.* 2 vols. Berlin, 1892–1893. In English: *The Working Man's Programme.* Tr. E. Peters. London, 1884.

———. *Franz von Sickingen: eine deutsche Tragödie.* Berlin, 1926.

Lefèbvre, Henri. *La Proclamation de la commune.* Paris, 1965.

Lenin, Vladimir Il'ich. *Staat und Revolution: Die Staatstheorie des Marxismus und die Aufgaben des Proletariats in der Revolution.* Wien, 1929. In English: *State and Revolution.* New York, 1932.

Lepelletier, Edmond. "Histoire de la Commune de 1871," *Mercure de France* (1911).

Lester, Richard A. *As Unions Mature: An Analysis of the Evolution of American Unionism.* Princeton, 1958.

Lippmann, Walter. *Herald Tribune* (Paris), December 7, 1966, p. 4.

Lips, Julius. *Die Stellung des Thomas Hobbes zu den politischen Parteien der grossen englischen Revolution.* Leipzig, 1927.

Lipset, Seymour Martin. *Agrarian Socialism: The Cooperative Commonwealth Federation in Saskatchewan: A Study in Political Sociology.* New York, 1968.

List Gesellschaft. *Planung ohne Planwirtschaft.* Basel, 1964.

Loewenstein, Karl. *Political Power and the Governmental Process.* Chicago, 1957.

Lorimer, Frank. *The Population of the Soviet Union.* Geneva, 1946.

Luxemburg, Rosa. *Massenstreik, Partei und Gewerkschaften.* Hamburg, 1906. In English: *Mass Strike, the Political Party and the Trade Unions with the Junius Pamphlet.* New York, 1971.

———. *Reform or Revolution.* Tr. Integer. New York, 1937.

———. *Die Russische Revolution 1918.* Ed. Ossip K. Flechtheim. Frankfurt-am-Main, 1963. In English: *The Russian Revolution and Leninism or Marxism.* Ann Arbor, Mich., 1961.

Maistre, Joseph Marie de. "Etude sur la souveraineté," in *Oeuvres complètes.* 14 vols. Lyon, 1884–1887.

Mallet, Serge. *La Nouvelle Classe ouvrière.* Paris, 1963.

Mannheim, Karl. *Ideology and Utopia: An Introduction to the Sociology of Knowledge.* London and New York, 1952.

———. "The Problem of Democratization as a General Cultural Phenomenon," in *Essays on the Sociology of Culture.* London, 1956.

Marcuse, Herbert. *One Dimensional Man: Studies in the Ideology of Advanced Industrial Society.* Boston, 1964.

Marquart, Frank. "New Problems for the Unions," *Dissent*, VI, 4 (Autumn, 1959), 375–388.

Marx, Karl. "Der Achzehnte Brumaire des Louis-Bonaparte," *Die Revolution* (1852). Reprinted in Karl Marx and Friedrich Engels, *Werke.* Frankfurt-am-Main, 1966. In English: *The Eighteenth Brumaire of Louis Bonaparte.* Moscow, 1967.

———. "Address of the General Council of the International Working Men's Association on the Civil War in France, 1871," in *The Civil War in France.* New York, 1962.

———. *Capital.* Tr. Eden and Cedar Paul. 2 vols. London, 1962.

———. *Critique of Hegel's 'Philosophy of Right.'* Ed. Joseph O'Malley; tr. Annette Jolin and Joseph O'Malley. Cambridge, England, 1970.

———. *Early Writings.* Tr. T. B. Bottomore. New York, 1964.

———. *Enthüllungen über den Kommunistenprozess in Köln.* Zürich, 1885.

———. *Grundrisse der Kritik der politischen Ökonomie.* Berlin, 1953. In English: *The Grundrisse.* Ed. and tr. David McLellan. London and New York, 1971.

———. *Herr Vogt.* Berlin, 1953.

———. *Der Historische Materialismus: Die Frühschriften.* Eds. S. Landshut and I. P. Mayer. Leipzig, 1932.

———. *Kritik des Sozialdemokratischen Programms von Gotha.* Berlin, 1946. In English: *The Socialist Programme.* Tr. Eden and Cedar Paul. Glasgow, 1919.

Mason, Edward S. *The Corporation in Modern Society.* Cambridge, Mass., 1960.

Matthöfer, Hans. "Die Bedeutung der Mitbestimmung am Arbeitsplatz und im Betrieb für die politische Bildungsarbeit der Gewerkschaften," *Die Neue Gesellschaft*, I, 15 (1968).

Mavor, James. *An Economic History of Russia.* 2 vols. New York, 1965.

Mayer, I. P. *Alexis de Tocqueville: A Biographical Essay in Political Science.* Tr. M. M. Bozman. New York, 1940.

Mehring, Franz. *Die Lessing-Legende.* Berlin, 1963. In English: *The Lessing Legend.* Abr. tr. A. S. Grogan. New York, 1938.

Meinecke, Friedrich. *Die Idee der Staatsraison in der neueren Geschichte.* Berlin, 1925. In English: *Machiavellism: the Doctrine of raison d'état and its Place in Modern History.* Tr. Douglas Scott. London, 1957.

———. *Weltbürgertum und Nationalstaat: Studien zur Genesis des deutschen National-staates.* München, 1911.

Melman, Seymour. *Decision-Making and Productivity.* New York, 1958.

Merton, Robert K. *Reader in Bureaucracy.* Glencoe, Ill., 1952.

———. *Social Theory and Social Structure.* New York, 1959.

Meyer, Alfred G. "The Functions of Ideology in the Soviet Political System: A Speculative Essay Designed to Provoke Discussion," *Soviet Studies*, XVII, 3 (January, 1966), 273–285.

Michels, Robert. *Zur Soziologie des Parteiwesens in der modernen Demokratie: Unter-suchungen über die oligarchischen Tendenzen des Gruppenlebens.* Leipzig, 1925. In English: *Political Parties: A Sociological Study of the Oligarchical Tendencies of Modern Democracy.* Tr. Eden and Cedar Paul. New York, 1915.

Mills, C. Wright. *The New Men of Power: America's Labor Leaders.* New York, 1948.

Mirkado, Ian. "Trade Unions in a Full Employment Economy," in *New Fabian Essays,* ed. R. H. S. Crossman. London, 1953.

Mises, Ludwig von. *Bureaucracy.* New Haven, 1944.

————. *Kritik des Interventionismus: Untersuchungen zur Wirtschaftspolitik und Wirtschaftsideologie der Gegenwart.* Jena, 1929.

Möser, Justus. *Patriotische Phantasien.* Berlin, 1778.

Moetteli, Hans. "Rechnungswesen und Industrie," in *Rechnungsführung in Unternehmung und Staatsverwaltung: Festgabe für Otto Juri.* Zürich, 1946.

Mombert, François. "Contribution à une théorique des incidences de l'impôt sur les sociétés," *Revue de science financière* (juillet, 1962), 437–460.

Montchrétien, Antoine de. *L'Oeconomie politique patronale. Traicté de l'oeconomie politique.* Ed. and intro. Th. Funck-Brentano. Paris, 1889.

Moore, Jr., Barrington. *Soviet Politics—The Dilemma of Power: The Role of Ideas in Social Change.* Cambridge, Mass., 1959.

More, Sir Thomas. *De optimo reipublicae statu deque nova insula Utopia.* Glasgow, 1750.

Morstein-Marx, Fritz. *Einführung in die Bürokratie.* Neuwied, 1959. In English: *The Administrative State: An Introduction to Bureaucracy.* Chicago, 1957.

Mosca, Gaetano. *Elementi di Scienza politica.* Turin, 1923. In English: *The Ruling Class.* Tr. Hanna D. Kahn. London and New York, 1939.

Nabholz, Hans. "Zur Frage nach den Ursachen des Bauernkrieges 1525," in *Gedächtnisschrift für Georg von Below.* Stuttgart, 1928.

Naville, Pierre. "Critique de la bureaucratie," *Cahiers internationaux de sociologie* (1953).

Neumann, Franz. *Behemoth: The Structure and Practice of National Socialism.* London, New York and Toronto, 1942.

Newcomer, Mabel. *The Business Executive: The Factors that Made Him, 1900–1950.* New York, 1955.

Nomad, Max. "White Collars and Horny Hands," *Modern Quarterly* (Autumn, 1932).

Novalis [pseud. of Friedrich von Hardenberg]. *Die Christenheit oder Europa.* Stuttgart, 1947. In English: *Christianity in Europe.* Tr. J. Dalton. London, 1844.

————. "Glauben und Liebe oder Der König und die Königin," in *Novalis, Auswahl und Einleitung.* Ed. Walter Rehm. Frankfurt-am-Main and Hamburg, 1956.

Opel, Fritz. *Der Deutsche Metallarbeiter-Verband während des Ersten Weltkrieges und der Revolution.* Hannover, 1962.

———— and Dieter Schneider. *Fünfundsiebzig Jahre Industriegewerkschaft.* Frankfurt-am-Main, 1966.

Ostrogorski, Moisei Iakovlevich. *La democratie et l'organisation des partis politiques.* 2 vols. Paris, 1912. In English: *Democracy and the Organisation of Political Parties.* Tr. F. Clarke. London, 1902.

Pareto, Vilfredo. "Réponse à René Johannet," *Cahiers Vilfredo Pareto*, 2 (1963).

Parkinson, C. Northcote. *Parkinson's Law and Other Studies in Administration.* Boston, 1957.

Patton, Arch. "Top Executive Pay: New Facts and Figures," *Harvard Business Review*, XLIV, 5 (September–October, 1966), 94–97.

Peacock, Alan T. and Jack Wiseman. *The Growth of Public Expenditure in the United Kingdom.* Princeton, 1961.

Perlmutter, Hovard V. "Menschliche Aspekte der internationalen Unternehmung," *Neue Zürcher Zeitung,* December 28, 1967.

Pipes, Richard. *Karamzin's Memoir on Ancient and Modern Russia; A Translation and Analysis.* Cambridge, Mass., 1959.

Pirenne, Henri. *Economic and Social History of Medieval Europe.* New York, 1937.

————. *Medieval Cities.* New York, 1956.

Pirenne, Jacques. "L'administration civile et l'organisation judiciaire en Egypte sous la Ve dynastie," *Annuaire de l'Institut de philologie et d'histoire orientales et slaves,* III (Bruxelles, 1935), 363–386.

Ploss, Sidney I. *Conflict and Decision-Making in Soviet Russia: A Case Study of Agricultural Policy 1953–1963.* Princeton, 1965.

Poirson, Auguste. *Histoire du règne de Henri IV.* 2 vols. Paris, 1856.

Polanyi, Karl. *The Great Transformation.* Boston, 1957.

Pollock, Friedrich. *Automation.* Frankfurt-am-Main, 1964. In English: *Automation: A Study of Its Economic and Social Consequences.* Tr. W. O. Henderson and W. H. Chalonet. New York, 1957.

Popitz, Heinrich, *et al. Das Gesellschaftsbild des Arbeiters.* Tübingen, 1957.

Presthus, Robert. *The Organizational Society: An Analysis and a Theory.* New York, 1965.

Pross, Helge. *Manager und Aktionäre in Deutschland: Studien zum Verhältnis von Eigentum und Verfügungsgewalt.* Frankfurt-am-Main, 1965.

Pyat, Felix. *La Commune* (Paris), March 24, 1871.

Reigrotzki, Erich. *Soziale Verflechtungen in der Bundesrepublik.* Tübingen, 1956.

Reinhard, Ewald. *Karl Ludwig von Haller, der "Restaurator der Staatswissenschaft."* Münster, 1933.

Ritter, Ulrich Peter. *Die Rolle des Staates in den Frühstadien der Industrialisierung.* Berlin, 1961.

Rosenberg, Hans. *Bureaucracy, Aristocracy and Autocracy: The Prussian Experience 1660–1815.* Cambridge, Mass., 1958.

Rubel, Maximilian. *Karl Marx: essai de biographie intellectuelle.* Paris, 1971.

Rühle, Otto. *Die Aktion* (September, 1920).

————. *Illustrierte Kultur- und Sittengeschichte des Proletariats.* Berlin, 1930.

————. *Der Mensch auf der Flucht.* Berlin, 1932.

————. *Mut zur Utopie: Baupläne für eine neue Gesellschaft.* Ed. Henry Jacoby. Reinbeck-bei-Hamburg, 1971.

Rühle-Gerstel, Alice. *Der Weg zum Wir.* Dresden, 1927.

Ruggiero, Guido de. *Geschichte des Liberalismus in Europa.* München, 1930. In English: *The History of European Liberalism.* Tr. R. G. Collingwood. London, 1927.

Ryapolov, Gregory. "I was a Soviet Manager," *Harvard Business Review*, XLIV, 1 (January–February, 1966), 117–125.

Saint-Simon, Louis de Rouvroy, Duke de. *Memoires*. Paris, 1947. In English: *The Memoirs of the Duke of Saint-Simon on the Reign of Louis XIV and the Regency*. Tr. Bayle St. John. London, 1900.

Salin, Edgar. "Kartellverbot und Konzentration," *Kyklos*, 2 (1963).

———. "Von den Wandlungen der Weltwirtschaft in der Nachkriegszeit," *Weltwirtschaftliches Archiv* (January, 1932).

Salomon, A. *Alexis de Tocqueville, Autorität und Freiheit: Schriften, Reden und Briefe*. Zürich, 1935.

Salz, Arthur. *Macht und Wirtschaftsgesetz: Ein Beitrag zum Erkenntnis des Wesens der Kapitalistischen Wirtschaftsverfassung*. Berlin and Leipzig, 1930.

Say, Jean-Baptiste. *Traité d'économie politique*. Paris, 1803. In English: *A Treatise on Political Economy*. Tr. C. R. Prinsep. London, 1821.

Schaff, Adam. *Marxismus und das menschliche Individuum*. Zürich, 1966.

Schapiro, J. Salwyn. "Alexis de Tocqueville, Pioneer of Democratic Liberalism in France," *Political Science Quarterly*, LVII, 4 (December, 1942), 545–563.

Scheler, Max. *Ressentiment*. Tr. William W. Holdheim. New York, 1961.

Schelsky, Helmut. *Wandlungen der deutschen Familie in der Gegenwart: Darstellung und Deutung einer empirisch-soziologischen Tatbestandaufnahme*. 2 vols. Stuttgart, 1955. In English: *Changing Family Structures under Conditions of Social and Economic Development*. Tr. of Volume I. The Hague, 1958.

Schenck, Ernst von. "Überwindung der bloss formalen Demokratie," in *Zweites Europäisches Gespräch: Arbeiter, Manager und Kultur*. Köln, 1951.

Scherr, Johannes. *Blücher, seine Zeit und sein Leben*. 2 vols. Leipzig, 1865.

Schieder, Wolfgang. *Anfänge der deutschen Arbeiterbewegung*. Stuttgart, 1963.

Schlesinger, Jr., Arthur M. *The Age of Jackson*. Boston, 1953.

Schmalenbach, Eugen. *Der freien Wirtschaft zum Gedächtnis*. Köln and Opladen, 1949.

Schmoller, Gustav Friedrich von. *Umrisse und Untersuchungen zur Verfassungsgeschichte*. Leipzig, 1898.

Schumpeter, Joseph A. *Capitalism, Socialism and Democracy*. New York, 1950.

———. *History of Economic Analysis*. New York, 1954.

———. "Science and Ideology," *The American Economic Review*, XXXIX, 2 (March, 1949), 345–359.

Seidman, Joel, et. al. *The Worker Views His Union*. Chicago, 1958.

Shonfield, Andrew. *Modern Capitalism: The Changing Balance of Public and Private Power*. London, New York and Toronto, 1965.

Siebel, Wiegand. "Rationalität und Normenorientierung in der Organisation," *Zeitschrift für die Gesamte Staatswirtschaft*, CXX, 4 (October, 1964).

Silagi, Denis. *Jakobiner in der Habsburger Monarchie: Ein Beitrag zur Geschichte des aufgeklärten Absolutismus in Oesterreich*. Wien, 1962.

Sismonde de Sismondi, Jean Charles Léonard. "Du Prince dans les pays libres ou du pouvoir executif," *Annales de législation et d'économie politique*, I (1822).

———. "Observations," *Annales de législation et d'économie politique*, I (1822).

Sloan, Jr., Alfred, P. *My Years with General Motors*. New York, 1964.

233

Smith, Adam. *An Inquiry into the Nature and Causes of the Wealth of Nations.* London, 1776.

Sombart, Werner. *Sozialismus und soziale Bewegung im 19. Jahrhundert.* Jena, 1897. In English: *Socialism and the Social Movement in the 19th Century.* Tr. Anson P. Atterbury. London and New York, 1898.

Sonnemann, Ulrich. *Die Einführung des Ungehorsams in Deutschland.* Hamburg, 1964.

Spanheim, Ezéchiel. *Relation de la Cour de France en 1690.* Ed. Emile Bourgeois. Paris, 1900.

Spencer, Herbert. *The Man Versus the State.* London, 1884.

Spitzer, Alan B. "The Bureaucrat as Proconsul: The Restoration Prefect and the *Police Générale,*" *Comparative Studies in Society and History,* VII, 4 (July, 1965), 371–392.

Stahl, Friedrich Julius. *Die gegenwärtigen Parteien in Staat und Kirche.* Berlin, 1868.

Stammer, Otto. "Politische Soziologie und Demokratieforschung," *Kölner Zeitschrift für Soziologie und Sozialpsychologie,* VIII (1956).

Stawar, André. *Libres essais marxistes.* Tr. from Polish, Jerzy Warszawski. Paris, 1963.

Stöcklein, Paul. *Joseph von Eichendorff in Selbstzeugnissen und Bilddokumenten.* Hamburg, 1963.

Strauss, Eric. *The Ruling Servants: Bureaucracy in Russia, France—And Britain?* New York, 1961.

Strauss, Leo. *The Political Philosophy of Hobbes, its Basis and its Genesis.* Tr. Elsa M. Sinclair. Oxford, 1936.

Sumner, B. H. *A Short History of Russia.* New York, 1943.

Talès, C. *La Commune de 1871.* Paris, 1924.

Tarsis, Valery. *The Bluebottle.* Tr. Thomas Jones and David Alger. New York, 1963.

Thompson, E. P. *The Making of the English Working Class.* New York, 1964.

Thucydides. *The Peloponnesian Wars.* Tr. Benjamin Jowett. New York, 1962.

Tingsten, Herbert. *The Problem of Democracy.* Totowa, N. J., 1965.

Tocqueville, Alexis de. *L'Ancien régime et la révolution.* Ed. I. P. Mayer. Paris, 1964. In English: *De Tocqueville's L'Ancien régime.* Tr. M. W. Patterson. Oxford, 1956.

———. *De la démocratie en Amérique.* 4 vols. Paris, 1835. In English: *Democracy in America.* Tr. Henry Reeve. New York, 1841.

———. *Oeuvres complètes.* 9 vols. Paris, 1864–1866.

———. *Souvenirs.* 6th ed. Paris, 1944. In English: *The Recollections of Alexis de Tocqueville.* Tr. Alexander Teixeira de Mattos. London, 1896.

Toennies, Ferdinand. *Thomas Hobbes Leben und Lehre.* Stuttgart, 1896.

Toynbee, Arnold. *Study of History.* Vols. I–VI. London and New York, 1947.

Treitschke, Heinrich Gotthard von. *Politik.* 2 vols. Leipzig, 1899–1900. In English: *Politics, by Heinrich von Treitschke.* Tr. Blanche Dugdale and Torben de Bille. New York, 1916.

Trevelyan, George Macaulay. *History of England.* London, 1964.

Triesch, Günther. *Die Macht der Funktionäre.* Düsseldorf, 1916.

Trotsky, Leon. *Geschichte der Russischen Revolution; Februar Revolution.* Berlin, 1931. In English: *History of the Russian Revolution.* Tr. Max Eastman. New York, 1932.
————. *Die Russische Revolution 1905.* Berlin, 1923. In English: *The Revolution of 1905.* New York, 1931.

Tschudi, Laurent. "Kritische Grundlegung der Idee der direkten Rätedemokratie im Marxismus." Diss. Basel, 1952.

Tyler, Gus. *A New Philosophy for Labor.* New York, 1959.

U. S. Congress. Senate. *Industrial Prices and their Relative Inflexibility,* by Gardiner C. Means. Seventy-fourth Cong., First Sess., S. Doc. 13. Washington, 1935.

U. S. Department of Labor. *Manpower Report of the President.* March, 1966.

Valéry, Paul. *Regards sur le monde actuel.* Paris, 1945. In English: *Reflections on the World Today.* Tr. Francis Scarfe. London, 1951.

Van de Vall, Mark. *Die Gewerkschaften im Wohlfahrtstaat.* Köln and Opladen, 1966.
————. "The Workers' Councils in Western Europe: Aims and Results," in *Proceedings of the Seventeenth Annual Meeting of the Industrial Relations Research Association.* Chicago, 1965.

Vialatoux, Joseph. *La Cité de Hobbes. Théorie de l'état totalitaire: essai sur la conception naturaliste de la civilisation.* Lyon and Paris, 1935.

Villiger, Andreas. *Aufbau und Verfassung der britischen und amerikanischen Gewerkschaften—Wachstum und Strukturentwicklung der Gewerkschaftsbewegung: Probleme der innerverbandlichen Demokratie.* Berlin, 1966.

Viollet, Paul Marie. *Histoire des institutions politiques et administratives de la France.* 4 vols. Paris, 1890–1912.

Wagner, Adolph. "Finanzwissenschaft und Staatssozialismus," *Zeitschrift für die gesamte Staatswissenschaft* (1887).

Walter, Hans. "Parkinson im Industriebetrieb," *Frankfurter Allgemeine Zeitung,* November 28, 1958.

Webb, Sidney and Beatrice. *The Consumers' Cooperative Movement.* London, 1921.

Weber, Alfred. "Bürokratie und Freiheit," *Die Wandlung,* December 20, 1946.
————. *Die Krise des modernen Staatsgedanken in Europa.* Berlin, 1925.
————. *Kulturgeschichte als Kultursoziologie.* Leiden, 1935.

Weber, Marianne. *Max Weber: Ein Lebensbild.* Tübingen, 1926.

Weber, Max. *Gesammelte Aufsätze zur Soziologie und Sozialpolitik.* Tübingen, 1924.
————. *Gesammelte politische Schriften.* München, 1921.
————. *Schriften zur theoretischen Soziologie, zur Soziologie der Politik und Verfassung.* Ed. Max Graf zu Solms. Frankfurt-am-Main, 1947.
————. *Wirtschaft und Gesellschaft.* Tübingen, 1922. In English: *Economy and Society: An Outline of Interpretive Sociology.* Eds. Guenther Roth and Claus Wittich; tr. Ephraim Fischoff *et al.* New York, 1968.
————. "Wissenschaft als Beruf," in *Gesammelte Aufsaetze zur Wissenschaftslehre.* Tübingen, 1922. In English: "Science as a Vocation," in *From Max Weber: Essays in Sociology.* Ed. and tr. H. H. Gerth and C. Wright Mills. New York, 1958.

Weill, Georges. *La France sous la monarchie constitutionnelle (1814–1848).* Paris, 1912.

Weitling, Wilhelm. *Das Evangelium des armen Sünders.* Birsfeld, 1846.

Wells, H. G. *A Modern Utopia.* London, 1905.

Whyte, Jr., William H. *The Organization Man.* New York, 1956.

Wittfogel, Karl A. *Oriental Despotism: A Comparative Study of Total Power.* New Haven, 1959.

Wolzendorff, Kurt. "Der reine Staat: Skizze zum Problem einer neuen Staats-epoche," *Zeitschrift für die gesamte Staatswissenschaft,* LVII, 1 and 2 (August, 1920).

Zbinden, Hans. *Neue Zürcher Zeitung,* August 27, 1965.

INDEX